Poetry and the Realm of Politics

FRONTISPIECE, Mary, Queen of Scots, pointing to her own execution. Engraving by J. Couvay (b. Arles, 1622), 'cum privilegio Regis Christiani'.

Poetry and the Realm of Politics

Shakespeare to Dryden

HOWARD ERSKINE-HILL

CLARENDON PRESS · OXFORD
1996

Oxford University Press, Walton Street, Oxford OX2 6DP
Oxford New York
Athens Auckland Bangkok Bombay
Calcutta Cape Town Dar es Salaam Delhi
Florence Hong Kong Istanbul Karachi
Kuala Lumpur Madras Madrid Melbourne
Mexico City Nairobi Paris Singapore
Taipei Tokyo Toronto
and associated companies in
Berlin Ibadan

Oxford is a trade mark of Oxford University Press

Published in the United States
by Oxford University Press Inc., New York

British Library Cataloguing in Publication Data
Data available

Library of Congress Cataloging in Publication Data
Erskine-Hill, Howard.
Poetry and the realm of politics :
Shakespeare to Dryden / Howard Erskine-Hill.
Includes bibliographical references and index.
1. English poetry—Early modern, 1500–1700—History and criticism.
2. Political poetry, English—History and criticism.
3. Politics and literature—Great Britain—History—17th century.
4. Politics and literature—Great Britain—History—16th century.
5. Shakespeare, William, 1564–1616—Political and social views.
6. Dryden, John, 1631–1700—Political and social views. I. Title.
PR535.H5E77 1996   821'.309358—dc20   95–10829
ISBN 0–19–811731–0

1 3 5 7 9 10 8 6 4 2

Typeset by Pure Tech India Ltd, Pondicherry
Printed in Great Britain
on acid-free paper by
Bookcraft Ltd,
Midsomer Norton, Bath

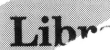

TO

PEMBROKE COLLEGE, CAMBRIDGE,
THE COLLEGE OF SPENSER AND
SIR JOHN HAYWARD

Acknowledgements

I HAVE incurred many debts in the planning and writing of this book. The late Philip Brockbank encouraged me to develop my interest in Shakespeare and Bodin, as did the late G. R. Hibbard who also kindly read the first three chapters of the book and gave me the benefit of his advice. Professor Wallace MacCaffrey also read these chapters and guided me on the reign of Elizabeth I. Others who read these chapters in earlier or later draft are Dr David Womersley, Dr Richard McCabe, Professor Anne Barton, Professor George Dekker, Mr Bryan Milnes, and Mr Robert Douglas-Fairhurst: I am particularly grateful for their help. Dr Blair Worden advised me on those chapters which consider republican ideas, and Professor Earl Miner kindly read in draft most of my discussion of Milton and Dryden; so did Professor Patricia Meyer Speacks. Professor Joseph Loenstein discussed certain Spenserian and Miltonic matters with me. Mr Richard Sharp, of Worcester College, Oxford, gave me invaluable advice on the illustrations of the book. I am most obliged to these kind colleagues and friends. None of them necessarily agrees with my arguments, and none, of course, is responsible for errors and omissions remaining in the book.

My debts to various institutions are no less important to acknowledge. I am exceptionally grateful to the National Humanities Center, North Carolina, for electing me into one of its Olin Fellowships for the academic year 1988-9. The whole of this book and the greater part of its sequel, *Poetry of Opposition and Revolution*— both parts of a single work at that time—were written up at the National Humanities Center, with the incomparably kind and efficient assistance of all its staff. Three more months at the Center would, I believe, have enabled me to complete what in ordinary Cambridge conditions took me several further years to do. I am also most grateful to Cambridge University and to Pembroke College for granting me sabbatical leave. I am grateful to the staff of the Cambridge University Library, the Bodleian Library, and the British Library (happily for me still in Bloomsbury). I am particularly grateful to Pam Judd, Assistant Librarian of Pembroke College Library. I acknowledge permission to publish a print of Oliver

Cromwell from the Ashmolean Museum, Oxford; and am grateful for the photographic services of the Ashmolean and the Cambridge University Library.

Finally, I want to express my thanks for a great deal of personal and academic kindness from senior and junior members of the College to which this book is dedicated.

H.H.E.-H.

19 July 1994

Contents

List of Illustrations

Abbreviations and Short Titles

Annals	William Camden, *Annals (Annales rerum Anglicarum et Hibernicarum regnante Elizabethae* (1615, 1627)), trans. R. Norton (3rd edn., 1635)
Complete Works	William Shakespeare, *The Complete Works*, ed. Stanley Wells and Gary Taylor (Oxford, 1986)
A Conference	Robert Parsons (with others?), *A Conference About the Next Succession of the Crowne of England . . . Published by R. Dolman* (1594)
EC	*Essays in Criticism*
ELH	*English Literary History*
Evelyn	John Evelyn, *Diary*, ed. E. S. De Beer, 6 vols. (Oxford, 1955)
'Hayward's Troubles'	Margaret Dowling, 'Sir John Hayward's Troubles Over His Life of *Henry IV*', *Library*, 4th ser., 11 (1931)
History of Italy	William Thomas, *The History of Italy* (1549), ed. George B. Parks (Ithaca, NY, 1963)
JEGP	*Journal of English and Germanic Philology*
Ben Jonson	*Ben Jonson [Works]*, ed. C. H. Herford and Percy and Evelyn Simpson, 11 vols. (Oxford, 1925–52)
MLN	*Modern Language Notes*
MP	*Modern Philology*
A Pithie Exhortation	Peter Wentworth, *A Pithie Exhortation To Her Majestie for Establishing Her Successor to the Crowne* (1598)
Poems	John Milton, *Poems*, ed. John Carey and Alastair Fowler (1968)
POAS	*Poems on Affairs of State*, ed. G. de F. Lord *et al.*, 7-vols. (New Haven, 1963–75)
Prose Works	John Milton, *Complete Prose Works*, ed. Douglas Bush *et al.* (New Haven, 1953–82)
PMLA	*Publications of the Modern Languages Association of America*
Six Livres	Jean Bodin, *Les Six Livres de la république* (1576) trans. Richard Knolles (1606), ed. K. D. McRae (Cambridge, Mass., 1962)
RES	*Review of English Studies*
TLS	*Times Literary Supplement*

Works   John Dryden, *Works*, ed. E. N. Hooker, H. T.
                         Swedenberg, *et al.*, 20 vols. (Berkeley and Los
                         Angeles, 1961–).
Works of Spenser   Edmund Spenser, *Works, A Variorum Edition*,
                         ed. Edwin Greenlaw *et al.*, 11 vols. (Baltimore,
                         1932–57)

A Note on Texts

IN choosing editions of works frequently quoted from in this book I have tried to be guided by considerations of simplicity and accessibility. This does not mean that I have neglected to consult other editions or first printings, especially where variation might affect the arguments of the book. Quotations from Shakespeare, for example, are generally drawn from the one-volume *Complete Works of Shakespeare* (Oxford, 1986), but I have repeatedly consulted the New Arden and other editions. In several cases, as it will be seen, textual disagreement (for example between New Oxford and Folio) bears directly upon arguments that are here advanced. I should add that I have followed Shakespeare in his revision of Oldcastle to Falstaff in 1 Henry IV.

In references, place of publication is London unless stated otherwise.

Introduction

THE chief contention of this book is that there is a political compo-
nent, often involving contemporary political ideas and historical
circumstance, in some of the most powerful poetic works of six-
teenth- and seventeenth-century English literature, works which have
in the past been usually read for their aesthetic achievement and
generalized wisdom. I argue that this political component is an
eventual part of their aesthetic life, and that that, in its turn, is part
of that wider historical culture which it is the vocation of scholarship
to explore with as much imagination and disinterestedness as it can.

Poetry is the first term in my title, and my first purpose here is to
say what kind of poetry I intend to discuss, and why I begin and end
where I do.

It seemed clear to me that the book had to open with the mid-
Renaissance, in the period of Spenser and Shakespeare. To have
gone back beyond the establishment of a print culture to the great
medieval poets would have been to confront different problems of
communication and reception. While in the earlier sixteenth century
Skelton and Wyatt are distinguished forerunners of Spenser and
Jonson respectively in the composition of a poetry conscious of
issues in affairs of state, they are hardly comparable with Spenser
and Shakespeare in the sheer scope of their public and historical
awareness. The book, then, had to begin with either Shakespeare or
Spenser. To some extent, as I hope to show, it opens with both. But,
further, it was a priority that the 'Poetry' of my title should encom-
pass a significant body of dramatic poetry. If we seek to trace the
part of political awareness within the poetic presentation of human
experience we are bound to pay special attention to literary forms
which accommodate opposing or diverse forces and choices, for
example King Richard and King Henry within the text of Shake-
speare's *Richard II*. One of the greatest short political poems of the
seventeenth century, Andrew Marvell's 'Horatian Ode upon Crom-
well's Return from Ireland', does expressly that, and it is significant
how poignantly this text recalls the dramatic presentation of an
earlier age. Shakespeare's Histories, in their close yet paradoxical
relation with the public issues of the 1590s, offered (it seemed to me)

the richest and most vigorous early example of poetry of the realm of politics. I therefore resolved that Shakespeare should be the first poet for sustained discussion. Attention to drama is, however, a feature of the whole book, and the post-revolutionary tragedy of Milton[1] and Dryden is compared. There are ways in which drama may explore a historical dilemma which more univocal forms can hardly undertake.

Spenser, however, is the major introductory example of this book. Not only in his *Prosopopoia. Or Mother Hubberd's Tale* (1590) did he publish a poem of overt political intent—a poem which in a later era would have been included in collections of State Poems—but, in the two instalments of *The Faerie Queene* (1590, 1596), Spenser published a long poem of great complexity and subtlety, in which, as has always been accepted, contemporary political allusion plays an important but by no means systematic role. A probable influence on Shakespeare, *The Faerie Queene* exemplifies multiple historical allusion according to which not only do numerous fictional figures seem to suggest at different times numerous historical figures, but particular historical figures can be suggested by different fictional figures. As Spenser claimed in the letter to Ralegh, 'In that Faery Queene I meane glorie in my generall intention, but in my particular I conceiue the most excellent and glorious person of our soueraine the Queene, and her kingdome in Faery land. And yet in some places els, I doe otherwise shadow her.'[2] In Fairy Queen, Belphoebe, and Mercilla, different faces of Elizabeth I are figured; in Amoret (perhaps) and Duessa (v. ix), Mary, Queen of Scots. In two significant recent essays Richard A. McCabe has carried the whole question of political allusion in *The Faerie Queene* to a more sophisticated level, noticing, among other things, how the Duessa of Book I, despite being surrounded by figures of more specific historical allusion, can be read as an allegorical figure of religious falsity, whereas in Book V, canto ix the generalized allegory of the first instalment of *The Faerie Queene* gathers up the earlier hovering hints of identity in an unmistakable allusion to the trial of Mary, Queen of Scots; and how 'the Fairy Queen . . . discussed, desired, idealized, envisioned, fleetingly apprehended in a myriad of male and female surrogates', never

---

[1] The problem of the date of *Samson Agonistes* is discussed at the beginning of Ch. 7.

[2] Edmund Spenser, *Works, A Variorum Edition*, ed. Edwin Greenlaw *et al.* (Baltimore, 1932–58), *Faerie Queene*, I. 168.

appears in 'the poem that bears her name'. 'Spenser identifies the absence of the monarch . . . as the single factor most detrimental to the struggle for "civility" in Ireland'.[3] And just as certainly as *The Faerie Queene* offered a complex, glancing, shadow play of identity and half-identity, so was it read for its contemporary allusion by some of the real actors in the action it presented, such as James VI, King of Scots (possibly alluded to at VI. xii. 4). A poet himself, James correctly perceived in the second instalment of the poem a judgement on his mother, the Queen of Scots, which denied the chief goal of his diplomacy: the English succession.[4] His ambassador protested to Queen Elizabeth. *The Faerie Queene* was banned in Scotland.

These facts form the basis for one of the chief arguments of the present book. It is still commonly assumed that, where poetic texts make contemporary political allusion, they do so by becoming *romans-à-clef.* Dryden's *Absalom and Achitophel* (1681) is constantly cited as the exemplar of poetry of clear and systematic political allusion. (A theatrical example of the same thing is Middleton's *A Game at Chess.*) Many other such texts may be found in the later seventeenth- and earlier eighteenth-century collections of State Poems, and are represented in our time by George de Forest Lord's seven-volume selection, *Poems on Affairs of State.*[5] These poems are of great interest and sometimes brilliance. I have drawn on them as ancillary material most fully towards the end of this book, and at the beginning of its sequel, *Poetry of Opposition and Revolution.* But the very skill with which *Absalom and Achitophel* drew a single biblical/modern parallel, in which all salient details were incorporated into an allusive system, has misled generations of readers into thinking that this and only this is what poetry of important political allusion must be like.

Two unfortunate consequences have stemmed from this conclusion. First, other and often more subtle modes of political allusion have gone unrecognized because they did not supply an allusive parallel such as we find in *Absalom and Achitophel.* Thus a whole

---

[3] Richard A. McCabe, 'The Masks of Duessa: Spenser, Mary Queen of Scots, and James VI', *ELH* 17 (1987), 224–42; 'Edmund Spenser, Poet of Exile', Chatterton Lecture on Poetry, 1991, *Proceedings of the British Academy*, 80 (1991), 73–103.

[4] *Works* of Spenser, *Faerie Queene*, v. 244–5.

[5] *Poems on Affairs of State: Augustan Satirical Verse,* 1660–1714, ed. George de F. Lord *et al.*, 7 vols. (New Haven, 1963–75).

dimension of some of the greatest poetry in the English language has been belittled or occluded. Secondly, critical attention has been allowed to glide over the complex and intriguing interrelation of political and (for example) personal or devotional awareness in ambitious imaginative works. I have therefore not called this book (as I once proposed to do) *Poetry and Affairs of State*, lest readers should jump to the conclusion that it was a study of *Poems on Affairs of State* alone. I have not primarily sought to discuss that specialized, explicitly political, kind of poem. I have thus not discussed *Absalom and Achitophel* (which has had plenty of attention) but I have discussed Dryden's *Aeneid* version. I have not discussed *A Game at Chess* but I have discussed *Paradise Lost*. In *Poetry of Opposition and Revolution* I discuss not Defoe's *Jure Divino* but Pope's *Rape of the Lock*, not Wordsworth's Sonnets on National Independence and Liberty' but *The Prelude*.

This book reaches its end with a discussion of the post-revolutionary tragedy of Milton and Dryden. Each affords a wonderful example of a poet deeply involved in the high politics of his time, each surviving a major reversal in Church and State. These two poets did not inhabit wholly separate worlds, as is sometimes assumed, and their use of epic and drama to explore and comment on their times is a matter of great interest, bringing to an end that phase of poetry and the realm of politics which Spenser seems to inaugurate. The practice of glancing, or complex or multiple, allusion by no means ends with the century, however, and the later original poems and drama of Dryden form a basis for the political poetry of the early eighteenth century.

This is the place to note that the poets I chiefly discuss in this book, Spenser, Shakespeare, Jonson, Milton, and Dryden, are all drawn from what (since the recent creation of alternative canons) has come to be called the canon of English literature. This is to say that these poets, of different periods though they are, ideologically diverse though they are, out of favour though all but one of them have been, and artistically various though they are, represent some of the best and most serious poetry that England has ever produced. I subscribe to no single, immutable, canon of English poetry. The traditional canon has been modified in the past and will undoubtedly be so again. Simply, however, because of the different periods in which the poets here discussed rose to fame, and the consequently different circumstances in which this fame was sustained, challenged, or restored, they comprise a different kind of list from any created to satisfy late twentieth-century social priorities, or indeed from any list created at a single time. It is obvious that in the latter case literary and political analysis will be likely to reach conclusions replicating the priorities which originally prompted the selection. On the other hand, a canon at once accumulated and thinned out over the centuries is at least going to be essential to study of historical consciousness in the several periods in which the texts were produced, read, and remembered. Of course I argue that their status is higher than this, and that time teaches us to recognize exceptional aesthetic achievement. To the extent that this is the case will literary and political analysis of such texts prove rewarding. At the same time I have sought to illustrate, where possible and relevant, the voice of popular poetry. At one point I juxtapose Milton and Martin Parker.[6]

I turn now to the second term of my title, 'the Realm of Politics'. The first chapter of the book opens with a short consideration of William Camden, England's first major historian. Camden's idea of history is approximately what I mean by 'the Realm of Politics'. This is political history: the deliberations, decisions, and deeds of rulers, debates about their title to rule, change in the forms of government, war and revolution at home and abroad. This is what the poets discussed in this book would probably have understood by politics. I use the word 'Realm' partly to intimate that the theme of royalism, and its opposite, republicanism, will be pervasive, but partly also to disclaim some wider senses of the word 'politics' which might now be used to denote relationships of power anywhere within historical experience, in the family, for example, or in the workplace. Evidently the different senses of the word are connected; indeed some of the subtle interconnections will be displayed in what follows. My chief focus, however, is the governance of the body politic, and the way in which major poetry between the later years of Elizabeth and the later years of William III was aware of and intervened in discussion of this governance.

This book is therefore of a historicist rather than New Historicist trend. As I wrote in the Introduction to an earlier book,

---

[6] See Ch. 5. Martin Parker, the ballad-writer, is generally credited with the famous song, 'The King Shall Enjoy His Own Again'.

the history of a particular span of years is the totality of human experience in that time, and ... the corresponding historiography is the balanced factual and critical account of that experience. Traditional 'history'—the political situations and expedients of the past—and 'criticism'—the examination and assessment of works of art—have their place, with other kinds of investigation, in the complex synthesis which is the history of the civilisation of an age.[7]

After the nihilistic polemic of deconstruction the New Historicism performed a valuable service in recalling the attention of writers about literature to history, and in demonstrating the breadth and variety of cultural evidence. All the same, its often arbitrary combinations of historical and literary material produced striking displays rather than told us truths about the past.[8] Such combinations seem warranted only in terms of some posited underlying ideology, the easier to assume when this was by definition what could not be directly articulated at that time. A discriminate historicism is more likely to be useful, one which nominates a centre of interest, and seeks from the historical record in its full breadth and variety evidence proximate and relevant to that interest. Again, the concept of ideology is hardly to be dispensed with, but will be confined in this book to patterns of values and doctrines capable in principle of being articulated in writings of the period concerned. Once ideology is allowed an empirical basis, the notion of a single-periodideology collapses, and we are confronted instead with conflicting or overlapping world-views.

To attempt to illustrate, in the analysis of Shakespeare's Histories, the proximate evidence of Shakespeare's contemporaries, Camden and Jean Bodin, proves illuminating. The first is significant for his record of the problems and crises of Elizabeth I's reign, the second for his analysis of forms of government and kinds of monarchy, partly articulating as he does an ideology of royal government. To take a further example, the varieties of non-royalist judgements on the career of Oliver Cromwell are illuminating for the light they throw on the epic Milton began around the time of Cromwell's death.

[7] Howard Erskine-Hill, *The Social Milieu of Alexander Pope* (1975), 3.

[8] e.g. Stephen Greenblatt, *Renaissance Self-Fashioning* (1980); *Shakespearian Negotiations* (1988); *Learning to Curse* (1990); (ed.), *Representing the English Renaissance* (1988). A valuable guide and landmark for recent Shakespearian study is Brian Vickers, *Appropriating Shakespeare* (1993), which discusses some further kinds of New Historicism.

If literary critics sometimes feel themselves to be confronted by different historicisms, historians, more deeply imbued in the discipline of their subject, are more aware of the conflicting claims of specific historical hypotheses, and of different visions of different periods. The historiography which has percolated into literary studies is often rather antiquated, Macaulayan myths of political progress with a neo-Marxist overlay. Few historians now have faith in grand retrospective hypotheses of this kind as explanations of historical change, while, self-evidently, they cannot help us recapture that historical consciousness which must be the basis for any convincing interpretation of the politics of poetry. Revisionist history, on the other hand, in its resolve to subject historical circumstance to the closest scrutiny, and to see the past in the terms in which the past saw itself, offers a far more interesting if dauntingly detailed ground for the present project.

I have therefore inclined to follow recent historiography in seeing the later reign of Elizabeth I rather as a lucky survival from a series of unresolved problems than the crowning decade of an era of successful rule.[9] I have followed the new historians of the mid-seventeenth-century civil wars, from whose work (to make an obvious point) we must conclude that the Independent and republican position of men such as Milton was that of a dynamic minority rather than of any large or long-standing popular movement. It is now hard, and was to some fellow Independents hard then, to see Oliver Cromwell as a champion of parliamentary liberty—a point full of consequence for some of Milton's major poetry.[10] Where the Restoration, the Revolution of 1688, and their aftermath are concerned,

[9] I am especially in debt to Wallace T. MacCaffrey's trilogy on the reign of Elizabeth I: *The Shaping of the Elizabethan Regime, Queen Elizabeth and the Making of Policy, 1572–1588*, and *Elizabeth I: War and Politics, 1588–1603* (Princeton, 1968, 1981, 1992). See too Patrick Collinson, 'The Elizabethan Exclusion Crisis and the Elizabethan Polity', *Proceedings of the British Academy*, 84 (1993), pp. 51–92.

[10] Conrad Russell, *The Crisis of Parliaments* (Oxford, 1971), *Unrevolutionary England, 1603–1642* (1990), *The Causes of the English Civil War* (Oxford, 1990), *The Fall of the British Monarchies, 1637–1642* (Oxford, 1991), are notable in the large amount of distinguished new work on the middle decades of the 17th cent. Contributing importantly to newer views are Patrick Collinson, *The Religion of Protestants* (Oxford, 1982); Nicholas Tyacke, *Anti-Calvinists: The Rise of English Arminianism, circa 1590–1640* (Oxford, 1987); Kevin Sharpe, *The Personal Rule of Charles I* (1992); John Morrill, *The Revolt of the Provinces: Conservatives and Radicals in the English Civil War, 1630–1650* (1976); Blair Worden, *The Rump Parliament, 1648–1653* (Cambridge, 1974); G. E. Aylmer (ed.), *The Interregnum: The Quest for Settlement, 1646–1660* (1972).

I have followed recent historians who have challenged the long-lingering Whig triumphalist vision of those uncertain and precarious years, and of the unpredictable alternative futures of the 1690s.[11] The oblique and circumspect modes of Dryden's later verse emerge as a central response to the post-revolutionary era, rather than secularized accommodation or marginalized protest.

Seen in historical context Shakespeare's Histories tend towards a distinct view of royal succession. They do not simply support some Tudor Myth, since the very ground of Elizabeth's myth and concept of her regality was (however weak her actual claim) hereditary right. But in his first tetralogy and *King John* Shakespeare puts hereditary right to the test and finds it wanting. The second tetralogy then begins to explore through drama a Lancastrian view of succession, corresponding to Bodin's pragmatic recognition that lordly monarchs and even usurpers could found dynasties capable of growing into legitimacy through time. This has great significance for the later 1590s, with the ageing queen still refusing to name a successor, and the hereditary-right argument building up in support of James VI. If to be a political conservative in late sixteenth-century terms was to endorse indefeasible hereditary right (an issue that might be open to debate) then Shakespeare was not at this time a conservative.

Further, if I am right to see in the action of *Hamlet* and its source Belleforest a series of historical allusions, then that play sees fate rather than hope in the Stuart succession. A political change does come about in Shakespeare, however, as can be seen in *King Lear*, *Macbeth*, and the Late Plays. Dynastic legitimacy is now revalued; much Stuart ideology is now explored in a positive spirit, but there is not an absolute change. The English scene in Macbeth (V. iii) marks the limit.

Meanwhile, English poetry and drama registered much interest in the working of republican polities, whether modern Italian republics

---

[11] J. P. Kenyon, *Revolution Principles: The Politics of Party, 1689–1720* (Cambridge, 1977), seems to me the book which has most altered our view of the later 17th and earlier 18th cent., though J. G. A. Pocock, *The Ancient Constitution and the Feudal Law* (Cambridge, 1957), was a significant earlier pointer. Ronald Hutton has now given us *The Restoration: A Political and Religious History of England and Wales, 1658–1667* (Oxford, 1985) and *Charles the Second, King of England, Scotland and Ireland* (Oxford, 1989). New work on Queen Anne by Edward Gregg, on political controversy by Mark Goldie, and much new work on Jacobitism prompted and assisted by Dr Eveline Cruickshanks, have modified our picture of these times.

or republics of the ancient world. Shakespeare is to the fore in his double dramatization of Venice, first as a republic of laws, then as a maritime state militant against the Turk (*The Merchant of Venice* and *Othello*). The image of Venice, 'the Adriatique Wonder', is to be found in the poetry of the period, and its reputation as a harmonious and lasting polity continues into the statist debates of the later Interregnum when Harrington's *Oceana* (1656) appeared. Kingdoms and republics could relevantly be compared as commonweals, as Sir Thomas Smith's *De Republica Anglorum* (1583) suggests, and sometimes the difficult relations of the one, the few, and the many, in a kingdom, could most clearly be explored through the dramatization of a republic. So it is with Shakespeare's *Coriolanus*, a play about the natural elements of kingship and its dangers in a republican society. So it is with Jonson's *Catiline*; a tragedy written to mark the survival of a monarchy from conspiracy against it, it is nevertheless a republican play which casts such a cold eye on the signs of emergent kingship that one might almost suspect Jonson of transgressing that acceptably learned frontier within which legitimate ancient republics were deemed relevant to legitimate modern monarchies.

Nobody foresaw the outbreak of wars within the British kingdoms in the mid-seventeenth century, let alone the establishment of a republic based on London. Sought originally by neither side, these developments may have arisen as much from miscalculations in the period 1637–42 as from more long-term factors. This seems especially probable in the area of religious policy as it bore on the government of three different kingdoms. Milton's writings between 1640 and 1648 seem retrospectively to express a republican spirit but could no doubt have been compatible with a monarchical polity of some kind. Only in *The Tenure of Kings and Magistrates* (1649) does Milton emerge as an anti-monarchist, and thus by negative implication as a republican. But the great transformation of the 1650s was that of Cromwell, from the general 'still in the republic's hand' to the quasi-monarch whom some of his supporters desired to crown. The Milton of *The Second Defence of the English People* is the champion of republican liberty caught in a Cromwellian trap. Nothing is more striking, at the end of the decade, than Milton's support for the Rump of the Long Parliament, long expelled by Cromwell. 'He who has advised Sulla now advises the People' is the epigraph on the title-page of *The Readie and Easie Way to Set Up a*

Free Commonwealth (1660). Cromwell is important for *Paradise Lost*, begun around the year of the Lord Protector's death, as an example of strong, libertarian leadership leading to the betrayal rather than the extension of freedom. Revolutionary events in the mid-seventeenth-century realm of politics help to explain the difference of conception between the early sketch of 'Adam Unparadised' and the poem as published in 1667.

Reversal in the realm of politics—for Milton the revolution of 1660, for Dryden that of 1688—shows each of them writing in response to defeat and danger. Each reacted to the new circumstances in characteristic ways. Milton's literary strategy was to withdraw into the foundations of his biblical myth; contemporary allusions are to be found, but the reader is, as it were, left to travel a long way to make the appropriate historical applications. For his part Dryden abandons the clear and systematic allusion of *Absalom and Achitophel* in order to emit a play of historical and political reference so plentiful and paradoxical as to serve as both protective screen and complex response to complex times. The two poets have something in common also. Each draws on Virgilian epic, Milton through imitation, Dryden through allusive translation, as a framework within which an understanding of the new historical situation may be achieved. Each offers a vision of historic destruction in dramatic mode: *Samson Agonistes* and *Alexander's Feast*. But this particular comparison takes us a little beyond the boundary of the present book, and into the territory of its sequel, *Poetry of Opposition and Revolution*.

The post-revolutionary Dryden may have responded in more circumspect manner to the collapse of previous political order than Milton. The myth of the lost monarch in *Don Sebastian* enabled Dryden to express his fidelity to the old world while not denying the new: his tragic action does not culminate, like Milton's, in the destruction of the government and leadership of a state. In its extraordinary compression and urgency, Milton's tragic action leads directly to the vindication of a historical and religious providence. Dryden's more elaborated and romantic story affords space between defeat and death for individual devotion and contemplation. It is tempting to see in the two tragedies some exemplification of the militant Protestant and of the Roman Catholic visions of historical defeat in late Counter-Reformation Europe.

PART I

Shakespeare and the Succession of Kings

I

The Political Foreground

There is a history in all men's lives
Figuring the natures of the times deceasd;
The which observd, a man may prophesy,
With a near aim, of the main chance of things
As yet not come to life, who in their seeds
And weak beginnings lie intreasurèd.

(2 *Henry IV*, III. i. 75–80)

WHEN Shakespeare wrote these impressive lines of Warwick to King Henry IV he held in his mind, albeit perhaps briefly, the idea that the chronicle narratives he was then dramatizing could be in some measure prophetic. Unlikely to have believed in indefinite historical progress or regress, Shakespeare more probably considered that history in some way repeated itself. If the chronicled past were not a clear mirror of things to come, it yet revealed recurrent problems and principles of action; it showed dangers and disasters to which the present and future were unlikely to be impervious; at the most simple level, as has been long recognized, it warned and taught lessons.[1]

That warning and teaching were part of Shakespeare's concern is suggested by his choice of materials from the chronicles, which

---

[1] E. M. W. Tillyard, *Shakespeare's History Plays* (1944); Lily B. Campbell, *Shakespeare's 'Histories': Mirrors of Elizabethan Policy* (San Marino, Calif., 1947; London, 1964); Irving Ribner, *The English History Play in the Age of Shakespeare* (Princeton, 1957); M. M. Reese, *The Cease of Majesty* (1961); E. W. Talbot, *The Problem of Order: Elizabethan Political Commonplace and an Example of Shakespeare's Art* (Chapel Hill, 1962); H. A. Kelly, *Divine Providence in the England of Shakespeare's Histories* (Cambridge, Mass., 1970); Robert Ornstein, *A Kingdom for a Stage* (Cambridge, Mass., 1972); John Wilders, *The Lost Garden: A View of Shakespeare's English and Roman History Plays* (1978); C. G. Thayer, *Shakespearian Politics: Government and Misgovernment in the Great Histories* (Athens, Oh., 1983); Graham Holderness, *Shakespeare's Histories* (1985); Alexander Leggatt, *Shakespeare's Political Drama: The History Plays and the Roman Plays* (1988). Leggatt tellingly notes that 'Tillyard, though persistently attacked, will not go away' (p. x). But it is clear that the plays are now less seen as expositions of providence than as texts in which providential expositions are to be found.

ought on the face of it to be surprising. The canonical History Plays of the 1590s dramatize not one reign of a king who combined political success with an undisputed title to the throne. Yet the chronicles offered many examples. If 'The politike Conquest of William the first' showed too much of the conqueror and too little of the inheritor, the long reign of Edward I gave an example of a prince 'not only valiant but also politike, labouring to bring this divided Ile into one entier monarchie . . .' while Edward III, valiant, courteous, and temperate, reigned for forty years at least 'in high felicitie, and as one happie in all his dooings'.[2] Might it not have been expected that the long reign of Elizabeth, lacking neither valour nor policy, would have prompted the dramatic celebration of such royal heroes of the English past? And would not their reigns have afforded as good intrinsic dramatic material for the particular kind of theatrical and poetic entertainment which Shakespeare made of the History Play in the 1590s?

The answer is complex. Some dramatists responded to the time in this way. George Peele's *Famous Chronicle of King Edward* (1590–3) is an example, a drama with some strong patriotic features; another is *The Reign of King Edward III*, to which Shakespeare may even have contributed. But the general notion that the History Plays of the 1590s had a didactic relation to their times does not necessarily imply that they in effect depicted their times. The relationship may rather have been one of deliberate and significant contrast, yet such a contrast is in itself complex not simple. Thus when King Henry IV wished to urge a moral upon his erring son he contrasted him, in a familiar human way, with his own youth. At the same time this contrast was supported by comparisons likening the young Prince to the fallen Richard and the young Bolingbroke to the valiant but disaffected Hotspur, 'As thou art to this hour was Richard then | . . . And even as I was then is Percy now' (*1 Henry IV*, III. ii. 93–5). In the event neither contrast nor parallels were fulfilled as the King forecast, history was not to repeat itself in quite that way, yet the intelligence and relevance of his diagnosis remains striking. The King's words, in their linked pattern of similitude within dissimilitude, offer a brief model of how the Histories might relate to their own age.

---

[2] Raphael Holinshed, *The Chronicles of England, Scotland and Ireland* (1587), iii. 1, 317, 412.

Comparison between drama and times, however, must be based so far as possible on contemporary witness. Especially is this important with Queen Elizabeth who has enjoyed an exceptionally favourable reputation in the eyes of posterity. By contrast with the disasters between Crown and Parliament in the seventeenth century Elizabeth's tense relations with her Parliaments have seemed sheer harmony. In his *Remarks on the History of England* (1730–1) Bolingbroke appropriated into his Tory polemic the Country or Old Whiggish tradition in favour of Elizabeth, showing her (by contrast with the reigning Hanoverian line) to have been the exemplary patriot prince. The Whig Interpretation of History paid tribute to her; and it may seem that from the eulogistic allegories of *The Faerie Queene* to the work of Sir John Neale the golden reputation has passed without challenge. But golden ages rarely seem gold at the time, and certainly not from every angle. In an attempt to secure a closer view of the reign of Elizabeth, from which to approach the Histories, I propose to draw on the record of her contemporary, William Camden.

I

Camden's may be thought the most central single account available. His *Annales Rerum Anglicarum et Hibernicarum regnante Elizabetha* (1615, 1627; trans. into English by 1629) was written between 1608 and 1617, on the original encouragement of Lord Burghley, the Queen's Secretary from 1559–?99. From 1597 Camden was permitted to use Burghley's and the Queen's papers; he had himself lived through the years of his narrative, and seems to have been an eyewitness at the great state trials of the reign. His bias was neither towards the Puritan nor Papist interests in the state but was inclined, as one might expect, to agree with the policies of the Cecils. In one respect one might need to be wary of Camden as a witness: like the Cecils at the end of the reign he seems to have favoured the claim of James VI of Scotland to succeed Elizabeth and, putting together his narrative during the English reign of James, probably made that succession seem more certain and desirable than it appeared while Elizabeth lived, and to those outside the confidential statesmen's view. On the other hand, by writing after the event, and by not publishing the second part during his own life, Camden was able to

tell far more than he could have published at the time. The danger
of retrospective interpretation is thus outweighed by the possibility
of retrospective free speech.

What was Camden's conception of history? What were for him
the chief features of Elizabeth's reign? His announced method for
his History was archival, documentary, oral, and judicious.

I procured all the Helps I possibly could for writing it: Charters and Grants
of Kings and great Personages, Letters, Consultations in the Council-
Chamber, Embassadours Instructions and Epistles I carefully turned over
and over; the Parliamentary Diaries, Acts and Statutes I thoroughly perused,
and read over every Edict or Proclamation . . .
  Mine own Cabinets and Writings I also searched into: who though I have
been a studious Regarder and Admirer of venerable Antiquity, yet have I
not been altogether careless of later and more modern Occurrences; but
have myself seen and observed many things, and received others from
credible Persons that have been before me, men who have been present at
the transacting of Matters, and such as have been addicted to the Parties on
both Sides in this contrariety of Religion. All which I have in the Balance of
mine own Judgement (such as it is) weighed and examined, lest I should at
any time through a beguiling Credulity incline to that which is false. For the
Love of Truth, as it hath been the onely Incitement to me to undertake this
Work; so hath it also been my onely Scope and Aim in it.

For Camden the 'things proper to History' are 'Affairs of War and
Policy', 'Businesses of greatest Weight and Importance', 'not onely
the Events of Affairs, but also the Reasons and Causes thereof . . .'[3]
History, then, he saw as the realm of high policy. Little attention is
paid to social or economic affairs. Surprisingly little attention is here
paid by the author of *Britannia* (1586) to the life of the regions.
Again, his historical vision is not strikingly providential, but *po-
litique*, with a realistic and sophisticated grasp of the art of the
possible. Though a pious and orthodox Protestant he has nothing
like the grand providential perspective of Foxe or the chronicler
Hall. As he looked back at the reign of Elizabeth, year by year, he
saw a repeated series of attempts, often unsuccessful, to gain ad-
vantage and to guard against danger. At the very centre of his

[3] The passages are drawn from Wallace T. MacCaffrey's abridgement of the
Annales (*The History of the Most Renowned and Victorious Princess Elizabeth . . .
Selected Chapters* (1970), 4–6). All subsequent quotations are from the earlier
English translation by 'R.N. [Norton]' (3rd edn., 1635), with page references to this
version. On Camden, see Hugh Trevor-Roper, *Queen Elizabeth's First Historian:
William Camden and The Beginnings of English Civil History* (1971).

perspective and as the major issue of the reign, the great matter of the royal succession, with its ramifications in the several marriage proposals to the Queen, in foreign and home policy, in the dilemma over Mary, Queen of Scots, and above all in the prospect for England on the death of Elizabeth, seized Camden's attention. Next to this, military campaigns abroad, in the Netherlands, France, and Ireland, fill his pages; some of his most memorable narrative is of naval expeditions; and the sack of Cadiz surely equals the trial of Mary, Queen of Scots, in evoking in the annalist all that is intensely dramatic.

At the opening of his *Annals* Camden alludes to 'the most un-doubted Title to the succession' of the Lady Elizabeth.[4] His preced-ing Introduction, however, disclosed some of the problems of her title: that at one stage Henry VIII himself pronounced by authority of Parliament that his first two marriages were null and the Ladies Mary and Elizabeth illegitimate; and that though Henry later estab-lished them in the succession after Prince Edward the earlier act was never repealed.[5] The amazing vicissitudes of the succession question in Henry's reign were outlined in Holinshed with such marked discretion as was bound to raise questions in the reader's mind. Partisans of Lady Jane Grey had further arguments against the claim of Henry's daughters, while Mary I during the course of her reign affirmed (what Henry had banned by his will) 'that *Mary* Queene of *Scots* was the certaine and undoubted heire to the Crowne of England next after her selfe', a view likely to have been shared by all Roman Catholics who held that Henry VIII's marriage to Anne Boleyn had been illegitimate (Introduction, n.p.). Mary Stuart had indeed an exceptionally strong hereditary claim, being a direct descendant of Margaret Tudor, elder sister of Henry VIII. The French raised the issue in the first months of Elizabeth's reign. 'What was the meaning of their obligation to the Crown of Eng-land', they asked the English ambassadors treating for peace, 'when it was so uncertain who was the rightful possessor of that Crown?'.[6] Elizabeth's indignation when her ambassadors seemed to acknow-

[4] *Annals, Or, The Historie of The Most Renowned and Victorious Princesse Elizabeth, Late Queen of England . . . Translated into English by R.N.* (3rd edn., 1635), 2.
[5] J. B. Black, *The Reign of Elizabeth* (Oxford, 1936), 15.
[6] Wallace T. MacCaffrey, *The Shaping of the Elizabethan Regime* (Princeton, 1968), 42–3.

ledge this legal problem makes clear what is borne out by virtually all her subsequent announcements and acts of policy: that she maintained her title to its full strength, her hereditary right as next successor by nearness of blood to her father after Edward VI and Mary I, a title endorsed by both Henry's will and by Parliament. That even in her later years she was defensive on the matter is suggested by her famous rebuke to the importunate ambassador of the elected King of Poland in 1597, 'a young man, and lately advanced to the Crowne, not by ordinary succession of bloud, but by election'.[7] Elizabeth never conceded any mitigation of her right by blood. Her title was, nevertheless, deeply involved in the great religious conflicts of the time. At the end of her reign Sir John Harington was to make the *politique* observation that because, after Edward VI, the nation wished for Mary, it had also to wish a reversion to the old faith; and because, after Mary, it wished for Elizabeth it had necessarily and by the very nature of her title to accept a revolution back to Protestantism.[8]

The character of Elizabeth's title in relation to that of her cousin Mary, Queen of Scots, together with the sensational events north of the border that sent Mary a fugitive into England, was to form for Elizabeth an agonizing and irresolvable dilemma which stretched throughout the middle decades of her reign, was a central theme in Camden, and was reflected in at least two celebrated chronicle plays. Meanwhile Elizabeth's early Parliaments, appalled at the prospect for England if the Queen should die, urged her to marry, or at least declare her successor. When she seemed near death of smallpox in October 1562 her Council appear to have been hopelessly divided as to what to do in the event of her death. Some wished to proclaim the Lady Catharine Grey who inherited a right specified in Henry VIII's will; some backed the Earl of Huntingdon, 'the nearest Protestant male in line'; some moved towards the Catholic claimant—or so the Spanish ambassador believed.[9] Yet in her early years several marriage proposals were refused, or failed, above all with the Archduke Charles; and she wisely withdrew from the possibility of marriage with her favourite Robert Dudley. Faced with these problems both Queen and councillors turned to chronicle

    [7] *Annals*, 476–7; she said, in contemptuous Latin, 'non de iure sanguinis sed iure electionis, immo noviter electus' (Cecil to Essex, 26 July 1597; SP Dom. 264 75).
    [8] Sir John Harington, *A Tract on the Succession to the Crown* (1602; 1880), 103.
    [9] MacCaffrey, *Elizabethan Regime*, 108.

material to fortify them in their views. In 1561 Sackville and Norton's *Gorboduc* was performed before the Queen; drawn ultimately from Geoffrey of Monmouth it could hardly have given her more explicit warnings against a divided realm and a disputed succession. The authors were members of Elizabeth's first Parliament; and their well-known play, which has many common features with Shakespeare's *King Lear*, was part of a concerted political campaign to persuade the Queen to settle the succession or marry.[10] Elizabeth for her part, as Camden suggests, reflected:

how great danger would threaten her by having a Successour designed . . . Shee knew that the hopes of competitours would be better kept in, and themselves contained in their duty, while she held them every one in suspence and expectance, and proclaimed none. She knew that children, out of an over-hasty desire to raigne, had taken armes against their owne Parents; neither could there any greater kindnesse be expected from kindred . . . successours in a collatorall line had seldome been proclaimed . . . That the designation also in *England*, had ever beene the undoing of them that had been designed. For *Roger Mortimer* Earle of *March*, designed heire to the Crowne by King *Richard* the second, was in short time extinct: his sonne Edmund was for no other cause shut up in prison in *Ireland* full twenty yeeres, and there languished to death. *Iohn De-la-Poole Earle of Lincoln*, designed Successour by *Richard* the third, when his sonne was dead, was always suspected by *Henry* the seventh, and in the end . . . was slaine in the field; and his brother *Edmund* beheaded under *Henry* the eighth. (*Annals*, 69–70)

Precedent and example reached from what Camden, at least, recognized as the mythical origins of Britain to the lifetime of the Queen's father.

By 1566, the year to which Camden assigns these reflections, Mary, Queen of Scots, now widow of Francis II of France, had come to her native kingdom and, after pursuing or resisting various other marriage prospects, had married Henry Stuart, Lord Darnley, a young English nobleman, ostensibly Protestant but perhaps crypto-Catholic, who had himself some hereditary claim to the English throne. Elizabeth and Mary were each involved in the sixteenth-century pursuit of power in which, short of successful war, dynastic alliance was the most effective means to gain advantage. Elizabeth, the more circumspect and original as it seems in hindsight, pursued trimming and defensive tactics, playing one expectation off against

[10] Ribner, *English History Play*, 37–45; Reese, *The Cease of Majesty*, 70–4.

another, to preserve England's freedom and recently re-established Protestant Church. Mary, bold but more orthodox, made at first sight an intelligent choice. The Darnley match would produce children with an even stronger claim to the English throne than her own; it refrained from committing Scotland to alliance with a great continental power; the marriage was neither powerfully Papist nor Protestant. In addition it involved a moderate but satisfying defiance of Elizabeth's wishes; and, at least at first, Mary and Darnley seem to have been in love. The grave defects of character in the young man who was now Henry, King of Scots, who was soon to be plotting against her, were not yet apparent.

Neither, it would be said, were those of the Queen of Scots herself. In 1567 news out of Scotland stunned the whole of Europe. First the Queen's Secretary, David Rizzio, was murdered in the Queen's very chambers, the King being present and complicit. Next the house of Kirk o'Fields, where the King was asleep in bed, was blown up and the King, escaping the explosion, was strangled in the adjoining orchard. Immediately it was rumoured that this was the work of the Earl of Bothwell, a Protestant noble then high in favour with the Queen. A Parliament was called to investigate the murder and punish the culprits. Bothwell was arraigned but (his chief accuser intimidated from attending) was acquitted. Hard on the heels of this acquittal Bothwell was created Duke of Orkney, divorced from his wife, and, on 15 May 1567, married to the Queen. Mary said her lords, whether from underhand motives or no, forced this decision on her, arguing that she needed the guidance of a husband.[11]

Whether to be more impressed by the folly or the wickedness of these deeds it was hard to know. Rumour that Mary herself had connived at the murder by Bothwell of her own husband the King was soon fanned to an overwhelming flame. She and the Duke withdrew from their capital. Their troops soon confronted those of a confederate group of lords led by Mary's illegitimate brother the Earl of Moray, bent on the capture of the Queen and avenging the death of the late King. At the surrender of Carberry Hill Bothwell fled abroad; Mary submitted to captivity. Moray was now supreme, acting in the name of the infant Prince James who, between the murder of Rizzio and the murder of King Henry, was born into this unnatural scene. In prison and threatened with trial and execution,

---

[11] Lady Antonia Fraser, *Mary Queen of Scots* (1969), 382.

Mary 'resigned the Kingdome to her sonne', 'constituted *Murray* to be Vice-Roy', 'And forthwith signified to the Queene of *England* by *Throckmorton*, that she had resigned by constraint, and had against her will subscribed to the instrument of her resignation, by the advice of *Throckmorton*', who had persuaded her, 'that the resignation extorted in prison, *which is a iust feare*, was utterly voyd'.[12] Next year she escaped from her prison in Lochleven, raised an army, was defeated by the superior force of Moray at the Battle of Langside, and fled into England, arriving by boat at Workington in Cumberland on 17 May, and appealing to Elizabeth for help.

The truth behind these events may never be known. Partly because of the secrecy of those who planned the murder; and partly because two opposed campaigns of propaganda subsequently occupied the field of events. The first, in which the leading writer was the famous humanist and Latin poet George Buchanan, charged Mary in his *Detectio* (1571) with contriving and abetting the assassination of the King in order to replace him by her lover, Bothwell. Great stress was laid on the ugly skin disease (smallpox or syphilis) from which King Henry had suffered shortly before the murder, the consequence, it was alleged, of an attempt by Mary to kill him by poison. The brief period of mourning and the shockingly hasty marriage to Bothwell, with the King but three months dead—these points and a wealth of other circumstantial but inconclusive evidence including the forged or partly forged Casket Letters purporting to prove early complicity with Bothwell seemed enough to depose and perhaps execute Mary, to make way for the Regent Moray ruling in the name of the infant James. Mary was early compared with Queen Clytemnestra who murdered her royal husband Agamemnon so that her lover Aegisthus might usurp the throne; the comparison, perhaps first used by Robert Semphill, 'Scottish politician and ballad writer', carried the implication that Orestes or those acting on his part would ultimately avenge his royal father's murder.[13] A play of Orestes and 'Tragedie of the kinge of Scottes' was played before Queen Elizabeth in the winter of 1567–8, and may have been the drama we now know as *Horestes* by John Pikeryng, probably of Lincoln's Inn and later Speaker of the House of Commons and Lord Keeper. *Horestes* (1567), the first English revenge drama, was based

---

[12] *Annals*, 80.
[13] Marie Axton (ed.), *Three Tudor Classical Interludes* (Woodbridge, 1982), 29–30.

on Lydgate's story in the *Troy Book*, and, in its political aspect, was a distinct reminder of contemporary figures: Clytemnestra of Mary, Agamemnon of Henry, Egistus of Bothwell, Idumeus of Elizabeth or English counsel, and Horestes of James and his self-proclaimed party, the confederate lords. The drama is aware of the ill motive which might spur unnatural revenge by a son upon a mother, but sets against that the concept of judicial redress in a necessary act of state. As François de Belleforest was to put it in his story of Hamlet in 1582: '. . . ou le public est interesse, le desir de vengeance, ne peut porter, tant s'en faut tiltre de condemnation, que plutost est louable, et digne de recommendation et recompense'.[14] A major origin of English Revenge Drama was in fact this 'tragedie' of high politics and its exploitation in contemporary propaganda.

The other side of the case began with the messages to England and France which Mary sent immediately after marrying Bothwell. On her arrival in England she was persuaded to submit to a hearing at York between the claims of her accusers, Moray and the confederate lords, and the representatives of her own party in Scotland. Chief among these was John Leslie, Bishop of Ross, who at York accused Moray of rebellion against his sovereign, and who soon published, according to Camden with Elizabeth's encouragement,[15] *A Defence of the honour of . . . Marie Queene of Scotlande . . .* (1569). In this passionately indignant and often highly rhetorical work Leslie not only accuses Moray and the lords of rebellion, but roundly charges Moray of contriving the murder of the King by Bothwell, the subsequent marriage of the Queen, and the blackening of her character, so that he might depose her, and seize the power which as her bastard brother he felt and sometimes pretended should have been his own. This defence of Mary is accepted by Camden (*Annals*, 76–8).[16] Leslie urges Elizabeth to restore Mary to her kingdom, pointing out that Scotland had given refuge to the fugitive Henry VI, and that 'our noble Cordell' (Cordelia) 'sett up agayne in the Royall throne of our Britannie, her father driven from thence by hys two other unkynde and vnnaturall daughters' (The Author To The Gentle Reader). At a later point, drawing on the Scottish chronicler Boece, he likens Moray's crime to that of Dunwaldus in 'the tragical

---

[14] Israel Gollancz (ed.), *The Source of Hamlet* (1926), 260.

[15] *Annals*, 113.

[16] See too Trevor Roper, *Elizabeth's First Historian*, 13, 30–2.

hystorie' of his murder of kinge Duffus, in a passage which Shakespeare may have remembered when he wrote *Macbeth*.[17] Leslie's *Defence* not only asserted Mary's innocence of the murder but, in Part II (1571), the strength of her hereditary claim to the throne of England; and in Part III he defended descent through a female line, and the 'regiment of women' (recently challenged by John Knox against this interest of Mary), when hereditary succession gave them the title to a crown.

The terrible allegations against Mary were neither dispelled nor demonstrated. Her refuge in England grew into captivity; while for Elizabeth the advantage of having her rival and chief claimant to the succession in her power grew, equally, into a moral and political trap. The inherent importance of Mary as rightful Queen of Scots and lineal heir to the crown of England bore out, in a way, Elizabeth's doubts concerning designated successors. Knowingly or unknowingly Mary became the focus of successive plots, not at first against Elizabeth, but at the least seeking to create a base for future power and influence independent of Elizabeth's wishes. The Revolt of the Northern Earls was linked with a scheme that the Duke of Norfolk should marry Mary—a proposal to assure the future backed at one time or another by several of Elizabeth's councillors, Leicester not excluded. But Norfolk lacked the decision to act at the right moment, with the result that in the north the rebellion of the Earls of Northumberland and Westmorland was deprived of a crucial focus and support in the south. Northumberland and Westmorland now went into exile. Norfolk was under a cloud. Then there began to be discovered the elaborate ramifications of the Ridolphi Plot, not unconnected with the Northern Rebellion but aiming at the replacement of Elizabeth by Mary with the help of foreign troops. Now Norfolk was tried and went to his death. Northumberland was captured and executed likewise.

In 1570 Pope Pius V, by his Bull *Regnans in Excelsis*, had placed Elizabeth under papal interdict.[18] She was now declared a heretic, deprived of 'her pretended title to the Kingdome' and her subjects absolved from their oaths of allegiance and obedience to her.[19] Parliament now pressed Elizabeth to try to execute Mary, to deny her regality within England, and repudiate any claim in her or

[17] Geoffrey Bullough (ed.), *Narrative and Dramatic Sources of Shakespeare* (1957–75), vii. 441–2.
[18] *Annals*, 124–6.   [19] Ibid.

her successors to the English crown. Elizabeth, however, neither signed nor vetoed the formidable bill to this effect with which Parliament presented her. Parliament was prorogued and the matter deferred.

Impressed anew with the need to break England's isolation and assure the future, Elizabeth 'was driven to serious cogitations of marriage by a double feare, in regard of lacke of children; on the one side by doubt of contempt at home, and on the other side, by feare of attempts abroad. Against both which shee persuaded her selfe, and often spake it to others, that an Husband and children would bee most strong Bulwarkes'.[20] The match in view was now with Francis, duc d'Alençon, one of the younger brothers of Charles IX of France, Charles seeming at the time to be compromising with his Protestant subjects. But Alençon had the reputation in England of being hostile to Protestantism; he was unpopular, and Elizabeth once again found occasion to temporize and hold the marriage at bay. That was in 1573. Negotiations came to a head, however, in 1581, when Alençon had become the duc d'Anjou. The terms, as Camden sets them out,[21] are eloquent of the anxieties felt in England at the prospect of a close dynastic link with a powerful Catholic power. Anjou conducted a long wooing at the height of which the Queen drew a ring from her finger and put it on one of his. This was taken as a sign of betrothal: 'some leaped for ioy, some were astonished, and some were cast downe with sorrow . . . *Leicester* . . . fretted as if the Queene, the Realme, and Religion were now undone.' That evening the Queen's women wailed and terrified her with their anguish. After a sleepless night she summoned Anjou to her, and had a long private conversation: 'He at length withdrawing himselfe to his Chamber, cast the ring from him, and soone tooke it againe, taxing with one or two quippes the lightnesse of women, and the inconstancy of Ilanders.'[22]

Camden follows up this admirable narrative anticlimax with an extended exposition of the Queen's thoughts: it is in effect a royal soliloquy:

The Queene cast in her troubled minde the things which she had heard of *Burghley* and *Sussex*; that unlesse she married the Duke of *Anjou*, the *League of offence* could not be hoped for from the *French* King; that she alone was too weak to withstand the greatnesse of the *Spaniard*, who

[20] *Annals*, 169.   [21] *Annals*, 232–4.   [22] *Annals*, 235.

tendering his daughter in marriage to the King of *Scots*, would easily draw to the *Scottish* King's party all the Papists in *England*, all the fugitives, all the rebels, all that were weary of the present government . . . That the hope of good men which trusted upon the Queenes issue by this marriage would be frustrate, who now neglecting her, would cast their eyes upon some of the *Competitors* . . .

Among these most perplexed cogitations of marriage, into which the consideration of the times had out of a certaine necessitie often times cast her, some were of opinion that she was fully resolved in minde, that she might better provide both for the Common-wealth and her owne glory by an unmarried life, than by marriage; foreseeing that if she married a Subject, she should draw dishonour upon herselfe by disparagement, and give fire to domesticall grudges and commotions; and if a stranger, she should subject both her selfe and her people under a forreine yoke, and endanger Religion: Not forgetting how unhappie had beene the marriage of her sister Queen *Mary* with King *Philip* a forreiner; and how unluckye that marriage of her great grandfather *Edward* the fourth . . . (*Annals*, 235–6)

Nothing could better demonstrate the insecurity of Elizabeth's government, the crucial importance of the dynastic issue, and the relevance of historical examples to current decision.

From the pages of Camden the situation of England at this time seems daunting and treacherous. Conspiracies against the young King James in Scotland were matched by new conspiracies in England against Elizabeth and on behalf of the imprisoned Mary. But there was sinister dealing here; Camden tells how 'to grope men's minds there were used some subtle devises indeed, counterfeit letters were privily sent under the names of the Queen of *Scots* . . . spies were sent abroad every where to gather rumours, and lay hold of words . . .'[23] Mary was committed to new and more severe keepers '(as some thought) that being driven into despaire, she might be the more subject to dangerous counsailes and treacherous plots . . . and *Leicester* (who was thought to cast in his head to prevent the lawfull succession) sent privily certaine murderers (as some say) to take away her life'.[24] At the very time when Elizabeth had somewhat strengthened her situation by concluding a League of Amity with James, the evidence of 'a most dangerous conspiracy' or linked series of conspiracies against her was brought to light: the second and final great crisis of Mary, Queen of Scots, in England. The Babington Conspiracy, involving invasion from abroad, the

[23] *Annals*, 261–2.   [24] *Annals*, 269.

liberation of Mary, and the killing of Elizabeth was thus discovered. It quite defeated the Queen's difficult but hitherto successful policy of procrastination. Parliament, frustrated in its desire for the trial and execution of Mary earlier, could hardly now be denied. Though Mary repudiated the right of any English court to try her and insisted on her status as a free sovereign prince, she was brought to trial before a special commission. The verdict was a foregone conclusion. Despairing of assistance from Elizabeth, Mary had no doubt been driven to acquiesce in desperate measures, though how far she was accessory to the most violent designs of the conspirators cannot be known.

At this point Camden again attempts to enter into 'the Queene's wavering and perplexed minde . . . whether it were better to put her to death or spare her'. She considered the danger of either course and they appeared equal. For every argument of her own, however, Camden attributes ten or more to the courtiers, and all in favour of sentencing Mary to death. Most interesting are the examples they propounded 'at home in our owne Country' (for what is done by examples, is done more excusably)':

how the Kings of *England* for their owne security have borne themselves toward their owne kinsmen and Competitors; namely, *Henry* the 1. toward *Robert* his elder brother; *Edward* the 3. or rather his mother toward *Edward* the 2. *Henry* the 4. toward *Richard* the 2. *Edward* the 4 toward *Henry* the 6. and his sonne the Prince of Wales, and toward his owne brother *George* Duke of *Clarence*; *Henry* the 7 toward *Warwicke* the Duke of *Clarence* his young sonne; and *Henry* the 8. toward *De la Poole* Earle of *Suffolke*, *Margaret* Countesse of *Salisbury*, and *Courtney* Marquesse of *Excester*: All which were for light causes (if their faults were compared with hers) made away. And not onely Courtiers used these perswasions to the Queene, but certaine Preachers also more sharply, and some of the vulgar sort, either in hope or feare, more sawcily exercised their wits at their pleasure in this argument. (*Annals*, 338–40)

It is notable that this persuasion by precedent spilled over into the popular communication of the pulpit.

Staggered and perplexed, Elizabeth 'gave her selfe over to solitarines' muttering to herself '*Aut fer, aut feri*, that is, Either beare strokes, or strike, and . . . *Ne feriare, feri*, that is Strike, lest thou be stricken'. So different is the account of Camden's prose annals from the idealizing account to be published some ten years later in the

Faerie Queene, Books IV–VI.[25] Finally, by a writing to her Secretary, Davison, signed in her own hand, she ordered a warrant for Mary's execution to be drawn up under the great seal, to be kept in readiness, for there was then a yet further plot against her own life. The next day she countermanded the order, and when Davison told her the warrant had already passed the seal, rebuked him for his haste. The implication of this is that it was her intention to have the warrant kept secret but ready for instant use. Davison, however, acquainted the Council who, 'being apt to believe what they desired', gave the necessary orders for the long-imprisoned Queen to be executed at last.[26] Mary played the last act of her life in 'the Theatre of the whole world',[27] Camden's narrative of it being a high point in the literature of that age. When the news was brought to Elizabeth, 'who little thought it, that the Queene of *Scots* was put to death, she heard it with great indignation, her countenance and her words failed her, and with excessive sorrow she was in a manner astonished . . .'[28] Her Council was rebuked and Davison imprisoned in the Tower. This was the public explanation of what happened; Camden adheres to it consistently. His subsequent narrative of the trial and defence of Davison does, however, give ample evidence that Elizabeth wished both to execute the warrant and lay the blame on others. But Davison's explanation also affords evidence for a third interpretation: that Elizabeth in the end preferred that Mary should be assassinated. This is the conclusion of Sir John Neale, Elizabeth's warmest defender in our time.[29]

It is to be observed that the quoted examples of kinsmen and competitors of English monarchs made away with is a list of those assassinated. What was new about the death of Mary was the civil process. 'What disturbed Elizabeth most profoundly . . . was the

---

[25] But she, whose Princely breast was touched nere
   With piteous ruth of her so wretched plight,
   Though plaine she saw by all, that she did heare,
   That she of death was guiltie found by right,
   Yet would not let iust vengeance on her light;
   But rather let in stead thereof to fall
   Few perling drops from her faire lampes of light;
   The which she couering with her purple pall
   Would haue the passion hid, and vp arose withall.

(*The Faerie Queene*, v. ix. 50)

[26] *Annals*, 340.   [27] *Annals*, 313; See Frontispiece.   [28] *Annals*, 345.
[29] Sir John Neale, *Elizabeth I and Her Parliaments*, 1584–1601 (1957), 137–42.

sacrilege of subjecting an anointed Queen to public execution'.[30] Camden includes an Epitaph set up near Mary's tomb, 'and soone after taken away'. This ran in part: 'A new and unexampled kinde of tombe is here extant, wherein the living are included with the dead, for know, that with the sacred hearse of Saint Mary here lyeth violate and prostrate the majestie of all Kings and Princes'.[31] When, in the next century, Milton came to defend in *The Tenure of Kings and Magistrates* the trial and execution of Charles I he did not fail to cite the life and death of Mary, Queen of Scots, as a supporting precedent. Elizabeth, in self-defence, had struck a terrible blow at royal sovereignty.

With the death of Mary Stuart in 1587 we are close to the decade in which Shakespeare's History Plays were written. The historical experience as Camden records it, however, includes the one piece of consummate statecraft that the Queen salvaged from the wreck of these remarkable events: by her specific intervention it was provided that the sentence against Mary derogated nothing from any title in James to the English throne.[32] It also includes the expedition of that famous '*Spanish* fleet, being the best appointed of men, munition, and all manner of provision, of all that ever the Ocean saw, and called by the arrogant name of *Invincible* . . .'[33] This fleet was assailed three times by the English before coming to anchor before Calais. At that crucial juncture the Prince of Parma, Viceroy of the Netherlands, was not ready with his supply of flat-bottomed boats and provisions necessary for the actual invasion. An attack by English fire-ships and a further sea battle ensued when a strong west-north-west wind threatened to drive the Spaniards 'upon the sands and shallows neere *Zeeland*'; the English gave up the chase, the wind changed into west-south-west carrying the armada clear of the shallows, and by common consent they resolved to return to Spain 'by the North Ocean'. While the Spanish landing was still expected, Camden relates, the Queen reviewed her army at Tilbury, 'walking through the ranks of armed men . . . with a Leaders trunchion in her hand, sometimes with a martiall pace, and sometimes like a woman, incredible it is how much she strengthened the hearts of her Captains and Souldiers by her presence and speech'. Camden concludes, as he is also to do in his account of the sack of Cadiz, by marvelling that so many were lost from the stronger side, 'not an

[30] Neale, *Elizabeth I and Her Parliaments*, 13.   [31] *Annals*, 343–4.
[32] Ibid. 324; Neale, *Elizabeth I and Her Parliaments*, 135.   [33] *Annals*, 365.

hundred of the *English* being lacking, nor one small ship lost, save
onely that of *Cock's*: . . . *Venit, vidit, fugit.*'³⁴ Yet he continues on a
sombre note: 'As *England* was troubled with outward warre, so did
it travaille this yeere of an inward schisme also: (for schisme ever-
more springeth up most rankly in the heate of warre)' and he moves
into a discussion of Martin Marprelate and the Puritan urge for
innovation in religion.³⁵ Finally Camden's account, which has at-
tended frequently to the hostilities between Catholics and Protes-
tants in France, now focuses on French affairs as they develop into
full-scale civil war. Here were striking analogies with what until
recently the English had so feared, the conflict between religion and
hereditary right, for Henry III had no issue, Anjou who had wooed
Elizabeth was now dead without issue, and the next heir, the King
of Navarre, was a Protestant. Backed by Spain and the Pope the
Catholic nobility of France formed themselves into a League on oath
to oppose any Protestant on the French throne. In 1589 Elizabeth
assisted Navarre and Henry III against the League; the Catholics
talked of changing the form of their state from a monarchy; the
King, fleeing for safety to the Protestants, was assassinated by
Catholic monks; the Cardinal of Bourbon was proclaimed Charles
X of France; and England committed more money and troops in
support of Navarre's fight for the throne to which he was the lineal
successor.³⁶ Before the end of the year four thousand English troops
under Lord Willoughby had been among those who assailed Paris in
the interest of Navarre, Henry IV, and had done 'stout service' in
securing several French cities for the King. Soon fears began to arise
that Spain would intervene from the Netherlands on the side of the
League, and would secure ports and bases in Brittany. Anxious
attention began to be focused on Rouen to which in 1592 Elizabeth
was to dispatch a further force under the command of the young
Earl of Essex.

II

The problems and conflicts inherent in Elizabeth's reign were high-
lighted, from one side or another, by the political and religious
writers of her time. The clash between Buchanan and Leslie on the

³⁴ *Annals*, 366–71.   ³⁵ *Annals*, 374.   ³⁶ *Annals*, 385–7.

conduct of Mary, Queen of Scots, became a disagreement, at the theoretical level, concerning the nature of kingship. While Buchanan argued elsewhere that monarchs might be deposed if they violated their contract with their people, and that individuals might use violence against a tyrant, Leslie adhered firmly to the doctrine of indefeasible hereditary right. A strong Protestant light was thrown on this divergence by a book published before the sensational events of Mary's Scottish years: the important and influential *Actes and Monuments* of John Foxe, the Protestant martyrologist, first published in 1563, and ordered to be placed in parish churches along with the Book of Homilies and certain of Erasmus's Commentaries. It has long been recognized that in Foxe's exposition of the origins and history of Protestantism the reign of King John was of crucial importance, for in John could be found an example of an early English monarch who defied—at first with success—the spiritual and political authority of the Pope. To the 'apocalyptic nationalism' of Bale and Foxe,[37] John seemed a tragic forerunner of Henry VIII, Edward VI, and Elizabeth. As it happens, however, the example of John touched another nerve in Elizabethan consciousness, for in terms of indefeasible hereditary right he had had a less strong claim to the throne of England than his nephew Arthur, son of his elder brother Geoffrey, and designated successor of Richard I, the previous king. Foxe's elevation of John to a place of honour in the new myth of Protestant England thus constituted a revolutionary precedent for the setting aside of the *de jure* prince on grounds of religion. John Ponet in his *Short Treatise of Politic Power* (1556) and Christopher Goodman in *How Superior Powers Ought to be Obeyed* (1558) had recently set forth some of the grounds and modes of resistance to princes. Foxe does not greatly insist on this implication, but his few words on the crowning of John suggest a covenant rather than the recognition of absolute right, the Archbishop charging him 'not to presume to take on hym this dignitie' unless he was ready to serve God and the laws.[38] It is not until John has fought with the King of France, won, and captured Arthur, that we hear of the latter's claim to be 'the lawful heyre of the crowne'. The question of John's complicity in the death of Arthur is played

<hr/>

[37] Quentin Skinner, *The Foundations of Modern Political Thought* (Cambridge, 1978), ii. 107.

[38] John Foxe, *Actes and Monuments* . . . (1563), fo. 71ᵛ. (Foliation and pagination are inconsistent.)

down: 'the Lorde knoweth'.[39] All this occurs early in the reign; and no connection is proposed between these events and John's subsequent defiance of the Pope, or his suffering of invasion and rebellion.

In 1569 there was published *Certayne Sermons appoynted by the Queenes Maiestie . . . [The Book of Homilies]*. Its 'exhortation, concerning good order and obedience to Rulers and Maiestrates' makes the simplest possible appeal, stating that kings and magistrates derive their authority from God not Rome, and quoting Paul from Romans 13 concerning the duty of the Christian to obey the higher powers; 'the powers that be, be ordeyned of God'. Since princes and magistrates are 'Gods lieuetenauntes' it is wrong to disobey even a wicked or a pagan ruler, even in self-defence. Only if they command against the will of God may the subject disobey, and even then he may not rebel or 'withstand violently'. This Homily offers no guidance to the subject confronted by rival claimants to the throne, but makes it abundantly clear that at the present time and in England Elizabeth is Queen (she is twice named). These are not just the urgent and pragmatic injunctions of a precariously re-established Protestant monarchy, vulnerable to rebellion at home and invasion from abroad. They correspond in their simplicity to the earlier teaching of Luther that the ruler is absolute under God, though they do not incorporate his later belief that the subject might have grounds for resisting his prince. In 1571, after the Northern Rebellion, the 'Homilie against disobedience and wilfull rebellion' was added to the *Book of Homilies*. Its argument is the same as that of the earlier Homily, though it adds the point that if subjects reform their own conduct God will either remove an evil prince or reform him. It is, however, altogether more vehement, copious, and scathing. It notes that Lucifer was the first rebel, and does not hesitate to claim that rebels spread diseases by congregating together in the open. In the Sixth Part,[40] it adds to its biblical examples that of the reign of King John, placed under papal interdict for defending his 'auncient right' to appoint the Archbishop of Canterbury. It shows how the Pope pretended to dissolve the oaths of loyalty of John's subjects, and sent the Dauphin of France to depose 'their naturall soveraigne lorde the king of *England*'. John was obliged to submit, and in consequence England was unable to

[39] Foxe, *Actes and Monuments*, fo. 71ᵛ.
[40] As Lily B. Campbell has pointed out, *Shakespeare's 'Histories'*, 143-4.

rid itself of these 'most greedie Romish wolues' until Henry VIII,
Edward VI, and Elizabeth. This Homily goes a little way towards
meeting the problem of rival claimants: you must not support an
invading foreign prince backed by the Pope. But that is as far as the
Homilies help. It is hard to argue from them that Elizabethans
believed in obedience to the *de facto* ruler, for the *de jure/de facto*
distinction is unknown to the Homilies. Despite the effective use of
John's reign as a warning example, the rival claims of John and
Arthur are not even mentioned. The Homilies, influential as they
were, were not designed to go into the difficult questions of conflict-
ing title.

Leslie's approach was very different. To Leslie John was a usurper,
and his whole reign could be seen as the moral consequence of
that original wrong: 'The pitiful reigne of the said John who doth
not lament, with the lamentable losse of Normandie, Aquitaine, and
the possibilitie of the Dukedome of Britanie, and with the losse of
other our goodlie possessions in France, whereof the Croune of
England was robbed and spoiled by the unlawful usurping of him
against his nephew Arthur. Wel let vs leave these greuouse and
lothsome remembrances . . .'.[41] For Leslie, right lies 'where God and
the lawe hath placed it'; though kings were originally chosen for
their quality and worth now they are recognized by succession and
blood. As Arthur once was so is Mary now. As for Foxe, so, in a
very different light, for Leslie, the role of John is also the role of
Elizabeth.[42]

Only four years after this, those like Leslie—or like Elizabeth—
who adhered to the doctrine of indefeasible hereditary right received
powerful support from the great work of Jean Bodin, *Les Six Livres
de la république* (1576). Bodin comes out in favour of monarchy as
the highest form of government, of royal or hereditary monarchy
ordained by God and enshrined in law as the highest form of
monarchy, and of the king (in such a state) as the embodiment of its
sovereignty, to whom subjects owe obedience whether he rule well
or ill. The true royal monarch, however, is marked out by the lustre
of natural justice, brighter than the light of the sun itself; and
observes the laws of nature as his people observe the laws of their
prince, the law 'being on both sides a mistresse, or . . . a queene
raigning over both, it shall in the same bonds unite the subjects

---

[41] *A Defence*, Book II (Liege, 1571), fo. 29^v.
[42] Ibid., Book II, fo. 6.

among themselves, and together with their prince: whereof shall grow a most sweet harmony, which may with wonderful pleasure and felicitye blesse them both'.[43] Bodin's conclusions had particular weight for several reasons. First his earlier work, the *Methodus ad Facilem Historiarum Cognitionem* (1566), well known in England, had shown a distinctly constitutionalist emphasis, while in the later *Six Livres* it was clear that the bitter experience of civil war in France had driven him in the absolutist direction: his views thus had the relevance of being forged from the experience of recent troubles, and also had the special interest of referring to contemporary English history. Secondly, the *Six Livres* were perhaps the most ambitious survey of all forms and theories of government, ancient and modern, that had ever been made; Bodin's subtle and analytic mind seemed to have ranged over the totality of political evidence: this above all lent authority to his conclusions. Lastly, the very diversity of his materials drew him into a satisfying complexity of formulation, so that Bodin seemed the very opposite of the thinker who simply confronted the manifold difficulties of the real world with the repetition of a traditional view. Bodin's latest views had 'an immediate and extremely powerful influence'. As early as the 1580s Gabriel Harvey observed that ' "you cannot step into a scholar's study" without the chances, as he put it, being ten to one that you will find him reading either Le Roy on Aristotle or Bodin's *Six Books*'.[44]

No doubt the first point that struck readers of Bodin's *Six Livres* was its advocacy of royal monarchy; indeed the first, only partial, English translation, Charles Merbury's *Briefe Discourse of Royall Monarchie, As Of the Best Common Weale* (London, 1581) is well summarized by its title and does little justice to the range and *politique* complexity of Bodin's thought. To be specific, Bodin clearly acknowledges that different forms of government have been, at one time or another, the legitimate governments of different states. Rome, he sees, was legitimately a republic while in the process of transforming itself, under the Julian house, into the higher political form of a monarchy. Further, of the three kinds of monarchy that he distinguishes, royal monarchy, lordly monarchy,

---

[43] Jean Bodin, *Les Six Livres de la république* (1576), trans. Richard Knolles (1606), ed. K. D. McRae (Cambridge, Mass., 1962), 205; and Book II, chs. 2–4 generally.

[44] Skinner, *Foundations of Modern Political Thought*, ii. 300.

and tyranny, he allows that a state may be transformed from one to another. His definition of the 'lordly Monarchy' is of particular interest; it is 'that where the prince is become lord of the goods and persons of his subiects, by law of armes and lawful warre; gouerning them as the master of a familie doth his slaues.' Nimrod, the fabled first king, was a lordly monarch. Such a monarch is distinguished from the 'lawfull or royall' monarch by his not conceding to his subjects 'their naturall libertie, and proprietie of goods'. Bodin gives two examples, one medieval, one modern. William the Conqueror, having mastered England by force of arms, 'proclaimed, that the soueraigntie and proprietie of al his subiects goods, mouable, and immouable vnto him belonged'—though he later contented himself with the direct sovereignty, fealty, and homage. The Emperor Charles V, on the other hand, having 'subdued the great countrey of Peru, made himselfe to be Lordly Monarch thereof, causing all things to be holden of him . . .'. Both lordly monarchs and royal monarchs are to be distinguished from tyranny often by 'vniust warre', where, 'the prince contemning the lawes of nature and nations, imperiously abuseth the persons of his free-borne subjects, and their goods as his owne'.[45]

In Bodin's thought these distinctions rest primarily on how the monarch governs rather than on how he has succeeded to his throne. He can thus concede that a lordly monarch may become a royal monarch where a just conquest is followed by a restoration of the liberties of the subject.[46] Even a monarchy based on force and illegality may grow into a royal monarchy.[47] Bodin's recognition of the complexities of political reality leads him to give a wide variety of instances of how a royal monarch may succeed to his throne, for while judging 'descent by [hereditary] succession' to be the commonest mode, Bodin allows other forms of just succession: by law, as in France; by election, as in many northern kingdoms; by gift; or by testament, where he most interestingly instances Henry VIII's instatement of Mary and Elizabeth into the succession after Edward, by his final will.[48] Different from these modes of just succession was that of 'Henry of Lancaster the sonne of Iohn of Gaunt' who 'deposed Richard the eldest sonne of Edward the Blacke prince: alleaging that his father being by death preuented, he could not succeed Edward his grandfather in the kingdome: which yet was but

[45] Bodin, Six Livres, Book II, ch. 2, 200–3.   [46] Six Livres, ch. 3, 204.
[47] Six Livres, 205.   [48] Ibid.

an vniust quarrell pickt'.[49] John and Arthur are mentioned in the
same connection, and after full discussion Bodin here supports the
claims of the grandson against the brother of the king.[50]

Bodin's vast range of examples on the question of succession alone
contributed to his fame in a country where the problem of the next
succession continued to defy solution, and the Queen remained
immovably against any declaration, let alone any parliamentary
intervention, in the matter. This last was what that staunch Protes-
tant and parliamentarian Peter Wentworth proposed in his *Pithie
Exhortation To Her Maiestie for Establishing Her Successor To the
Crowne*, published in 1598, but evidently drawn up in 1587. From
the first he hoped that it could be presented to Elizabeth, by Parlia-
ment, by Burghley, or by the young Essex. He sought to build up a
campaign in its support, and his ideas must have begun to get
publicity, for in 1593 he was questioned by a group of the Privy
Council and imprisoned in the Tower, where he continued his
efforts by all means available to him. While the *Pithie Exhortation*
as published in 1598 may well differ from its earlier form, it is
important as a broad indication of the fears and the precedents
which were active in the minds of the more politically conscious
public when Shakespeare began to write his Histories.

Wentworth's examples, largely drawn from English and biblical
history, were most directly addressed to Elizabeth's known reluct-
ance to designate an heir. Henry VIII, he says, recalled the 'mischief
and man-slaughter continued in this Realme betwixt the houses of
York and Lancaster', by which the realm had nearly been destroyed,
and attributed those terrible civil wars to the fact 'that ther had not
sufficient care bene taken to mak publiklie knowne, and to establish
the right of succession'.[51] The Queen is exhorted to remember,
among other examples, the 'lamentable miseries of . . . civill dissen-
sion' after the death of Goborduc and his sons Ferrex and Porrex,
when 'the land was left without a certain known successor'.[52] A
foreign marriage is presented in a very bad light, for that of Mary I
had 'nearly cast out the old inhabitantes, and have had this Ile a
dwelling place for strangers'.[53] Finally he turns to Elizabeth's fear of
deposition by a successor, and we notice here how the problem is

[49] *Six Livres*, Book VI, ch. 5, 738.   [50] *Six Livres*, 740.
[51] Peter Wentworth, *A Pithie Exhortation To Her Majestie for Establishing Her
Successor to the Crowne* (1598), 19–20.
[52] *A Pithie Exhortation*, 30.   [53] *A Pithie Exhortation*, 75.

turned round from those reflections attributed to the Queen in Camden (see p. 19 above): there she feared *for* the successor, here she fears for herself. Edward II, says Wentworth, in an argument unlikely to have pleased the Queen, was not deposed by Edward III, but by the nobility and commons together for being unworthy to be a king.

And king Richard the sec. was deposed, not by one whome he had made his knowne successor, but by Henry the fourth: no successor to him by right, but an vsurper . . . as it doth appear in the storie by 28 articles objected against him at his deposing: wherein his nobility and commons shewed, that they liked rather to haue an vsurper to raigne over them, that would preserue the crowne & them, then a rightfull king that would perill the crowne and state also.

Wentworth is no less trenchant on the troubled reign of Henry VI:

. . . deposed by Edwarde the fourth, who had a present right to the crowne, and was neither heire apparent nor knowne successor vnto him: but he was deposed for the causes, for the which God is often angrie with princes, namelie (as witnesseth the storie) for being to much advised by the wicked counsell of William de la Poole, Duke of Suffolke, by whose meanes (as the historie saith) the good Duke of Glocester, the kings vncle, was put to death: and the countries that the crowne of England did then possesse in France, were delivered and loste: hee being the swallower vp of the kings treasure, wherby the warres were not maintained, and the expeller from the King of all good and vertuous counsellours, and the bringer in, and the advancer of vitious persons, common enemies & apparent adversaries to the publike weale. Heere be manie hard points discovered in a counsellour, the which a wise prince will narrowlie looke into: least anie of his be infected with anie of these faults. His wife also and others did likewise so over-rule him, so that the state was (by his evill governement) greatlie troubled & vexed, and the nobility much perilled. Nowe, King Edward the fift was murdered being but a childe, by his wicked and trayterous vncle Richard the third, who was neither his heire nor successour by right. (*A Pithie Exhortation*, 79–81)

From all this, Wentworth concluded, 'princes are in far more danger, succession not being established, then when it is setled'.[54] He makes a formidable case against Elizabeth's *fear* of a successor which may, in this period of setting and rising suns,[55] have been the chief obstacle to settling the future of England. He does not address

54 *A Pithie Exhortation*, 81–2.
55 *A Pithie Exhortation*, 87–9 for Wentworth's extended metaphor.

himself to Camden's insight that, by keeping the various claimants in hope, the Queen could preserve some advantage for herself and England even into her latest years.

The principles which underlie Wentworth's *Exhortation* are of some interest. He had once been a fierce opponent of the Stuart claim, but that was when Mary lived. It is telling that his campaign to settle the succession originates in the year after the execution of the Queen of Scots, for now there was an excellent opportunity to combine the desire for a Protestant successor with the argument from hereditary right. Wentworth's subsequent writings fully support this: his campaign was in fact to have the King of Scots made the official heir to the English throne. Wentworth's *Discourse Containing the Authors Opinion of the True and Lawfull Successor to her Maiestie* (also first published in 1598) does not hesitate to employ the argument of legal hereditary right; in fact it quotes John Leslie's argument against the impediment to the Stuart claim of Henry VIII's will.[56] He can even set hereditary right to the throne above the authority of Parliament. Yet Wentworth's treatment of his chronicle precedents shows his fundamental difference from Leslie. While Leslie sees political failure as the consequence of usurpation, Wentworth is inclined to see deposition as the result of misrule: he makes much of the faults of Richard II and Henry VI, little of Edward IV's right or Henry IV's lack of right. The execution of Mary had in fact produced a *volte-face* in political argument; Catholics were not now attracted to the hereditary strengths of the Stuart claim, James VI being a Protestant, some preferring the far-fetched hereditary title of the Spanish Infanta. On the other hand Protestants, who had agonized over the conflict of religion with the legal and hereditary argument when Mary lived, now had that powerful argument pointing in the direction of the future they desired. Nothing could better demonstrate the new importance and position of the concept of indefeasible hereditary right than the resort to it at this time by a man such as Peter Wentworth.

This ironical *volte-face*, more apparent in Wentworth's *Discourse* than his *Exhortation*, was partly caused and greatly heightened by the publication in 1594 of the brilliantly provocative *Conference About the Next Succession to the Crowne of Ingland . . . Published*

[56] Peter Wentworth, *Discourse Containing the Authors Opinion of the True and Lawfull Successor to her Maiestie* (1598), 8–9, 42.

by R. Dolman, written by the Jesuit Robert Parsons, possibly with
some collaborators, and dedicated to the Earl of Essex. In the new
situation with Mary dead and the best lineal claimant a Protestant,
Parsons opened up the whole question of the hereditary succession
of kings, stealing the clothes of some of the most radical Protestants
as he did so. In his first chapter he argues that: 'Succession to
Government By Neerness of Blood is Not by law of nature or divine,
but only by humane and positive lawes of every particular common
wealth and consequently may uppon iust causes be altered by the
same'.[57] He states that the British monarchy is mixed in form;[58] that
princes may be restrained or deprived;[59] that Richard II was deposed
by Parliament for misgovernment, that Henry IV was a 'notable'
king and Henry V 'the Alexander of Ingland'.[60] His work has a
distinct Lancastrian flavour, but he dwells on the main troubled
periods of English history, John and Arthur, and Edward II, as well
as the conflict between the Houses of York and Lancaster. He
argues that 'god' favoured the commonwealth's election of John,
when Arthur was defeated: but that later John did evil and was
deposed by the Pope at the request of the 'people',[61] and that Louis
the Dauphin was chosen instead, swearing fealty in London, thus
briefly uniting the crowns of France and England which might have
remained one.[62] Though he recalls the work of his co-religionist
Leslie in defence of Mary, Queen of Scots, Parsons drives to a very
different conclusion: that considerations of religion may be allowed
to determine the succession to a throne. Like Leslie in his *De
Origine, Moribus, et Rebus Gestis Scotorum*,[63] Parsons prints a
genealogical tree to illustrate the succession to the English throne.
But while Leslie's tree pointed unmistakably to the Stuart claim,
Parsons's genealogical table was designed to show the numerous
claimants with some hereditary right. The Spanish Infanta, in sup-
port of whose title Philip II had sent his Armada, was included, but
Parsons professed to think that, for a variety of reasons religious and
nationalistic, the title of the House of Hertford would in the end be
preferred.

[57] Robert Parsons, *A Conference About the Next Succession to the Crowne of
Ingland . . . Published by R. Dolman* (1594), 1.
[58] *A Conference*, 24.   [59] *A Conference*, 37–9.
[60] *A Conference*, 59–60; cf. *Henry V*, IV. vi. 30–2.   [61] *A Conference*, 56.
[62] *A Conference*, 57.
[63] Published in Rome in 1578; see H. N. Paul's valuable study, *The Royal Play of
Macbeth* (New York, 1950), 171–9.

It can be seen that all these British writers use chronicle material as a storehouse of example and precedent. The same is true of those passages in Camden where the Queen is shown resolving upon a course of action, or where her councillors urge a particular decision upon her. Such examples are the armoury of persuasion and may be deployed in one way or another, presented in one or another light, depending upon the argumentative end in view. And while all cite other periods of history, biblical, classical, and British, the reigns of John, Edward II, and of the Houses of Lancaster and York, occur more frequently than the rest. These reigns were controversial and in almost any argument about the succession they were either open for exploitation, or needed to be neutralized as significant counter-instances. In either case a parallel was briefly held in the mind: Elizabeth as John and Mary as Arthur; Elizabeth as John and Louis the Dauphin as Philip of Spain (Foxe); Elizabeth as Richard II and Mary, Queen of Scots, as Mortimer; Elizabeth as Richard II and some powerful subject (Huntington, Derby?) as Henry IV; Elizabeth as Henry IV and Mary, Queen of Scots, as Richard II; Elizabeth as Edward IV and Dudley as Elizabeth Woodville (Camden); Elizabeth as Henry VIII and James VI as Mary I and Elizabeth (Wentworth). An unwelcome parallel could be acknowledged by the need to refute it: Elizabeth as Richard II and James VI as Henry IV, Elizabeth as Henry VI and James VI as Edward IV (Wentworth). With the exception of Bodin who treats historical instances as evidence or illustration, these examples with their implied parallels are part of an overt effort at persuasion or self-persuasion. Their intention and significance is clear.

This is by no means the case, however, with all historical material of the period. Holinshed himself, Shakespeare's major source, is a special case as has been widely recognized. As a compilation from many different sources and the work of several different compilers it was, unlike Hall, not a book with an overall interpretation.[64] This does not mean that Holinshed was uncontroversial or bland. The material on Ireland in Elizabeth's reign was evidently censored (*DNB*), while the account of Henry VIII's marriages is so discreetly superficial as to be problematic. This demonstrates the great delicacy needed in publishing events of the present and recent reigns.

[64] Stephen Booth, *The Book Called Holinshed's Chronicle* (San Francisco, 1968); see also, however, Kelly, *Divine Providence in the England of Shakespeare's Histories*, ch. 6.

Wentworth draws explicitly on Holinshed;[65] it was a useful book for politicians, and might therefore also be abused. Where a single-minded historical work was concerned, a vigilant and suspicious government could be more interested in the author's intentions. An excellent instance of this is afforded by the last work to be discussed in this chapter: Sir John Hayward's *The First Part of the Life and Raigne of King Henrie the IIII* . . . (1599).

There has been much misdirected discussion of Hayward's 'troublesome little work',[66] chiefly through the attempt to show that Hayward's book influenced Shakespeare's *Richard II*. Rather it is likely that Shakespeare influenced Hayward; but, as Lily B. Campbell has concluded, the facts that Hayward's book about the deposition of Richard II was originally dedicated to the Earl of Essex ('Magnus si quidem es, et presenti judicio, et futuri temporis expectatione') as Camden noted;[67] that Hayward was interrogated about it not long before the Essex Rising; and that Essex's followers, as is well known, seem to have arranged for the performance of Shakespeare's *Richard II* on the eve of that rising, provide us 'with a clearly authenticated account of the Elizabethan recognition of history as a political mirror potentially dangerous',[68] whatever reservations we may have about the metaphor of the mirror.

Evidence of how historical material of this kind was read may throw a little light, albeit retrospectively, on how dramatized historical works might be intended. For a work such as Hayward's has at least this in common with a chronicle drama, by contrast with collections of chronicles, that it is a deliberate selection from a much larger stock of materials. In the interrogations of Hayward the question of selection was repeatedly insisted on by Sir Edward Coke:

1   he selecteth a storie 200 yere old, and publisheth it this last yere; intendinge the application of it to this tyme

2   maketh choice of that story only, a king is taxed for misgovernmt, his councell for corrupt and covetous [*sic*] for there priuate the king censured for conferring benefits of hateful parasites and fauorites, the nobles discontented, the commons groning vnder continuall taxation. herevppon the king is deposed, by an erle and in the end murdres [*sic*][69]

---

[65] *Discourse*, 78.

[66] *Richard II*, ed. Peter Ure, New Arden Series (1958), p. lxii.

[67] *Annals*, 530.   [68] Campbell, *Shakespeare's 'Histories'*, 188–9.

[69] Margaret Dowling, 'Sir John Hayward's Troubles Over His Life of *Henry IV*', *Library*, 4th ser. 11 (1931), 213.

Coke's charges became more explicit as the examination went on; his notes speak of Hayward's '(outward) pretence and his secret drift', of his pretension 'to wright a history past but entend to point at this very tyme'; and they ask 'to quo animo & to what end . . . he selecteth this (only) bloody story (out of all the rest) of the (unlawfull deposition of a lawfull kinge that had longe raignes [*sic*] by an erle . . .'.[70] Coke attempted to strengthen his case against Hayward by observing that the book did not even plainly follow the sources for the period of history selected, but imported into them details and remarks from other periods. Thus 'benevolences' as an expedient for raising funds was inserted from the reign of Richard III, while a speech of the Archbishop [of York?] to Bolingbroke had a strikingly modern and *politique* note in its allusion to deposers of kings and princes who had had good success.[71]

Finally, all kinds of detail seem to have struck Coke as possible allusions to Elizabeth. This may be thought surprising: surely the elderly, circumspect, intelligent, and politically successful Virgin Queen, heroine of the Protestant Cause in Europe, had little or nothing in common with the irresponsible, self-indulgent, twice-married Richard II? On the contrary, we have already seen how parallels between the two monarchs had occurred to several observers and writers and even Elizabeth herself. Coke is decisive in the detail he focuses on: first, 'a greate rebellion in Ireland' constituting a challenge inadequately met; subsidies demanded to finance the Irish Wars which other monarchs had nevertheless not needed when *they* put down the Irish; the extreme vulnerability of a prince without heirs, when neither armies nor strongholds are so strong defences as 'the multitude of children'; associations by which subjects swore to protect the monarch—such as had been established by Parliament in the immediate aftermath of the Babington Plot in 1586; and finally other expedients for raising funds which might not have been necessary had the 'greate officers' of the prince cleared themselves of their own debts.[72]

What Elizabeth and the government suspected, and Coke was urged to demonstrate, was that Hayward had employed an implicit historical parallel between Richard II and Elizabeth to urge the deposition of the childless and ageing queen by him who was great

---

[70] 'Hayward's Troubles', 215.   [71] 'Hayward's Troubles', 214.
[72] 'Hayward's Troubles', 213–15.

now and great in future expectation: Essex, 'an erle'. The so far unsuccessful attempt to put down the Irish Rebellion (a suspected sign of disloyalty and conspiracy on Essex's part), and the various financial measures mentioned, were all marks of a regime sinking into danger and corruption: a situation so grave that, in the words of Hayward's Bolingbroke, 'he that aymeth at a kingdome' was urged on in his ambition by 'neccessity' itself.[73] Such suspicions seem typical of the anxieties of Elizabeth as recorded by Camden and addressed by Wentworth. Hayward was not convicted of treason, however, his friend Bacon saying jestingly for the defence that felony rather than treason might be the appropriate charge, so much had he taken from Tacitus.[74] He was nevertheless kept in prison from the time of the Essex rising till the death of the Queen.[75]

The execution of Essex, the champion, the general, the generous patron, the great earl who might have become something greater still, was at least mourned by the common muse in two of the finest ballads of Elizabeth's reign:

> Abroad, and eke at home,
>   *gallantly, gallantly,*
> For valour there was none
>   like him before.
> In Ireland, France, and Spain,
>   they fear'd great Essex name—
> And England lov'd the same
>   In every place . . .

---

[73] Sir John Hayward, *The First Part of the Life and Raigne of Henrie the IIII* . . . (1599), 65–7.

[74] 'Hayward's Troubles', 218, 223.

[75] In 'A New History for Shakespeare and His Time', *Shakespeare Quarterly*, 39 (1988), 441–64, J. Leeds Barroll complains at the recent overconcentration on the Lambarde interview, at the expense of other evidence about the Essex revolt, and the activities of the players before and after. I hope to have met his demand for a variety of other political evidence concerning the precedent of Richard II. I do not assume that Elizabeth was alluding to Shakespeare's *Richard II* in her remarks to Lambarde. As it happens my argument is that Shakespeare's play is neither 'subversive' nor 'conservative'. I think, however, that the Lambarde interview and the examination of Sir John Hayward, at the time of the Essex revolt, will always constitute a flashpoint in the relationship between writing and high politics—similar, perhaps, to James VI's protest against *The Faerie Queene*, IV–VI. Hayward's importance is endorsed in illuminating new work on the Essex Circle by David Womersley: see 'Sir Henry Savile's Translation of Tacitus and the Political Interpretation of Elizabethan Texts', *RES* NS 42: 167 (1991), 313–42; and 'Sir John Hayward's Tacitism', *Renaissance Studies*, 6: 1 (1992), 46–59.

I have deserv'd to die, I know;
  but ne'er against my Countries right,
Nor to my Queen, was ever foe,
  e'en to my death, at my Good-night.

Farewell, Elizabeth, my gracious Queen!
  God bless thee with thy Council all!
Farewell, you Knights of Chivalry!
  farewell, my Souldiers stout and tall!
Farewell, the Commons great and small!
  into the hands of men I light;
My life shall make amends for all,
  for Essex bids the world good night.[76]

Of course Hayward denied Coke's imputations and (in the words of his Epistle Apologeticall) the 'secrete sences, which the deepe searchers of our time, haue rather framed then found'.[77] His works on William II and Edward VI (unpublished in his lifetime) suggest a consistent concern with problems of succession. He was in unexpected difficulty when the great man and favourite to whom he had originally dedicated his work became a gravely suspect figure. He used all his wits to clear himself of the charge that he had intended an 'application' of his narrative to the present time. Even if Hayward's denials were not disingenuous, however, Coke's suggestions surely tell us a great deal about the thoughts that might pass through the mind of a well-informed reader when a book such as Hayward's *Henry IIII* was read, or of a spectator when a play such as *Richard II* was performed. Camden alone would suffice to show that such parallels and applications were the very bread and butter of Elizabethan political commentary, sometimes though rarely of treasonable intent. It is clear from Camden and the other writers alluded to above that political allusion to the present times did not depend upon a complete realistic likeness between the figure presented and the figure alluded to; it turned rather upon certain salient common features, problems, or issues, in situations otherwise very different, which could remind contemporary readers or audiences of their own time.

[76] The first stanza quoted comes from *A Lamentable Ditty compos'd upon the Death of Robert Devereux . . .*; the second and third from *A Lamentable new Ballad upon the Earle of Essex his Death*; *The Roxburghe Ballads*, ed. William Chappell (1871), i. 564–74.
[77] 'Hayward's Troubles', 221.

A Lamentable new Ballad upon the Earle of Essex his Death.

To the tune of *Essex['s] last good-night.*

All you that cry O hone! O hone![1]
    come now and sing O hone![2] with me;
For why, our Jewel is from us gone,
    the valiant Knight of Chivalry:
Of rich and poore belov'd was he,—
    in time an honourable Knight,—
When, by our Lawes condemn'd to die,[3]
    He lately took his last Good-night.

      4

      8

FIG. 1. *A Lamentable New Ballad upon the Earle of Essex his Death*. The Earl of Essex was executed by Queen Elizabeth I in 1600. In one recorded version of this ballad, it is to be sung to the tune of 'The King's Last Good-Night'.

When Shakespeare based his History Plays of the 1590s on the English chronicles he was not basing them on a pristine field of information. Partly this was because the work he most used, the 1587 Holinshed, was itself a miscellaneous compilation of earlier works. Partly it was because, especially for the reigns Shakespeare chose, the ground had already been trampled up and down, quarried for evidence in political demonstration, plundered for instances to lend power to political rhetoric. English history was a common possession and in its chronicled form was being constantly put to use. Whether Shakespeare knew it or not—but surely he did know—his Histories were put together out of the precedents and warning instances of current historical discussion. Camden's account of the reign of Elizabeth reinforces this view.

2

The First Tetralogy and King John

So many passages remain in which Shakespeare evidently takes
his advantage of the facts then recent, and of the passions then
in motion, that I cannot but suspect that time has obscured
much of his art, and that many allusions yet remain
undiscovered which perhaps may be gradually retrieved by
succeeding commentators.

(Samuel Johnson, *Works, On Shakespeare*, ed. Arthur
Sherbo (1968), vii. 417)

WHEN Shakespeare chose to produce a sequence of plays on
the reign of King Henry VI he was choosing material of tradi-
tional and orthodox significance, of relatively recent relevance,
and of current topical interest. Traditionally, the reign was a terr-
ible example of misrule, political and military failure, and escalat-
ing civil war. Like *Gorboduc*, nearly thirty years earlier, the
Henry VI plays made their immediate impact by the kind of telling
contrast with the present which carried a grim warning. That
the reign displayed features 'for the which God is often angry
with princes', as Wentworth had recently argued, was clear to all,
though opinions might divide as to why these appalling develop-
ments had occurred. Despite the obvious theme of order and disor-
der to which Tillyard most notably drew attention, no clear
providential explanation is prominently advanced in the text. The
great providential scheme of Hall, showing how England suffered
for the deposition of Richard II, is nowhere explicit. Those
who comment upon England's woes attribute them firmly to evi-
dent short-term causes, for example the unscrupulous ambition
of the great nobles and the weakness of the inexperienced young
king.[1]

---

[1] E. M. W. Tillyard, *Shakespeare's History Plays* (1944), 161–73; H. A. Kelly,
Divine Providence in the England of Shakespeare's Histories (Cambridge, Mass.,
1970), 246–53.

I

At first, at least, the overwhelming impression conveyed is the traditional judgement of Exeter:

> 'Tis much when sceptres are in children's hands,
> But more when envy breeds unkind division:
>
> (*1 Henry VI*, IV. i. 192–3)

Wentworth's summary of the Henry VI story had added the point that the King was overruled by his wife.[2] It is here that the subject had recent relevance, for Henry's marriage to Margaret of Anjou well conveyed what many English including Elizabeth herself had feared in the prospect of a foreign match, the last great promotion of such, the unpopular Anjou (Alençon) wooing, having occurred eleven years before *1 Henry VI* was first performed in 1592. The spectacle of a too pliable English king and a too commanding French queen addressed anxieties that, in a great foreign match, the free English sovereignty of Elizabeth would be impaired. Even the name of the match—Anjou—may be thought to have been an advantage for the dramatist in his choice of this chronicle subject. If the point about the name seems strained, it is worth noting that Shakespeare appears to have exploited another such opportunity with the Duke of Alençon (the New Arden editor gives the English form: Alanson), one of the French nobles who with René (Reignier), Duke of Anjou and titular King of Naples, appears regularly in support of the Dauphin, later King of France, throughout *1 Henry VI*. The most recent duc d'Alençon had been a suitor for Elizabeth's hand before he became duc d'Anjou: well known at the English court and in London, he was a prominent political figure who, though a devoted Catholic, sought to assist the revolt of the Protestant Netherlands against Spain. He was considered *politique* to the point of duplicity but hardly a successful military leader. This is his character in Camden.[3] The chronicle story allowed Alençon to be presented quite unfavourably: suddenly beaten back by the English in I. ii; among those who (in the Folio stage direction) escape from the English in their shirts in II. i, where the fault is declared to be that of Joan de Pucelle and the 'Duke of Alençon' (l. 61); in III. v where he declines Talbot's challenge to come down from the walls

---

[2] *A Pithie Exhortation*, 80–1.   [3] *Annals*, 168–9, 242.

of Rouen to fight and later flies; and in v. vi where he is termed by
York: 'Alençon, that notorious Machiavel' (l. 74) in preparation for
his urging 'policy' on the French king to make a truce he does not
mean to keep (ll. 159–64). This provocatively contemporary line
clearly prompts the audience to find something in common between
a recent Alençon and the Alençon of the chronicles.[4] If, as Geoffrey
Bullough and the Oxford editors allow, *1 Henry VI* was written
later than 1590, a further contemporary allusion turning on a name
was probably to the death on 18 November 1590 of Talbot, sixth
Earl of Shrewsbury, Earl Marshal of England, praised by Camden
for his military prowess and 'fidelity' in doubtful and treacherous
times.[5] The choice of chronicle material featuring the valiant life and
death of the first Earl of Shrewsbury afforded the opportunity of a
complimentary bow to a great Elizabethan, recently dead, through
dramatization of his famous ancestor.[6] To these instances of prob-
able contemporary allusion may be added the well-known case of
Shakespeare's offence to the descendants of Sir John Oldcastle, in
the original version of *1 Henry IV*.

The great topical interest of *1 Henry VI*, however, arose from the
fact that by the end of 1589, with Alençon dead and Henry III
murdered, the earlier Catholic–Huguenot conflicts broke out into
full-scale civil war, with two strongly supported claimants to the
throne, the Protestant Henry IV and the Catholic 'Charles X'. This
situation was what had seemed to threaten England when the next
heir to the throne had appeared to be Mary, Queen of Scots. As
Camden records, Elizabeth now supported the Protestant claimant
with troops and money, and Bullough may be right to see the play
reflecting England's further interventions under Norris and Essex.[7]
For the first time in a century and a half the wars which led to the loss
of the French realm of the English crown were powerfully recalled.
Sixteenth-century England was a post-imperial state, the last of the
French possessions, Calais, having gone under Mary. Both the Cath-

---

[4] The New Arden editor notes the contemporary allusion here though he is
otherwise misleading, since Gentillet did not translate *Il Principe* but attacked
Machiavelli, and the Alençon who became King Henry III was not he who wooed
Elizabeth *c.*1580; *1 King Henry VI*, ed. Andrew Cairncross, New Arden Series
(1962), 124.

[5] *Annals*, 395.

[6] This has been suggested by Emrys Jones in his admirable study, *The Origins of
Shakespeare* (Oxford, 1977), 120–1.

[7] *Narrative and Dramatic Sources of Shakespeare*, iii (1960), 24–5.

olic Leslie and the Protestant Wentworth draw regretful morals on the loss of these possessions (see Chapter 1, pp. 32, 36); Parsons was to do the same, and Hayward was even to suggest that it might not be out of the question that England's French realm could be regained.[8]

Of abiding relevance but highly topical too, in view of Peter Wentworth's initiative, was the question of succession. It continues through the Henry VI plays into *Richard III* even after the ominous scenes of civil war had changed their ground from France to England. Here is the major contemporary theme dominating the traditional materials and political wisdom of Shakespeare's earlier Histories. It is of great interest to see how Shakespeare dramatizes the growing conflict between the House of York and the House of Lancaster, in his shaping and colouring of his chronicle sources, for it is in this way that the concept of indefeasible hereditary right which was in the end to give the English throne to the Scottish party is put to the touch: the test that the historical experience of earlier reigns afforded those who sought to foresee their own future.

Within the context of the wider action, the crucial scenes are *1 Henry VI*, II. iv and v; *The First Part of the Contention of . . . York and Lancaster* (*2 Henry VI*), II. ii, III. i; and v. i; *Richard Duke of York* (*3 Henry VI*), I. i and I. ii. The first of these, not based on any chronicle source and thus, perhaps, showing Shakespeare's intent the more clearly, is the Temple Garden scene. It gives the origin of the York–Lancaster quarrel in so far as it presents the earliest dispute between the great protagonist of the Yorkist cause and his earliest opponents. The subtlety of the scene lies in its character in relation to the *concept* of law and right, without directly disclosing the particular issue in connection with which law and right are invoked. This may concern Richard of York's status as son of the Earl of Cambridge executed for treason under Henry V, and seems not to concern (as ll. 41–60 of the following scene show) the deeper issue of York's claim to the crown. Shakespeare thus dramatizes the psychology that can generate a grievous civil conflict before he specifies the cause or the rationalizations which are to sustain the different sides. The acted symbolism of the scene is of the plucking of the white and red roses, and since York opens by invoking 'truth' (ll. 2 and 5) while in response Suffolk declares he will frame the law unto his will (ll. 8–9), it seems fair to suppose that the party of the white

---

[8] Sir John Hayward, *An Answer to Dolman* (1603), 48.

rose, 'this pale and maiden blossom' (l. 47), is that of innocence and right, that of the red rose bloodshed and force. This impression is fortified when the agreement that Vernon should give a casting vote is repudiated by the party that does not get it, and when the lawyer backs York. But of course Somerset and Suffolk lay claim to truth and right also, and as the dispute mounts into anger Shakespeare is able to sound ominous variations on the emblems of white and red:

RICHARD PLANTAGENET. And, by my soul, this pale and angry rose,
  As cognizance of my blood-drinking hate,
  Will I for ever, and my faction, wear . . .
SUFFOLK. Go forward, and be chok'd with thy ambition!

(ll. 107–9, 112)

Despite its clear imagery and bold language the scene has intimated with some delicacy that the incipient conflict is fundamentally to be one between law and force, right and possession; but it has also shown that ambition, hatred, and latent violence spurs on both sides. Shakespeare has begun from a simple contrast of concept and emblem and shown how the heat of competitive emotion has complicated that simplicity so that each colour seems to invade the other.

The relation of II. iv with II. v has a distant resemblance to I. ii and I. iv of *Hamlet*; in each we are first shown the emotion of the protagonist, York's ambition and Hamlet's suspicion, before its proper object and justification have been revealed to him; and only after are we shown the protagonist directly confronted by his destiny. In *1 Henry VI*, II. v York's instinctive sense of his higher rank and his belief that his grievance is greater than that of his antagonists receives justification in a scene in which the dramatist boldly reshapes explanatory matter from his chronicle sources. Even Hall whose whole narrative gives the fullest exposition of the Yorkist claim to the crown offers, at this point, the briefest of passages on the death of the last Mortimer, Earl of March, how his inheritance passed to York, and how York subsequently claimed the crown. Shakespeare draws together material from other parts of Hall and perhaps Holinshed to frame a lengthy and elaborate account of how to be the heir of the last Mortimer might be thought to be king *de jure*. By a bold and simple dramatic decision this necessarily extended explanation is turned into the deathbed speech of an old man who has languished years in prison, delivered to the very person whom it most concerns. Thus the lengthy genealogical account, which must always have been hard for an audience to assimilate, is given theatrical power from the very circumstances in which it is made. The account itself depends wholly on the concept of strict hereditary kingship; indeed it presses the theory of indefeasible hereditary right to a genealogical extreme, turning as it does on descent from the third rather than the fourth son of Edward III, and twice depending from marriage to females of the title-bearing line. The Yorkist title is thus always complicated to explain, and it is explained several times during the course of the Henry VI plays. On the other hand it rationalizes York's ambition in terms of the theory of kingship which Queen Elizabeth never for a moment abandoned, which Bodin preferred before all other forms of government, and to which Wentworth had so recently turned in his campaign to settle the English succession. Read in the context supplied by Camden the scene does seem to recall the most prominent recent instance of a long-imprisoned bearer of hereditary right, Mary, Queen of Scots, whose claim had stemmed from a marriage, by James IV of Scotland, to the elder daughter of Henry VII. But if Mortimer was a reminder of Mary (as the historical Mortimer seems to have been to Elizabeth), then York suggested James, and the House of Lancaster the Elizabethan regime; the parallel just emerged, no doubt, to fade from the audience's mind. Seen from another angle York's situation resembled that of several young contemporary English noblemen— Derby, Hertford, even Essex—who will have wondered whether their indirect hereditary claims to the English throne might not commend them more to the political nation than the son of Mary, Queen of Scots; or the Spanish Infanta. Radically reshaped as it is, the chronicle story briefly reflects certain aspects of contemporary high politics before moving on.

There is a dramatic secrecy about the scene arising from the revelation of long-hidden wrongs, the ritual passing on of an almost forgotten right, and the politic recognition of current reality:

MORTIMER. With silence, nephew, be thou politic.
  Strong-fixèd is the house of Lancaster,
  And like a mountain, not to be remov'd.
  But now thy uncle is removing hence,
  As princes do their courts . . .

                (ll. 101–5)

But York now sees his ambition as part of a historical pattern, which had begun with the rising of 'The Percies of the North' under Henry IV and continued with that of York's father the Earl of Cambridge under Henry V—efforts which now seem, from a Yorkist point of view at least, not rebellions but attempts to restore the right.

The parallel to this scene in *The Contention*, II. ii, marks the further emergence of the Yorkist claim. In another garden setting York now puts his case to Salisbury and Warwick; it is an even fuller genealogical explanation, broken up by a few questions and objections, but accepted at the end. Stress is laid once again on descent by the female line and through marriage; no Salic Law inhibits York's claim; no Salic Law had inhibited Elizabeth's. The dialogue develops the problem of how to think about the currently reigning House of Lancaster. In *1 Henry VI*, II. v, Mortimer's word for Bolingbroke's assumption of power was 'usurpation' (l. 68) and York's for Henry V's execution of the Earl of Cambridge 'bloody tyranny' (l. 100). Now in a new public situation the words are softened, even perhaps altered: we hear instead of deposition and 'force' which, in Bodinian terms, presents the princes of the House of Lancaster as closer to lordly monarchs than tyrants. Indeed these terms link back to some of those used of English rule in France, in *1 Henry VI*: 'conqueror' (Talbot of Henry V; III. v. 40), 'lordly nation' (Pucelle of the English; III. vi. 62). York's original wrath at Mortimer's revelations has now cooled and he is persuading others to his cause. Though he has made a most emphatic statement of his claim to Warwick, and to Salisbury, veteran of Henry V's wars, the scene ends with an echo of Mortimer's counsel of policy and concealment. But now a course of action is specified and it does not sound pretty. It is to let York's two great enemies, Somerset and Suffolk, destroy 'the good Duke Humphrey' (l. 74) and through that themselves. Only so can a comparatively weak pretender make way against a strongly established dynasty.

The elaborate cunning with which York works towards his goal is strikingly exemplified in his next step: sent by policy to put down an Irish rebellion he is doubly politic in response. ' 'Twas men I lacked' (III. i. 345), but now he has them, and meanwhile raises up in John Cade of Kent a false 'Mortimer' to create trouble in England and test how well affected the commons may be to the Yorkist claim. Shakespeare follows Hall and Holinshed in giving prominence to this conspiracy, though by omitting or playing it down Shakespeare could have made the *de jure* claimant seem less cold-blooded and cunning. But policy is employed on the other side too. Returning with his troops and the time-dishonoured claim that he wishes only to remove evil councillors (Somerset) from the King, York is tricked in turn, dismissing his men only to find Somerset not dismissed as promised. He narrowly escapes imprisonment; Salisbury defends the breaking of his oath to Henry VI; and at the First Battle of St Albans the Yorkist cause achieves its first regular military victory in the field.

In *Richard Duke of York* (*3 Henry VI*), I. i, Shakespeare renews his dramatic investigation into the problems of the succession of kings. Here he transforms York's long oration to Parliament that he found in Hall (but which may perhaps have influenced York's discourse to Warwick and Salisbury in *The Contention*, II. ii) into a dialogue between York, Henry, and other nobles. Here York physically occupies the throne, and is challenged for so doing by King Henry VI in orthodox terms:

> Thou factious Duke of York, descend my throne,
> And kneel for grace and mercy at my feet;
> I am thy sovereign.

> (ll. 74–6)

The first challenge to the command thus made by the reigning King is from Warwick, and is purely military: all present are reminded that the Yorkists have just been victorious in the battle. The debate proper, however, opens in response to York's defiant question to King Henry: 'Will you we show our title to the crown? I If not, our swords shall plead it in the field' (ll. 102–3). In reply King Henry sums up the apparent situation:

> Thy father was, as thou art, Duke of York;
> Thy grandfather, Roger Mortimer, Earl of March.
> I am the son of Henry the Fifth,
> Who made the Dauphin and the French to stoop,
> And seized upon their towns and provinces.

> (ll. 105–9)

Henry's argument is twofold. Unlike York he is the son of the last king. Further, that king had been warlike and a great conqueror. The idea of conquest, which will apply not only to Henry V's famous victories in France, but also to the rise of Henry IV in

England, is thus effectively introduced. In Bodinian terms, at least, the concept of conquest is not, like that of tyranny, evil by defini- tion. Both Henry and York appeal to this idea. Out of the noisy altercations that follow Henry's words he speaks again, appealing to the Plantagenet descent they both have in common, but going on to ask the common-sense *de facto* question: 'Think'st thou that I will leave my kingly throne, I Wherein my grandsire and my father sat?' (ll. 125–6) and concluding with the affirmation that his title is better than that of York. Asked to make that good in argument the mild Henry can only respond that: 'Henry the Fourth by conquest got the crown' (l. 133) and is answered at once by York calling that conquest rebellion. Nothing in the chronicle sources anticipates the damaging admission Henry now makes in an aside: 'I know not what to say—my title's weak' (l. 135), and if this is a mark of his inner integrity it tells the more strongly for the Yorkists. Henry has now one resort left. Having argued unsuccessfully from descent, from possession, and from conquest, he can still attempt to derive his title from Richard II if Richard could be thought to have voluntarily 'Resign'd the crown' (l. 140) and adopted Bolingbroke his heir. Since it has already been argued that this resignation was the consequence of rebellion and force, Warwick now meets the point in a new way: in strict hereditary descent no abdication can hinder the claim of the next heir; just over a century later Dryden was to make the same point about the same king,[9] and it may be remembered that Elizabeth, even when confronted by Parliament's condemnation of Mary, Queen of Scots, had intervened to prevent the barring of any title in James. If Mortimer rather than Boling- broke had been Richard's true heir, Henry VI's claims to the stronger title would fail (ll. 125–50).

But the drama lends all these arguments a certain unreality. One battle in an English civil war has already been fought, and has shown the usual dire generation of revenge:

CLIFFORD. King Henry, be thy title right or wrong,
  Lord Clifford vows to fight in thy defence.
  May that ground gape and swallow me alive
  Where I shall kneel to him that slew my father!

(ll. 160–3)

---

[9] John Dryden, 'The Good Parson', ll. 113–15, in *Poems*, iv. 1739; ed. James Kinsley (Oxford, 1956).

Further, though in late sixteenth-century terms York has proved he has the better title, yet demonstration must be backed by force. In an ironical echo of Richard's constrained resignation of the crown the sudden appearance of armed men in Parliament prompts Henry to propose compromise: that he should live as king if he acknowledges York and *his* posterity as next heirs to the throne. As Clifford at once points out, Henry thus disinherits his own son. Nevertheless the compact is made and York takes an oath to maintain it. At this juncture the union of the two noble houses of Lancaster and York might have been achieved, to the great good of England, had not the warlike instinct of most Lancastrians, hatred, lust for revenge, and above all the manlike resolution of the Queen, meant that Henry's supporters disobeyed his decision.

Among the consequences of Shakespeare's having rejected as material York's oration to Parliament is the loss of just about the most powerful opportunity offered by the chronicle sources to express Hall's providential scheme. It is a most interesting decision by the dramatist. What he achieves, on the other hand, is an opening up of the problems of royal succession, a trying out of different grounds for a valid royal title (inheritance, conquest, designation, and bequest), and an exposure of the moral wrongs, and human and political difficulties, involved in any attempt to reverse a long-standing usurpation. The scene may be thought to possess a rather pat and *politique* character, rehearsing in rapid dialogue the chief Bodinian modes by which a dynasty may be founded and maintained. Shakespeare thus shows his awareness of contemporary succession theory but the scene is not among the more dramatically powerful of the Henry VI plays.

The immediate aftermath of this scene is a spontaneous oathbreaking on both sides. Henry cannot hold his queen or the northern Earls to the compact; York for his part is easily persuaded to break faith. He is especially swayed by the sophisticated argument of his younger son Richard that oaths are valid only if made in the presence of a magistrate, and that since Henry is a usurper, and thus no true magistrate, the oath is not binding. Samuel Johnson, who had his own reasons for thinking seriously about oaths of allegiance, took the trouble to refute this specious and sophisticated argument, while upholding Salisbury's right, in *The Contention* (2 *Henry VI*), v. i, to abandon an oath which was only later proved to have been made to an usurper.[10] This argument of the young Richard III-to-be carries to a further extreme that rather modern and academic air which has often characterized York's claims. This at all events is the aspect of the situation which Shakespeare chooses to stress, making no use of those points in the chronicles which show that York knew Henry would not be able to keep the bargain, or which record that York had procured an absolution from the Pope for his oath-breaking (the latter a potentially popular Protestant point, like Glouces-ter's seeing through of the false miracle in *The Contention*, II. i). Here, no sooner has York resolved to break his oath than he realizes he is already surrounded by the troops of his foresworn enemies. He goes out to fight, is defeated, captured, ridiculed, and stabbed to death. He dies choked with his ambition; but it is, in the context of the action and argument presented, hard to think of him as simply rebellious or evil.[11]

The remainder of *Richard Duke of York* displays the terrible escalation of civil war in a way partly reminiscent of *Gorboduc*, or *King Lear*. But with this dreadful difference. While in *Gorboduc* the royal line has completely destroyed itself, thus leaving the ravaged land defenceless before the advance of the predatory foreign in-vader, Albany; while in *Lear* two possible leaders, Albany and 'Legitimate Edgar' survive the slaughter; here Shakespeare shows the final triumph of the legitimate royal line, the proper guardians of the land, in a welter of blood. At the Lancastrian defeat at Tewkesbury, Prince Edward, son of Henry VI, is repeatedly stabbed, while Richard of Gloucester, who has slowly emerged as the subtlest and most ruthless Yorkist, posts away to murder the saintly usurper Henry VI in the Tower. In the final scene York's eldest son, the young Edward IV, recounts the harvest of deaths reaped to secure his throne, Gloucester pays hypocritical homage, and thus begins the 'lasting joy' of York.

---

[10] Samuel Johnson, *Works* (New Haven and London, 1968), viii. 598–9. The great question of Johnson and the Oaths has, for the first time, been fully discussed, by J. C. D. Clark, *Samuel Johnson . . .* (Cambridge, 1994), ch. 4.

[11] Irving Ribner in *The English History Play in the Age of Shakespeare* (Princeton, 1957; rev. 1965), 108–10, takes it for granted that 'Shakespeare censures rebellion against the *de facto* ruler'. Shakespeare's attitude is arguably more complex. While he displays the horror of civil conflict, nobody succeeds in disproving York's title, and nobody argues that there is a higher political duty than to observe this title. Shakespeare may implicitly censure the means York chooses to attain his end, while accepting their virtual inevitability in the political world.

The emergence of Richard of Gloucester in *Richard Duke of York* is important in many ways. If Alençon was the unsuccessful 'Machiavel' of the first part of the chronological trilogy, Richard is the increasingly successful and self-proclaimed 'Machiavel' of the third part (III. ii. 193). No Talbot-like figure stands against him here; the nearest is the young Clifford, lacking Talbot's loyalty and locked into constancy by his revenge and hatred. Richard has been borne forward into the political world as a fierce supporter of the legitimist cause of his father and elder brother. Because the House of Lancaster was 'strong-fixed' and like a mountain not to be removed the Yorkists could advance, at first, only through policy and concealment. In retrospect it seems that out of experience of these means was borne Richard as a new Sinon and Machiavel (or Catiline), and it is in the scene where, applying these names to himself, he discloses in soliloquy his own ambition for the crown, that the first qualities of the humorous Vice are seen in him: 'Can I do this, and cannot get a crown? | Tut, were it farther off, I'll pluck it down' (ll. 194–5). His dry demonic wit here rises, *Richard Duke of York* and *Richard III* being, by this token, closely bound together. The Richard of *Richard III* is by any definition the dramatization of a tyrant; and it is thus that the first tetralogy of Histories brings us face to face with the dreadful paradox that out of the politic legitimist crusade of York could be born, like the killers from the belly of the auspicious Trojan Horse, the utter illegitimacy of the tyrant Richard III. By comparison with him the compassionate though wavering usurpation of Henry VI seems happy, and even the manlike bloodthirstiness of Margaret of Anjou less deliberately evil.

It is to Lily B. Campbell that we owe the very salient point, not acknowledged by the New Arden editor of *3 Henry VI*, that Sinon, Catiline, Machiavel, and Richard III occur as linked names in the recusant *Treatise of the Treasons Against Queen Elizabeth, and the Crowne of England* . . . (1572), an attack, according to Camden,[12] on Lord Burleigh and Sir Nicholas Bacon.[13] When it is noted that the unamended quarto text of *The True Tragedie* reads 'aspiring *Catilin*' for 'murderous Machiavel' at III. ii. 193, it is hard to think Shakespeare did not remember the *Treatise of the Treasons*, dangerous and scarce though it probably was. Shakespeare may only have

[12] *Annals*, 167.
[13] Lily B. Campbell, *Shakespeare's 'Histories': Mirrors of Elizabethan Policy* (San Marino, Calif., 1947), 321–6. *Treatise of Treasons*, fos. 83–5.

remembered and put to use this collocation of names. But if they were employed to analogous effect to *The Treatise*, they must have warned against the ambition of the Queen's councillors. This will not have been an allusion on Shakespeare's part to a publicly known royal person such as Alençon, the imprisoned Mary, Queen of Scots, or James VI. Any contemporary allusion to the danger that some of Elizabeth's councillors might, under cover of the cause of hereditary legitimacy, seek to reach the throne themselves, and thus subvert the very cause they seemed to serve, would, presumably, have been chiefly apparent to those factions which closely studied the late Elizabethan court and distrusted the potent influence of the Cecils, who seem to have been attacked, in this same year, in the publication by Spenser of his *Mother Hubbard's Tale*.[14] Such a faction would be looking for a leader-like figure, not necessarily with the best title to the crown, to succeed the ageing Elizabeth, and prevent the further rise of the *regnum Cecilianum* in the person of the shrewd, ambitious, misshapen Robert Cecil, leader of the Commons and new Secretary to the Queen.

Particular allusion, if it can here be credited, is hardly necessary to point the general moral, though it would sharpen it. The moral is that a royal and legitimist crusade such as York's, with the best contemporary political credentials and supporting in effect the Bodinian notion of Royal Monarchy, could, if forced into the adoption of politic and treacherous means, betray its own end and give birth to a monster. So far we can say that Shakespeare's first tetralogy has a pointed political message. Beyond that we see that drama does not usually take sides on specific historical issues, and does not here. Rather it acts out the opposing arguments and exposes the human and practical implications of principle. So it is in these four plays. In terms of the very texts themselves we cannot read the tetralogy, as the New Arden editor appears to do, simply as the story of a

---

[14] *The Works of Edmund Spenser, A Variorum Edition*, ed. Edwin Greenlaw, Charles G. Osgood, and Frederick M. Padelford (Baltimore, 1932–47); *Minor Poems*, ii. 579–80. For a later record of an association of Robert Cecil with Richard III, see Calendar of State Papers Domestic, lxix. 67: 'Richard D. of Glo. Robert E. of Salisburie. The anagram whereof is silie burs.

> Whiles two RRs both crouchbacks stoode at the helme
> The one spilt the bloud royall, the other the realme'

Quoted by Barbara De Luna, *Jonson's Romish Plot* (Oxford, 1967), 211, who explains that 'Burs' is a hump as well as a bourse, and that 'silie burs' is an anagram of Salisbury.

rebellion against a king. Henry VI cannot be thought of simply as *the* king, when from the first these plays show so much interest in what circumstances give, or do not give, kings a valid title, and when Henry himself owns in an aside that 'my title's weak'. Richard of York is no rebel but, in the contemporary theoretical terms of kingship held by Elizabeth herself, king *de jure*. Unfortunately no providential power brings on in peace the triumph of his right. This requires policy, cunning, duplicity, armed might, tenacity, and extraordinary resolution, all the means of the fallen world. It can be seen that the first tetralogy does not conform to the later and more familiar pattern in which a *de jure* but ineffective king is opposed by a born leader who becomes king *de facto*. That political configuration may seem more probable and natural. The reign of Henry VI, on the contrary, embodied paradoxes and problems. The false king seemed pious and saintly, yet never sufficiently his own master to do what his nature increasingly seemed to prompt: abdicate unconditionally. The true king, justifiably aggrieved at the outset, and never evil, never tyrannous as Richard of Gloucester would become, is wholly consumed in the cunning and force with which he has pursued his goal. It is clear that a Richard of Gloucester could emerge from a historical process of this kind.

It is this too which links *Richard III* to the Henry VI plays. Though a providential play, endorsing order and reprehending civil war, its providential features bind it to the preceding dramas in a limited way. They avenge the tyrannous and unnatural deeds of Richard III; and many of these deeds are themselves seen by that lingering revenge figure Margaret of Anjou as retribution for wrongs done her and the House of Lancaster; but neither underlines a providential scheme like that found in Hall or urged by Tillyard, which stems from the original deposition of Richard II. Only the somewhat adventitious scene between Henry VI and the young Richmond (*Richard Duke of York*, iv. vii. 67–76), of which Johnson said: 'Shakespeare knew his trade',[15] links with *Richard III* through Hall's grand argument. It is not the business of *Richard III* to recall *Richard II*. *Richard III* does two different things. First, it deals a terrible blow to the doctrine of indefeasible hereditary right. Not only does it show that the single-minded pursuit of a royal title *de jure* can, the world being what it is, lead straight to tyranny. It

---

[15] *Works*, viii. 607.

also shows, in a bloody political paradox, what Parsons would very shortly point out in 1594: that, having murdered all those nearer to the throne than himself, Richard III 'might in reason seem to be lawful king, both in respect that he was the next male in blood after his said brother, as also for that by diverse acts of parliament his title was authorized'.[16] In a tetralogy which has recited the logic and modes of that concept more explicitly and often than its chronicle sources, this terrible consummation can hardly be ignored. Though in strict logic the concept is not damaged, yet as the examination of Sir John Hayward was to show, the ending of the action was where people looked for the main significance. In these plays indefeasible hereditary right makes a bad end. Richmond has a less lineal claim than Richard, though his proposal to marry Elizabeth of York acknowledges the importance of such a title. In the atmosphere of *Richard III* we see Richmond as a liberator rather than a king from over the water. Secondly, however, *Richard III* is a different style of play from the Henry VI plays. The audience cannot but have a quite different relation with Richard III than with any major figure of the earlier Histories. This is entirely the consequence of the Vice-like humour and demonic wit of Shakespeare's stage tyrant. The monstrous theatricality of Richard, together with his dry intelligence, takes some of the evil out of his wickedness: he plays Herod and we relish his performance. *Richard III*, linked as it is with its predecessors in the tetralogy, is in several senses a less serious political play than they are. But it does at least give the lie to the *Book of Homilies*. The worldly knowledge and humour of the vice, however, are to be differently employed in the later Histories of *King John* and Parts 1 and 2 of *Henry IV*.

II

For those in the 1590s who dramatized the reign of King John there were two clearly contrasted opportunities. It was possible to construct an orthodox and unproblematic play about John as he was presented in two of the most widely disseminated of all Elizabethan publications: Foxe's *Actes and Monuments*, and the 1571 'Homilie

---

[16] Robert Parsons, *A Conference About the Next Succession to the Crowne of Ingland . . .* (1594), 61.

against disobedience and wilfull rebellion'. Placed in every parish church, these works stressed John as the early Protestant hero, Foxe, as we have seen, saying little about John and Arthur, while the 'Homilie against disobedience' totally ignored that aspect of John's reign. Some would have been fortified in accepting the interpretation of these texts by recollection of John Bale's drama of *King Johan* (developing through different versions between 1537 and 1561) which had drawn clear parallels between Henry VIII's conflict with the Papacy and that of John. This tradition thus concentrated on John as would-be supreme head of the Church in England, as a nationalistic defier of the supranational claims of the Roman Catholic Church, and as the victim of invasion by continental powers urged on by the Pope, which occasioned a rebellion of the English nobility against their native king.

In the 1590s this orthodox play was never written—significantly enough. *King Johan* was never brought up to date; or rather was brought up to date so radically that the orthodox tradition on John was completely reassessed. This was the second opportunity for those planning a drama on his reign. It was seized by both the author of *The Troublesome Raigne of King John of England* (published 1591) and Shakespeare, whenever they composed their plays, and whichever was written first.[17] Both dramatists were concerned with the idea of succession, both were concerned with conflicting titles to the throne, both boldly resolved to dramatize the issue of legitimacy neglected by Bale, Foxe, and the 'Homilie against disobedience', but to which Leslie and Bodin had drawn attention, and about which much could be found in Holinshed. If the later date of *John* is accepted, it is possible to argue that it may respond to the provocative remarks on that reign in Robert Parsons's *Conference About the Next Succession to the Crowne of Ingland* . . ., published in 1594 and dedicated to Essex. Unlike his fellow Catholic Leslie (whom he had read), Parsons was not indignant on behalf of Arthur. For Parsons, John did not possess the lineal right, but his early success against France and Arthur showed that God favoured the

---

[17] These are matters still in dispute. E. A. J. Honigmann, in his Arden edition of Shakespeare's *King John* (London, 1954), pp. xi–lviii, argues for the early date of 1590–1, and sees *The Troublesome Raigne* as derivative from Shakespeare. Few have agreed; and some prefer a date between 1593 and 1596. Ribner, *The English History Play*, 119–20, displays a representative reaction. The Oxford editors assign *John* to 1596.

commonwealth's 'election' of John, who put Arthur to death to make his own title more clear.[18] Later, however, John was guilty of misgovernment, and was deposed by the Pope at the request of the 'people': here Parsons strongly supports the Dauphin Louis who was chosen king and swore fealty in London. Had the situation not changed again (Parsons argued) England and France might have been united under one crown from that day.[19] The *Conference* is always bold and surprising; and these views effectively support the grand argument of its Civilian Lawyer, that rulers are not made by divine or natural law, but by 'humane and positive lawes of every particular common wealth'.[20]

Shakespeare's chief stroke of art in *John*, as all accept, is the telescoping of the reign so that the conflict with Arthur and the conflict with the Pope could just overlap. They are made to do so in a sinister, Machiavellian, and modern way. Thus the claims of hereditary right and the claims of the Papacy do not originally join together (as they did in Leslie's propaganda on behalf of Mary, Queen of Scots). They do so only when Pandulph, the Pope's representative, foreseeing that the triumphant John will try to have the captive *de jure* claimant Arthur assassinated, argues that then the title *de jure* will descend to the Dauphin Louis, who is thus urged to persist in his hostility to a *de facto* English monarch also under Papal interdict. Subsequent and foregoing events show how the hereditary principle is used as a means to ends other than that of legitimate kingship. It is now perceptibly detached from the interests of the Catholic Church, as was apparent in the contemporary world where in England the Protestant Wentworth made it the key argument in his campaign to settle the succession, and in France Catholics resisted Navarre's *de jure* claim to the throne. Parsons's *Conference* boldly called attention to this rift.

But this is to anticipate. As the York and Lancaster story unfolded from the invented scene of the plucking of the white and red roses (*1 Henry VI*, II. iv) so this drama of legitimacy and illegitimacy unfolds from I. i, an invented scene of extraordinary boldness and verve, and quite iconoclastic vigour. It flares into life as the emmissary of the King of France challenges John's right to the English throne, John meeting the challenge and resolving on war. In terms of hereditary succession it is far more clear than it was in *Henry VI*

---

[18] Parsons, *Conference*, 194.   [19] *A Conference*, 56–7.
[20] *A Conference*, 1.

who has the better title to the throne: it is Arthur, whose cause Philip of France has espoused. While John, like Elizabeth, braves out his title to the full: 'Our strong possession and our right', his mother Eleanor, though his constant supporter, pointedly riposts with the true case: 'Your strong possession much more than your right' (ll. 39–40). All this is dispatched in a mere 43 lines, to give place to the adjudication by John and Eleanor of the dispute between the younger but legitimate and elder but allegedly illegitimate sons of the late Sir Robert Faulconbridge. There is some broad stage comedy: God has stood up for bastards in that this 'bastard' is not only 'A good blunt fellow' (l. 71) but a fine figure of a man, and far more like Richard Cœur de Lion, his rumoured father, than his own feeble-looking legitimate brother. John gives conventional judgment: since the 'bastard' was born in wedlock he is legitimate heir, but Eleanor daringly throws everything back on his natural qualities and real parentage. Urged on by her, the 'bastard' resolves to avow bastardy and be the known natural son of the late king. At this John knights him as 'Sir Richard and Plantagenet' (ll. 161–2).

This part of the scene is a fine acted parable. John and Eleanor in effect avow the illegitimacy of their own position by making a bastard of Faulconbridge and recruiting his support. Their stand is in favour of possession and strong natural qualities, against argument, law, and ecclesiastical authority. They are further supported by the Bastard's cynical insights into the interest which usually lies behind argument, law, and authority: 'Commodity, the bias of the world' (II. i. 575), perceptions that he expresses with his characteristic bluntness. The Bastard's soliloquy on 'Commodity' which may be thought to rival the real Machiavelli in its grasp of *realpolitik*, is occasioned by that peace and marriage alliance with which John of England and Philip of France symmetrically make up their symmetrically expounded and defended differences. Its free reflection and plain language contrast effectively with the more formal and embellished language and symmetrical speeches and manœuvres that have gone before. The case of Arthur who claimed all, and of John who denied all, have been laid aside for self-interest. Into this formal peace now intrudes the Papal Legate to introduce the more familiar Elizabethan theme of John's reign. At once John assumes the defiant Henrician stance; he is supreme under God and will permit no 'Italian priest' to meddle with his Church. With the characteristic speed of this play Pandulph responds with curse and excommunication; further, he pledges (what the Pope of John's day did not, but the Pope of Elizabeth's day did) that the killer of the *de facto* monarch shall be canonized (III. i. 102–5).[21] King Philip is now urged to break his faith with John to show himself a true son of the Church. As before two sides sought to win Angier, now in a changed but similar configuration two sides seek to win Philip. Pandulph's argument seems especially sophistical, though Johnson defends it.[22] At length the French king yields, breaking his oath to John and making ready for war. Arthur's claim is thus resumed, but as a by-product of Pandulph's diplomacy.

At this point it is right to consider the contemporary political allusion latent and emergent in Shakespeare's dramatic narrative. At the moment when Pandulph speaks of canonizing the killer of John a fuse of allusion is lit which points first to Henry III of France, a Catholic but assassinated by a Catholic fanatic in 1589 for opposing the League, which actually campaigned for the assassin's canonization. This leads back further to the long-standing and well-known situation of the Queen, who had since 1571 been in exactly the peril with which Pandulph threatens John. Finally the trail of allusion returns to John who, the 1590s audience would recall before the play had ended, had been assassinated by a Catholic fanatic despite his having humbled himself to the Pope in the meantime. John is the Tudor monarch-to-be; and not only in his conflict with the Pope, but also in his confrontation with a *de jure* claimant to his throne. For Arthur is very much a reminder of the Stuart claim; he is the relatively weak title-bearer whose strong theoretical claim, though barred by a will (II. i. 192) is supported by a great Catholic power. As we have seen, the case for Mary, Queen of Scots, had been argued in terms of the right of Arthur.[23] These are major allusions, already clear by Act III, though the latter part of the play is to develop and bear them out. It is then interesting that the Papal Legate's denunciation of John breaks what might have seemed a fair compromise between *de facto* and *de jure*, a point relevant to the ever-widening gap between Elizabeth and Mary. (If the later date for *John* is assumed, King Philip's breaking of his oath with England

[21] See III. i. 103 n. and p. xxix of New Arden edn.
[22] Johnson, *Works*, vii. 419.
[23] This was first observed by Campbell, *Shakespeare's 'Histories'*, 142–3; her more convincing points are incorporated in Honigmann's introduction to the New Arden edition, pp. xxvii–xxix.

and reversion to full obedience to the Catholic Church recalls the decision of England's Protestant ally Navarre, King Henry IV, to change his faith in order to secure his kingdom.) There is one further allusion, which would already have been clear by this stage of the play. It concerns the well-known figure, Sir John Perrot, Lord Deputy of Ireland for the period 1584–8, an impetuous commander, notorious for his blunt and disrespectful speech, and the reputed natural son of King Henry VIII whom he physically resembled.[24] Camden reports him saying of Elizabeth that she was 'illegitimate, fearful & curious, that she cared not for military men, that she had hindered him from reducing *Vlster* into order, and that she would one day stand in need of his helpe.' He also noted that he was 'a man most averse from the Popish Religion'.[25] In March 1591 Perrot was arrested for treason, with the Chancellor, Hatton, against him, but Burleigh and Essex in his favour. He was condemned, protesting his innocence to the end, and challenging (it was said) the Queen to 'suffer her brother to be offered up as a sacrifice to the envy of my flattering adversaries'. For whatever reason Elizabeth did not sign the order for his execution and he died a natural death in prison in November 1592. It may be thought that the Bastard was simply modelled on Perrot rather than alluding to him, but in a drama so concerned with the Henrician stand against Papal power, and its precedent in John, allusion to a natural son of Henry would seem particularly consistent and effective, allowing 'Cœur de Lion' to refer back to Elizabeth's royal father.

In the second half of *John* we see the poised symmetries of the earlier acts give way to an increasingly dizzying and dangerous see-saw of events. Pandulph wins over King Philip but John wins the subsequent battle and captures Arthur: the point which Parsons's *Conference* claimed showed God favouring John. But this is the moment when John resolves to plunder (or reform) the monasteries; on his way back to England he attempts to commission Arthur's death by heavy hints to Hubert; next King Philip's 'whole armada' against England is scattered by a tempest (III. iv. 1–3). Mary was dead before a later Philip's armada sailed against Elizabeth—indeed her death was a cause of its sailing—but the series of contemporary allusions continues strong and consistent. It has been recognized

[24] See G. B. Harrison, *An Elizabethan Journal . . .*, i. *1591–94* (1928), 393, 16, 125–8, 143–5, 178–9.
[25] *Annals*, 410.

that *John* uses 'armada rhetoric' and evokes the emotion of an England which had recently survived the Armada threat. Here Pandulph's persuasion of the Dauphin to persist with the war against England on behalf of his own claim to its throne is an interesting parallel to Philip of Spain's sending the Armada on behalf of the Infanta (Mary being then dead). Act IV is dominated by the attempt to make away with or blind Prince Arthur. Here Shakespeare is expanding on the hints as to Arthur's end to be found in the chief chronicle sources. More than with the dying Mortimer in *1 Henry VI* he is able to play on the pathos and vulnerability of the imprisoned title-bearer. Spenser, alluding to Mary, Queen of Scots, on trial, showed how she evoked '*Pittie*, with full tender hart'.[26] Shakespeare picks up this current of emotion and gives it less qualified expression: Arthur is innocent of conspiracy but, as Pandulph saw, was bound to be a focus of conspiracy against John. Thus far the general allusion of Arthur to Mary and John to Elizabeth is seen to continue; but when Hubert and John clash over whether or not the King commissioned Arthur's death, John saying: 'I had mighty cause | To wish him dead, but thou hadst none to kill him' and Hubert replying: 'Here is your hand and seal for what I did' (IV. ii. 206–7, 216), another of those brief but clear details is communicated which would be superfluous if they did not have contemporary point. (We may compare Eleanor's assertion, II. i. 191–2, that she can produce a will barring Arthur's claim, which can only have been mentioned to allude to Henry VIII's attempting to bar the Stuart claim; and we may note how in Sir John Hayward's examination Coke kept insisting on the detail that it was an *earl* who deposed Richard II, Essex being an earl but Bolingbroke a duke). The words 'hand and seal' in the context of the time refer to Elizabeth's order for the execution of Mary (her hints in favour of assassination having fallen on deaf ears), and her subsequent blaming of Secretary Davison for having exceeded her orders. The Davison allusion has sometimes been questioned, though accepted by the New Arden editor. I think nobody who reads through Camden's account of the episode can doubt that Shakespeare refers to it here. Neither is Shakespeare, any more than Camden, unmasking a piece of cold hypocrisy: the dangers to John and Elizabeth from Arthur and Mary were so great, whatever course they took, that their

[26] *Faerie Queene*, v. ix. 45.

repudiation of Davison after Mary's death, and of Hubert after Arthur's supposed death, has an evident emotional validity. What Camden saw, Shakespeare understood, and in drama had the means to convey: that rulers are rarely consistent and single-minded. Even the Bastard, bold asserter of illegitimacy and *de facto* power, appears stunned when he sees Arthur's dead body on the stones: however his lines are pointed, he seems for a moment to recognize in 'this morsel of dead royalty' 'The life, the right, and truth of all this realm' (IV. iii. 144–5), and it is surely strained to argue that this refers only to the revolt against John that he now foresees.[27]

Act IV opened on a newly crowned and confident John; Act V shows him with such confidence as submission to Pandulph can give him, but with the invasion previously intended by King Philip now really on English soil, and in tremendous strength (IV. ii. 110–12). Louis the Dauphin has invaded England as swiftly as John previously invaded France: the drama, having previously seemed to mirror the scattering of the Spanish Armada in the dispersion of Philip of France's fleet, now on the stage fulfils all the Armada fears. John is helpless and his nobles, incensed at the death of Arthur, have revolted against him. In the finest and most significant political irony of the play—more telling even than the truce which occasioned the Bastard's 'commodity' speech—the sometime politic and far-seeing Pandulph baldly announces to the Dauphin that John has submitted to the Pope: 'Therefore thy threat'ning colours now wind up' (V. ii. 73); the invasion can be called off. The Dauphin's response demonstrates the arrogance, and here naïveté, of papal authority over princes. A great invasion, with the ambitions it naturally generates, cannot so easily be abandoned; besides Louis rightly argues, as Pandulph once argued, that the doctrine of indefeasible hereditary right (never more than a handy weapon for papal diplomacy) does now make Louis *de jure* king. In this appalling crisis for John and England, the embodiment of the fears of the 'Homily against disobedience', the Armada nightmare come true, the Bastard remains faithful. (As Perrot said of Elizabeth: 'she would one day stand in need of his helpe'.) So does the wronged Hubert. At the eleventh hour England is delivered, partly by the remainder of faithful support for John, partly by Melun's disclosure of Louis's

[27] See IV. iii. 142–3 n. and 154 n. of New Arden edn.

intended treachery to his English supporters, partly by fortune (or Providence) when the Dauphin's supplies are sunk in the Goodwin Sands (v. v. 10–13). But in the dizzying turn and return of events, John himself, like the recent Henry III of France, has been poisoned by Catholic fanaticism. The 'burning quality' of the poison (v. vii. 8) is in its way the fit death for a ruler compounded more of air and fire than the baser elements: his impetuous life is 'a scribbled form, drawn with a pen | Upon a parchment, and against this fire | Do I shrink up' (v. vii. 32–4). John, the royal hero of Foxe, seems almost to endure that death by fire which the Protestant martyrs would later suffer, as the *Actes and Monuments* recorded. But John's is not a completed faith; he is the tragic precursor, the type, at his best, of what Henry, Edward, and Elizabeth would achieve and maintain. Violent fires soon burn themselves out: his valiant hubris is soon chastised and quenched. John's tragedy is to have tried to do what was right according to Henrician standards, before history was ready and the time ripe. England is left with the Bastard's sentiments: first his confidence that Prince Henry, following his father, shall 'put on | The lineal state and glory of the land' (v. vii. 101–2), thus permitting John's usurpation to found a regular monarchy; secondly, and famously, that England need fear no conquest if 'to itself' 'it rest but true!' (v. vii. 118). With commodity the bias of the world, honest national self-interest (perhaps what he twice calls 'fair play') is the best basis for loyalty, he says.

John is Shakespeare's most explicitly political play in that it comes closest to setting up a consistent series of specific contemporary allusions, and to being, in this direct way, what Lily Campbell has called 'a political mirror'. Less crowded with incident than the Henry VI plays, it is, I believe, as coherent a drama as *Richard III* while more evidently a political problem play. By contrast with the first tetralogy *John* does not sway our judgement by examples of misrule. John is a more effective *de facto* king than Henry VI, Arthur a less destructive *de jure* king than York. But where misrule is absent, perfidy and treachery are present, and nearly all on the side of the *de jure* claimants and the Papacy. The one example on the other side, the plot to assassinate Arthur, is, however, a particularly ruthless piece of *realpolitik*. Yet *John* is a drama which seems to take sides. Fully aware of the concept of indefeasible hereditary right, and of the supranational pretensions of the Papacy, it suggests that each is in the end only governed by self-interest. The character who sees and says this most plainly is he who plays 'the devil' (II. i. 135), the Bastard, in whom the Vice's cynical knowledge of the world does not here animate a tyrant such as Richard III, but heartens the Tudor patriot.

3

The Second Tetralogy and After

THE likening of King John to the Protestant Tudors was orthodoxy for their era until dramatists of the 1590s injected into the comparison the volatile contemporary ingredient of Arthur and the succession question, played down or ignored by Foxe and the *Book of Homilies*. The comparison between Elizabeth and Richard II, as we have seen from Camden and Peter Wentworth, was compelling though it involved no orthodoxy and appealed to various viewpoints, from those of the Queen herself to the judgements of subjects discontented with her rule, or anxious about the future. The examination of Sir John Hayward—after Shakespeare's completion of the second tetralogy—seems to show a nervous tendency on Elizabeth's part to identify with a king whom some thought it had been right to depose; while her well-known announcement to William Lambarde: 'I am Richard II. know ye not that?'[1] is further and exceptional evidence that, whatever its significance, Elizabeth did see a link between herself and Richard in the aftermath of an unsuccessful revolt against her.

I

What content did these various comparisons hold, prior to the composition of *Richard II*, probably in 1595? Before the execution of Mary, Queen of Scots, Elizabeth seems to have thought of herself as Richard and Mary as Mortimer, as she deliberated whether to designate a successor; much later, when Mary was condemned to death, courtiers urged that Elizabeth should act towards Mary as Henry IV had to Richard. Wentworth declared Richard to have been deposed, not by a declared successor by right, 'but an vsurper' and thus, on the face of it, Elizabeth was urged not to fear finding herself in Richard's position. But (Wentworth continued more ominously and subtly) the nobility then 'liked rather to have an vsurper to raigne

---

[1] *Richard II*, ed. Peter Ure, New Arden Series (1956), p. lix. See Ch. 1 n. 3 above.

over them, that would preserve the crowne & them, then a rightful king that would perill the crowne and state also'.[2] His warning to Elizabeth is clear enough. Wentworth's campaign links with a point that emerged from the examination of Hayward, and is relevant to Elizabeth earlier than 1601: she lacked that most strong defence of any throne, 'the multitude of children'. Here we are at the heart of the connection between the two monarchs.

One implication of Wentworth's comment on Richard II and Henry IV is that the former imperilled the crown in ways other than the failure to designate a successor; for Richard had after all named Mortimer. Wentworth was thinking of examples of misrule, drawn up in the parliamentary articles objected against the King at his deposition. This is more difficult ground for a comparison between Richard and Elizabeth; in these respects no simple parallel or allegory can be entertained. Nevertheless the apparently popular stage play *Thomas of Woodstock* (*c.*1591?) makes such vehement and sweeping charges of misrule against Richard II as at least to prompt the question whether some writers of the 1590s did not attack Richard II in order to communicate their sense that, childlessness apart, the Elizabethan regime was going the same way as Richard's had gone. That sense could only imply an apparently weak monarch, with blood on her hands, unpopular councillors and favourites, a military crisis in Ireland, and deeply resented expedients for raising the funds to resolve it. The final stroke to be added to this sketch of Richard's image in the 1590s comes from the subtle and provocative Parsons. The Civilian Lawyer of his *Conference* is roundly in favour of deposition when kings misrule: Richard had been 'an euel king', 'a tyrannical, obstinate euel prince' with his feet set on the head of the realm. He had had Woodstock murdered. Like Edward II Richard was deposed by Parliament, and in his place 'by free election was chosen for king the noble knight Henry, Duke of Lancaster, who proved afterward so notable a king as the world knoweth . . .'.[3] The *Conference* rounds off the argument by pointing out that all the depositions of kings in English history had proved happy for England, that 'God concurred' in them, and that it would be quite impossible to challenge their legality so many years later.

---

[2] Peter Wentworth, *A Pithie Exhortation To Her Majestie for Establishing Her Successor to the Crowne* (1598), ch. 1.

[3] Robert Parsons, *A Conference About the Next Succession to the Crowne of Ingland . . .* (1594), 40, 59, 60.

Set against these various views, of varying relevance to the Queen's last years, *Richard II* yields up some of its political character. Misrule is an important factor in the action, but comparison with *Woodstock* or with the sweeping conclusions of Parson's *Conference* shows Shakespeare giving a qualified picture of the King. The assassination of Woodstock, Duke of Gloucester, is the dominant action of the earlier drama: we see its cause, planning, and completion. *Woodstock* shows Richard utterly in the hands of parasites, wasting his wealth, issuing blank charters to raise funds, farming out the kingdom to his favourites, and finally delegating his powers to them and dividing England into three, with the best portion going to the greatest favourite. In Elizabethan dramas of kingship, from *Gorboduc* to *King Lear*, delegation and division were the most ominous possible signs—the equivalent, perhaps, of the triggering off of a nuclear war during the Cold War period.

Richard II displays nothing like this; and where it has common features with *Woodstock* it either removes them from the central focus, or adds a measure of justification. The murder of Woodstock is clearly attributed to Richard by Gaunt (i. ii. 37–41) and, indirectly, by York (ii. i. 183); it sounds like the act of a tyrant, which is certainly the case in *Woodstock*, but here the circumstances are unexplained, and the deed is in the past. Gaunt justifies his inaction in the matter partly on grounds of his own complicity, partly on the unimpeachably orthodox grounds of non-resistance to God's deputy even when tyrannous. Again, the expedients for raising funds, farming out the realm, and blank charters, receive briefer mention in *Richard II*, but not so brief as to exclude a new factor: in Shakespeare's text the reason for these undesirable devices is to finance the Irish war to which the King will go in person (i. iv. 41–51). Shakespeare thus gives a good end to dubious means, and depicts Richard as engaging in kingly action rather than simply spending great sums on a lavish court. But it is apparently his previous waste which now renders the dubious means necessary. The third instance of misrule is of course the confiscation of Bolingbroke's inheritance on the death of his father, Gaunt (ii. i. 156–63). Here too, arguably, the end is good, but this act is a great deal more serious than Richard's other ways of raising funds. As York protests, this is to deny the hereditary principle which makes Richard himself king (ii. i. 195–209). It is a denial of Bolingbroke's common-law rights. This speech makes it clear that in Bodinian terms

Richard is a royal monarch, inheriting his crown by descent and law, who now acts as a lordly monarch. That is one who 'is become lord of the goods and persons of his subiects . . . as the master of a familie doth his slaues'.[4] Not for nothing does Northumberland, seething with resentment at all these measures, announce that 'we shall shake off our slavish yoke. . . .' (II. i. 293). On the point of misrule, therefore, Shakespeare shows Richard hampered by his past misdeeds but attempting to disentangle himself from them. He is imperilling his crown, as Wentworth said,[5] but is struggling by wrong means to face up to his responsibilities. He is a very different figure from the King Richard of *Woodstock* though it is true there that some awareness of his crimes and follies was dawning towards the end,[6] even if we do not know what was to have been the consequence of Richard's military defeat at the end of that play.

The deposition is to *Richard II* as the murder is to *Woodstock*: the main action that is displayed almost from its beginning to its end. Bodin, as we have seen, declared that it was an 'uniust quarrell' on Bolingbroke's part against Richard,[7] but saw it as a contention that, the eldest son having predeceased the king, the crown should go to the eldest surviving son rather than to the son of the dead eldest. This argument seems never to have entered the English tradition concerning Richard. Conspicuous in the English tradition is the parliamentary ratification of the deposition, with all the instances of misrule duly enumerated; and this of course is the basis of the

[4] Jean Bodin, *Les Six Livres de la république* (1576), trans. Richard Knolles (1606), ed. K. D. McRae (Cambridge, Mass., 1962), 200.
[5] Wentworth, *Pithie Exhortation*, 79–80.
[6] Ed. George Parfitt and Simon Shepherd (Nottingham, 1977), v. iv. 2864–70; T. J. L. Cribb, 'The Politics of *Richard II*', unpublished paper communicated to me by the author, 5–6; and J. H. Hexter, 'Property, Monopoly and Shakespeare's *Richard II*', in P. Zagorin (ed.) *Culture and Politics* (Berkeley and Los Angeles, 1980), 1–24. My own discussion of Richard at this point is most in debt to Samuel Schoenbaum, ' "Richard II" and the Realities of Power', *Shakespeare Survey*, 28 (1975), 1–13. See too P. A. Jorgensen, 'A Formative Shakespearian Legacy: Elizabethan Views of God, Fortune and War', *PMLA* 90 (1975), 222–33; Zdenek Stribrny, 'The Idea and Image of Time', *Shakespeare Jahrbuch*, 110 (1974), 129–38; and id., 'The Idea and Image of Time in Shakespeare's Second Historical Tetralogy', *Shakespeare Jahrbuch*, 111 (1975), 51–66; Robert P. Merrix, 'Shakespeare and the New Bardolaters', *Studies in English Literature*, 19 (1979), 179–96; John Alvis and Thomas G. West, *Shakespeare as a Political Thinker* (Chapel Hill, NC, 1981); Hugh Grady, *The Modernist Shakespeare* (Oxford, 1990); Anthony Miller, '*Henry IV Part I* and Renaissance Ideologies', *Sydney Studies in English*, 16 (1990–1), 35–53; Phyllis Rackin, *Stages of History* (1991).
[7] *Six Livres*, 738.

argument of the Civilian Lawyer in Parsons's *Conference*. This equally is ignored by Shakespeare: *Richard II* does not agree with the *Conference* that the King was deposed by Parliament for misrule. Once Richard is back from Ireland he is never formally charged with misrule; those who depose him do not give this as a reason for their action. Though not forgotten the matter is kept in the background. Bolingbroke's message to Richard that he has returned only to reverse his banishment and secure his inheritance (III. iii. 31–60) implies past injustice; Carlisle's argument that if criminals are not condemned unheard the King should not be deposed unheard (IV. i. 114–20) implies charges that are never in fact brought; finally the reliable because largely choric Garden Scene directly blames Richard for misgovernment. Far more prominent than these moments and their implications, however, is the question of power and support on each side: Bolingbroke's strength and Richard's weakness, which it is the prime purpose of the magnificently structured III. ii to drive home.

When Richard, in this scene, has learned most but not all the dreadful news concerning the ebbing away of his support, he can say:

> Cover your heads, and mock not flesh and blood
> With solemn reverence. Throw away respect,
> Tradition, form, and ceremonious duty;
> For you have but mistook me all this while.
> I live with bread, like you; feel want,
> Taste grief, need friends. Subjected thus,
> How can you say to me I am a king?
>
> (III. ii. 167–73)

He needs friends: there is the point. It is not a point against the divine right of kings, that is to say, against the divine commission of the Bodinian Royal Monarch. The Bishop of Carlisle, the most steadfast defender of Richard's royal title, in whom Bolingbroke himself sees 'High sparks of honour' (v. vi. 28) and Johnson was to judge 'brave, pious, and venerable',[8] twice makes the point that 'The deputy elected by the Lord' (III. ii. 53) must embrace the means that heaven yields (III. ii. 27–8).[9] He corrects Richard's professed belief

---

[8] Samuel Johnson, *Works* (New Haven and London, 1968), vii. 446.

[9] With the additional 4 lines printed in the 1597 First Quarto, ll. 176–81. Cf. the one-volume Oxford edition of Shakespeare, *The Complete Works*, ed. Stanley Wells and Gary Taylor (Oxford, 1986), 445 D. Shakespeare may have dropped these lines in revision, as conjectured. One can only say that their relevance to the concept of kingship in the 1590s (and again in the 1630s and 1640s) is obvious. They cannot be ignored.

that God will necessarily defend his 'deputy' against the 'shrewd steel' of his enemies (III. ii. 55–62). The *de jure* king must therefore study how to sustain power and seize the occasion that heaven affords. It is a lesson which Richard learns too late to save himself: but his awareness of it informs all his later role in the play.

Power, and the tradition, form, and ceremonious duty which in Richard's case have originally seemed at one with it, are in this play frequently dramatized by the use of theatrical height. In the lists at Coventry it is clear that the King and his nobles are situated above the combatants. (This is the point of I. iii. 54, while l. 123 makes it probable that Richard ascended again after embracing Bolingbroke, as common sense suggests.) From that height Richard hears the formal challenges of the tournament, arrests the combat at the last moment, metes out sentences to the combatants, commanding them to swear oaths against their wishes, and finally mitigates the sentence against Bolingbroke whose response: 'How long a time lies in one little word' (l. 206) underlines the power of the King at this point. With this scene we compare the next where the King is aloft: III. iii, where the balcony is the decayed battlements of Flint Castle (ll. 31–3). Here the King can put up no resistance; while Northumberland is sent to him with fair words, Bolingbroke parades his troops 'without the noise of threat'ning drum' before his eyes, a display of silent might. If Richard will revoke his banishment and restore his lands, he promises, he will be loyal. 'If not, I'll use the advantage of my power' (ll. 50; 35–47). To the perhaps wishful imagination of Bolingbroke the royal figure on the battlements seems like the sun about to be dimmed by cloud; to York, with a strong sense of Richard's inherent sovereignty, he 'Yet' looks like a king: he has all the fair show of authority and power (ll. 60–70). And indeed Richard, though 'bereft of friends' (l. 83) as he concedes, defies them for the moment with the full power and logic of his royal title (ll. 71–99). Insincere courtesies are exchanged. Nobody is deceived. Bolingbroke attends in the 'base court' and, invited to come down, Richard dramatizes in words and action his second significant descent to greet his cousin:

> Down, down I come, like glist'ring Phaethon,
> Wanting the manage of unruly jades.
> In the base court: base court, where kings grow base
> To come at traitors' calls . . .

> (III. iii. 177–80)

Nothing could be more chilling in the circumstances than the consistent language of loyalty on the rebels' part. Richard is impressive here, among other reasons, because he will have no truck with this false show. The conclusive end of this scene asserts what will be repeated in later scenes concerning the nature of the King's deposition:

RICHARD. For we must do what force will have us do.

(III. iv. 206)

The drama of power has thus been visually and theatrically conveyed: the acted images of height and depth, ascent and descent, are incorporated (and transformed) in the King's later image of the two buckets of the well: 'That bucket down and full of tears am I, | Drinking my griefs, whilst you mount up on high' (IV. i. 178–9). Johnson noted the implication: 'the usurper the "empty" bucket'.[10] The same comparison, though with a clear moral against Richard, is stressed by the choice of a word: 'Here, cousin, seize the crown' (l. 171) the King cries, and we remember his 'we do seize to us' and 'we seize into our hands' (II. i. 161, 210) when, so much earlier as it now seems, he unlawfully confiscated Bolingbroke's patrimony.

  Richard II is then a drama about power and force. It splits the 'fair show' of royalty from its power. Richard chiefly suffers this split, in his mind. Bolingbroke, who never declares a purpose to supplant Richard before he constrains Richard to resign, is the figure of force, but the King seeks to fight by force too, and fails partly by chance (III. ii. 65–70), partly because he has understood too late that a true king needs friends and troops and support. Thereafter he can only respond with words; yet in the ceremonious figure of the falling King is gathered all the logic, eloquence, and imagery of Royal Monarchy. His arguments against resistance and deposition are also found in the mouths of Carlisle, Gaunt, and York. These totally orthodox arguments are not countered by any others: as they advance to power Northumberland and Bolingbroke simply ignore them. In large measure these images and arguments form the moral and political outlook of the play though it is also full of understanding as to how rebellion *can* come about, unjustifiable though it may be. The Bolingbroke of the end is thus a quintessentially *de facto* king. One wrongful implication of the deposition is, however,

[10] Johnson, *Works*, vii. 447.

here deliberately ignored by Shakespeare: its depriving Mortimer of his right (as pointed out by Exeter in *Richard Duke of York*, I. i. 146–7). Thus the fudging words of *Richard II*'s York (still borne in mind): 'Richard, who with willing soul | Adopts thee heir . . . | Ascend his throne, descending now from him' (IV. i. 99–102), appear to possess a rudiment of fitness where the childless Richard is concerned. This is precisely the situation which Camden shows Elizabeth to have so feared if she were to designate an heir. Here it is plain, as often pointed out, that there is in Richard a general allusion to Elizabeth, though by no means a realistic, or an allegorical, representation of her. The eloquent, formal, ceremonious Elizabeth, childless and likely to be the last of her line, deliberately played the queen (as James I, for example, did not play the king).

Richard, like her in all these respects, like her also in his Irish troubles and in the unpopularity of the means to which he resorted to put down Irish rebellion, is filled by Shakespeare with the *idea* of lineal royalty, kingship by divine election and human law, Royal Monarchy. It proves as powerful a dramatic and theatrical idea as the idea of intelligent tyranny in Richard of Gloucester, or of realistic patriotism in the Bastard. But set effectively against it is the new *de facto* king, Bolingbroke, a figure of strength not lacking in the quality of intelligent mercy, as his treatment of Carlisle and Aumerle shows. But here too there is a plain allusion; and here we see how incisive and analytic a political drama *Richard II* is. For if John, Hubert, and Arthur allude to Elizabeth, Davison, and Mary, the similar situation at the end of this play (V. iv–vi and especially V. vi. 34–47), which Shakespeare did not have to include in the way he does, must carry, though more briefly, the same allusion. It is perhaps the mark of this play's greatness that, just when so much of vulnerable Elizabethan royalty seemed invested in the figure of Richard, the tables turn, and we see in Bolingbroke the Tudor Queen, with none too secure a title, whom the apparently inexorable logic of events had brought to the point of hoping for the assassination, but in the end signing the death warrant, of her competitor and heir. The play shows us Elizabeth as Richard II, but also Elizabeth as Henry IV. Just over a century later Dryden, another poet for whom the example of Richard II was crucial, translated the *Aeneid* so as to see in Aeneas both James II and William III.

10

Judged in context *Richard II* is no celebration of Lesleian indefeasible hereditary right. Turning to the opposite political extreme, however, we see that it does not conform to Parsons's contention that Richard was evil, or justly and by due force deposed for misrule. It ignores Bodin's specific and academic interests in the claim of Bolingbroke against Richard, but in a more central way responds fully and powerfully to the Bodinian notion of the Royal Monarch. It deploys in no merely dutiful way the arguments of the *Book of Homilies* against armed resistance to princes even when guilty of injustice. But it makes clear that Richard's nobles were not driven to such desperation that rebellion was their only resort. Richard II is no Richard III. We do not hear of the concept of necessity, which plays so striking a part in Hayward's account of the deposition in *Henry IIII*, nor of the duty of the subject to the state transcending that to the prince. *Richard II*, if anything, explores as only a play can the paradoxes in Peter Wentworth's statement that Richard was deposed by 'an vsurper' but one whom the nobility 'liked rather . . . to raigne over them, that would preserve the crown & them, then a rightful king that would perill the crowne and state also'. But with this exception: Shakespeare shows the *de jure* king attempting to surmount his early crimes and errors. The real moral of the play, perhaps, is to recommend patience on the part of subjects towards erring princes.

II

In the playing of the King by Falstaff and Hal, in the first Tavern Scene of *1 Henry IV*, Falstaff can say:

Depose me. If thou dost it half so gravely, so majestically both in word and matter, hang me up by the heels for a rabbit sucker, or a poulter's hare.

(II. v. 438–41)

The speech nicely catches the relation between *Richard II* and the two parts of *Henry IV*. Seen from the wider world of the two later plays *Richard II* appears a grave and majestical prologue to an extended drama which has much in it that is serious and noble but which can also and characteristically remind us of ordinary everyday life, of poulterers' shops. A little earlier in the same scene Falstaff has regaled Hal with the high political news: a new rebellion is afoot, 'Worcester is stolen away tonight. Thy father's beard is turned white with the news. You may buy land now as cheap as stinking mackerel' (II. v. 361–3). This is not an idiom we hear in *Richard II*, and it throws matters of rebellion and deposition into an entirely new light. The language is not only a sign of human distance from these events: it is a mark of a new kind of interest in them. Falstaff has immediately seen the stock exchange aspect of an imminent breakdown of government. These points need early emphasis, for a concern with revolutions in high politics in these plays almost always opens out into a relatively realistic portrayal of national life. The present argument concerning the succession of kings thus takes on greater human substance than it has previously borne. It is hardly necessary to demonstrate this important feature of Shakespeare's *Henry IV* and *Henry V* dramas, for it is now widely recognized that their 'high' and 'low' life scenes are not merely contrasting and complementary, but integral in their dramatization of national life, and absolutely necessary to the grand new theme of these plays: that of the education of a prince and, one may add, the education of a new royal line.[11]

For while everywhere in *1* and *2 Henry IV* Bolingbroke is referred to as the King, if one thing is clear from the relation of these plays to *Richard II* it is that he secured the throne by force, force partly acquired by his having courted popularity. In Bodinian terms Henry is not, in the fullest sense, a Royal Monarch but a Lordly Monarch: we may recall that Bodin's two chief examples of Lordly Monarchs were William the Conqueror in England and the Emperor Charles V in the New World. A recurrent theme in Bodin's thinking about Lordly Monarchy is the problem of what Machiavelli termed 'new principalities' in chapter 6 of *The Prince*. At the same time we have seen that Bodin's basic distinctions between Royal, Lordly, and Tyrannous Monarchs focus rather on the nature of their rule than their manner of acquiring it. It is thus that Bodin's thought permits the evolution of political forms, from republic to monarchy even, certainly from Lordly Monarchy to Royal Monarchy. Here, it may be thought, Shakespeare's theme of education has its widest relevance. In *1 Henry VI* and *The Contention* Prince Edward, the lineal heir of the *de jure* royal line, though brave and loyal to his father, is demonstrably unready for the throne, as his handling of his

[11] Irving Ribner, *The English History Play in the Age of Shakespeare* (Princeton, 1957; rev. 1965).

marriage displays. Both he and his brother Richard have been trained in civil war rather than government; and it shows. In *1* and *2 Henry IV* Shakespeare not only offers a daring new embodiment of the traditional concept of the education of the Christian prince; he also brings this to the deeper historical notion of the possible, but by no means inevitable, slow incorporation of a new dynasty into the institution of monarchy and the wisdom of rule: the transformation of a usurping and Lordly line into a Royal Monarchy.

If this hypothesis is to be examined, however, it will be necessary not to think of Worcester, Northumberland, Hotspur, and their supporters as 'the rebels'. They may, on the contrary, be legitimists, like York, Warwick, and Salisbury in *The Contention*, but seeking here to set right a more recent historical wrong. In the dramatization of their views we first hear of pride in Hotspur and malevolence in Worcester (i. i. 90–8). In the scene in which Henry first confronts the discontented group, attempting to assert his authority over it, Worcester resents the scourge of greatness upon his house, 'And that same greatness too which our own hands | Have holp to make so portly' (i. iii. 12–13). That is the nub of the matter, psychologically speaking. Henry is openly angry and sarcastic, very different from the silent figure in *Richard II*, and from him we hear that the 'noble Mortimer' of i. i. 38 is 'the foolish Mortimer' and finally 'revolted Mortimer' (i. iii. 79, 91): what develops is a quarrel about the honour and future of the Percys' kinsman in which Henry's manner is high-handed and threatening. Into the seething resentment thus provoked Worcester drops the germ of the *de jure* argument: was Mortimer not proclaimed 'By Richard, that dead is, the next of blood?' (l. 144). This is new to Hotspur and new to us; it gives him a new image of Henry, whom he now begins to call not just 'ingrate and cankered Bolingbroke' (l. 135), a first reaction, but 'this subtle King' (l. 167) and 'this vile politician Bolingbroke' (l. 239). It is notable that Hotspur, though warm to defend his kinsman Mortimer, can give an account of Northumberland's and Worcester's role in the deposing of Richard and enthroning of Henry which might not have displeased Richard himself (ll. 156–83). What emerges from these two scenes is that anger against a king who behaves less gratefully than the kingmakers hoped mounts a political argument in its support; and this makes a strong impression on Hotspur.

The strange Welsh scene, partly comic, partly wonderful, introduces a most sinister sign in its curiously innocent atmosphere: the division of the kingdom (III. i. 67–137). What Richard was rightly condemned for attempting in *Woodstock*, is being attempted here in his memory. The malcontents are here shown in a very irresponsible light. And it is significant that in the next act the three parts of the opposition to Henry cannot unite in time for the expected battle. As this approaches, the real danger and seriousness of the situation begins to come home to the combatants, lending a dramatic urgency to the exchange of arguments which first takes place. To Henry's offer to redress grievances and pardon those in arms against him Hotspur responds with scepticism. There follows a restatement of what is dominant in the 'griefs' of the insurgents: how dependent on them Henry once was, how proud he now seemed to those who 'Did give him that same royalty he wears' (IV. iii. 57). It is a deeply understandable but quite irrational ground for resisting the *de facto* monarch, who is at least, as Blunt has reminded them, 'anointed majesty' (IV. iii. 42). But it is also Hotspur who, coming to the point, advances, uniquely in the *Henry IV* plays, the genuine *de jure* and also common law argument:

> [Henry] . . . suffered his kinsman March—
> Who is, if every owner were well placd,
> Indeed his king—to be engaged in Wales,
> There without ransom to lie forfeited.
>
> (IV. iii. 95–8)

He concludes that Henry's own title is 'Too indirect for long conti- nuance' (l. 107). This is his answer to Blunt, not Henry himself. The impetuous Hotspur yet reserves the deliberated answer for the following morning and the mouth of Worcester. And in the chill and ominous dawn of the next day Worcester attends at Henry's camp to give what should be the official as well as the most politic and wise explanation of why he and his friends are in arms. It is significant that Worcester has nothing to say concerning Mortimer as the true king. His impressive speech once again rehearses his family's resentment that the king whom they (and fortune) have made should play the king to them. He adds the charge of oath- breaking which Hotspur too had mentioned (v. i. 30–71). Henry repeats his offer which Worcester himself is to call 'liberal and kind' (v. ii.); Hal predicts that it will be rejected by the sheer confidence of Hotspur and the Douglas (v. i. 115–16); it is in fact rejected because Worcester dares not repeat it to Hotspur, lest he accept it.

Worcester's grim knowledge of the world tells him that without a victory treason would always now attach itself to his name, and that Henry has been foresworn before. His reasons for remaining in arms against Henry are now sheer *realpolitik*; only Hotspur has expressed a justifying argument. The emotion that drives each of them on is outrage that their erstwhile colleague should assume kingly authority over them now. Thus the Battle of Shrewsbury is joined, Falstaff putting into a few words what we may conclude all felt, and saying something as expressive as many a long speech: 'I would 'twere bed-time, Hal, and all well' (v. i. 125).

In the Introduction to 2 *Henry IV* Rumour speaks of 'the flame of bold rebellion' (l. 26). It is a nicely poised mention for the word has more authority from this choric figure than the mouths of Henry and his party. On the other hand the choric figure is Rumour. In the excellent scene in which the news of his son's defeat is finally brought home to Northumberland the question of this 'word "rebellion" ' is most interestingly raised. Welcoming the rising of the Archbishop of York Morton says that he 'Turns insurrection to religion. . . . Derives from heaven his quarrel and his cause' whereas before 'that same word "rebellion" did divide' the body and soul of their party (I. i. 190–208). It is an important admission of the psychological effect of *de facto* kingship on people's minds—or is it, further, an implied admission that Northumberland and his party are in fact rebels? Remembering the role of the Bishop of Carlisle in *Richard II*, though remembering also that in *1 Henry IV*, I. iii. 259–64, Northumberland was to creep into the Archibishop's bosom, we await with interest Shakespeare's handling of this churchman. The conclave of the Archbishop's party, however, opens at the point where 'the occasion of our arms' (I. iii. 5) has been granted, and the debate turns from ends to means. As they resolve to take up arms against Henry, the Archbishop utters trenchant judgements on the times, and in a biblical image that Wordsworth was to use in writing about the French Revolution and the crowning of Napoleon, compares the land, which has put down Richard and now longs for him back, to a dog that craves to eat its own vomit (ll. 87–108).[12] When the Archbishop's forces confront those of Henry, at Gaultree Forest, he again dwells on the sickness of the time and the sinfulness of man, and claims to 'find our griefs

---

[12] 2 Pet. 2.22; *The Prelude* (1805), x. 934–5.

heavier than our offences' (IV. i. 69). As before the case of the insurgent nobles comes down to grievances rather than title, Hotspur's speech before Shrewsbury being the single exception. It is then the case that, whatever the significance of Mortimer in Yorkist arguments in the Henry VI plays, the groups which here take up arms against the *de facto* monarch scarcely resort to the available legitimist principle. In the Henry VI plays genealogical arguments were reiterated; reiterated in these plays are the complaints of aggrieved kingmakers. Whether to come to your king with an army and a list of griefs constitutes rebellion might be debated; it is very like coming with an army to remove evil councillors: there is a measure of coercion involved. The opposing party in the Henry IV plays is to this extent rebellious, though it need not have been had it consistently and wholeheartedly denied Henry's right. The indispensable principle of kingship was, however, most evident in the person of Henry. And in Henry that principle, vulnerable yet necessary, is endowed with a resolute and indeed ruthless will to resist coercion. This is shown in the energy with which Henry fights the Battle of Shrewsbury and the cool treachery with which, on Henry's behalf, Prince John secures in the interests of necessity of state the capitulation of the rebels at Gaultree Forest.[13]

If the resentful and angry Henry of *1 Henry IV*, I. i and iii is a dramatic revelation after the Bolingbroke of *Richard II* who so silently gathered power, the Henry of III. ii, the first intimate exchange between the King and his eldest son, is a further revelation still. Here for the first time Henry begins to speak of how he came to the crown. The scene is obviously one of those which concerns the education of the Prince in the person of Hal, but as Henry looks back on the political course which has brought him where he is we begin to see that it also concerns the education through experience of the Lordly Monarch who has seized the crown. The scene, in fact, forms a sequence with III. i and IV. iii of *2 Henry IV*. It springs from Henry's rebuke to Hal's apparently disorderly conduct and touches ominously on the possibility of divine punishment of Harry 'for some displeasing service I have done' (III. ii. 5) and then, almost casually, makes an extraordinarily frank admission: 'Opinion, that did help me to the crown . . .' (l. 42). He does not talk of Richard's misrule. He talks of how Richard made his presence cheap. It is

[13] See *2 Henry IV*, ed. A. R. Humphreys, New Arden Series (1966), 237–40.

convincing psychology that he should read back into the king he overcame the errors he now sees in his own son. 'The skipping King' (l. 60) is hardly to be found in *Richard II* though perhaps in *Woodstock*. *Richard II* does, however, confirm Bolingbroke's 'courtship to the common people' (i. iv. 23) 'As were our England in reversion his' (l. 34): what distinguished his behaviour from his alleged picture of Richard was his intelligent cultivation of popular opinion, by contrast with thoughtless public display. This is the lesson which Henry greatly enlarges on to Hal. Its political significance can hardly be underestimated, for though at this stage Henry sounds no note of guilt, he shows he has learned how popularity may successfully overcome hereditary right (ll. 39–91). We may well wonder what Shakespeare's original audience made of Henry's explanation, and whether his comparison of his presence to 'a robe pontifical | Ne'er seen but wonder'd at' (ll. 56–7) did not seem to strike a slightly spurious note. But this is not, of course, all Henry's thought on kingship in this scene. His praise of Hotspur, designed to urge Hal forward into similar martial activity, shows a concept of what could be 'worthy interest to the state' (ll. 98–9), seeing, or pretending to see, more potential value to the state in Hotspur than such an heir to the throne as Hal.

The vigorous didactic tone of this scene, fitting prelude to Henry's and Hal's success on the field of Shrewsbury, is succeeded in Shakespeare's series of retrospects by the troubled night scene of 2 *Henry IV*, iii. i. Once again highly conventional reflections, the soliloquy leading up to 'Uneasy lies the head . . .' (l. 31), touch on the possibility of crime and punishment. They move to a deeper level with the notion of the kingdom diseased (ll. 38–43), and one deeper still (it is I think a quite new moment in Shakespeare) at the outbreak of Henry's lament:

> O God, that one might read the book of fate,
> And see the revolution of the times . . .
>
> (ll. 44–6)

for here the bitterness and disappointment of historical process is expressed by the very man who has made a revolution. The new king, would-be founder of a new line, could hardly be more effectively humanized. Henry speaks first of 'how chance's mocks | And changes fill the cup of alteration | With diverse liquors!' (ll. 50–2) but his immensely dramatic recall of Richard's prophecy against

Northumberland suggests that history is not mere chance, indeed that there are laws allowing prediction.[14] In the disavowing parenthesis in which he now states he had then no design upon the crown he appeals to the opposite idea: not chance but 'necessity so bow'd the state | That I and greatness were compell'd to kiss' (ll. 68–9). Warwick picks up the notions of necessity and prophecy, giving them the psychological basis in *realpolitik* which had underlain what Richard said: '. . . thou, which know'st the way | To plant unrightful kings, wilt know again' (ll. 62–3). The dejected and intimate character of this scene flows in great measure from Henry's having learned this lesson in *realpolitik* through bitter and direct experience. But he takes back the concept of necessity, now sounding more like a law in the science of politics, and turns it into a stoic defence of action (ll. 87–8). Force will confront force once more; and at Gaultree Forest Prince John, exercising another element in the art of *realpolitik*, will disperse the danger.

But when, in IV. iii, King Henry's final victories are announced to him he is struck sick. Like the very first scene of *1 Henry IV*, this scene opens with Henry's plans for the crusade, but despite mention of all his practical preparations, his mind is really on his son. The long passage of advice to his younger sons, maxims from the art of the courtier, show with what concern the King is now thinking about the heir to the throne and the dynasty that he hopes to have established. The one is the means to the other. As the scene unfolds the King's fears are shown to go deeper. Advice to his sons on how to handle Hal is succeeded by a bitter, grief-stricken denunciation: no courtier's art could (it now seems) redeem the next king:

> therefore my grief
> Stretches itself beyond the hour of death.
> The blood weeps from my heart when I do shape
> In forms imaginary th' unguided days

[14] Shakespeare appears to forget that Richard's prophecy was not uttered when 'check'd and rated by Northumberland' (*Richard II*, IV. i. 68) but later, on his way to prison, when Bolingbroke was not present (V. i. 55–68). He surely cannot forget that, in *Richard II*, IV. i. 104, *before* Northumberland had rated and accused Richard, Bolingbroke had announced: 'In God's name I'll ascend the regal throne.' If the tetralogy is generally coherent, Henry's disavowal must be seen as either disingenuous, or sincere retrospective self-deceit. (See *2 Henry IV*, New Arden Series (1966) 93, ll. 72–4 n., for the New Arden editor's contrary view, which also ignores the political character of *Richard II*.) A later scene (*2 Henry IV*, IV. iii) tells us which interpretation to put on Henry's disavowal.

And rotten times that you shall look upon
When I am sleeping with my ancestors.

(IV. iii. 56–61)

Warwick's attempt to comfort him has something of the rationali-
zation we recall from the conclusion of Hal's first scene in *1 Henry
IV*: 'The Prince will, in the perfectness of time, | Cast off his
followers', having studied their immodesty (ll. 74–5). It is an import-
ant truth but hardly the whole truth. Warwick's obvious, courtier-
like desire to comfort the King without criticizing the Prince, does
not seem to succeed, though there may be an element of self-pity in
the ageing Henry which will not acknowledge comfort on this score.
He is comforted by news of Gaultree Forest but, the line of the
drama holding the interest as it turns, further good news, this time
of victory in battle, only writes his good fortune in 'foulest letters':
'O me! Come near me; now I am much ill' (l. 111). The young
princes confide their alarm to one another; the King is laid on a bed;
music plays, the crown is set beside him on his pillow—and the
theatrical emblem, with all its visual eloquence, has been prepared
for the very process of royal succession. The separation of the crown
from the King seems a premonition of his death: he no longer (it
seems) embodies monarchy, but rather it is the object of his contem-
plation.

Hal now arrives from the hunt, noisy and full of vigorous common
sense: a strong contrast with the solemn tableau, challenging its
hushed music. As Hal remains his thoughts slowly draw him into
the significance of what he sees: the stillness of his father's figure
confronts him with the separation of man and crown: '. . . this is a
sleep | That from this golden rigol hath divorc'd | So many English
kings' (ll. 166–8). The crown is now 'My due' (l. 172); these plays,
unlike the Henry VI plays, do not now countenance a legitimist
claim. With no spirit of impiety, selfishness, or riot, but with a full
sense of its responsibilities, Hal dons the crown as a 'lineal honour'
which 'God shall guard'. The Prince's last words before his exit
speak not primarily of himself, not of his father, but of the royal *line*
that, together, they seek to establish:

This from thee
Will I to mine leave, as 'tis left to me.

(ll. 177–8)

The scene of final reconciliation between king and heir which takes place when Henry awakes rehearses again his fears that anarchy will break out in the already strife-torn kingdom with the new reign; and it rehearses again the oft-propounded aim (last put by Warwick) of Hal's sudden reformation: 'The noble change that I have purposeèd!' (l. 283). The effect is to underline the fundamental interest of the kingdom in the imminent succession. The return of the crown with the prayer that it may be divinely guarded (ll. 272–3), and the heir's kneeling before the King, clearly implied in ll. 275–7, visually re-establishes the proper situation prior to the passing on of the crown. At this point the King plays a paternal and didactic role, the Prince an explanatory and submissive one. But no sooner is their reconciliation complete than, in the most intimate exchange we have yet witnessed between the two, the King adopts the confessional role, more deeply confessional and revealing than in any of the earlier confessional scenes. This is the culmination of their sequence. Now he says far more than that opinion had helped him to the crown:

> God knows, my son,
> By what bypaths and indirect crook'd ways
> I met this crown; and I myself know well
> How troublesome it sat upon my head.
> To thee it shall descend with better quiet,
> Better opinion, better confirmation;
> For all the soil of the achievement goes
> With me into the earth.
>
> (ll. 312–19)

The immediate impact of these lines is to show that, by the admission of the very man who took the crown, the crown was taken wrongly. The content and tone of this speech, by comparison with what he has said before, is quite different. Yet on closer inspection these words stop just short of confessing a crime. The title of a crown can be an elaborate and complicated matter, as the Henry VI plays and *Henry V* show, and that very complexity can afford an opening for hostile comment and resistance. Shakespeare appears to have blended two sources, *The Famous Victories* where, with a similar opening and tone, Henry confessed less ('For God knowes my sonne, how hardly I came by it')[15] and Daniel's *Civile Wars* with

[15] *2 Henry IV*, ed. Humphreys, 227.

its more explicit admission of guilt: in Daniel he speaks of getting the crown 'with bloud' and leaving it 'with horror' and of 'sinne'.[16] Shakespeare's refashioning of these sources (there is no close analogue in Holinshed or elsewhere, so far as is known) is brilliantly done: the words 'crook'd' and 'soil' carry the strong implication of guilt while sufficiently euphemistic to be psychologically convincing from a man who cannot be said to repent fully that he has become king. (Daniel, by comparison, seems to show a transient intention on Henry's part to restore the crown to some *de jure* claimant.)[17] This is borne out by Henry's deathbed advice to his heir. For the first time his goal of a pilgrimage to the Holy Land, which has received prominent mention throughout *Richard II* and *Henry IV*, is linked with his struggle to maintain the new royal line upon the throne ('. . . and had a purpose now | To lead out many to the Holy Land, | Lest rest and lying still might make them look | Too near unto my state' (IV. iii. 338–41). It has been suggested that Shakespeare has here followed Daniel in revealing duplicity of motive in Henry.[18] But Daniel's 'Machiavellian strain' is of the genuine kind: realist rather than treacherous. Henry's aim in the poem is 'T'appease my God, and reconcile my land'.[19] Each writer is, like Machiavelli, concerned with the means by which a new prince may establish himself, but if anything the secular motive is stronger in Shakespeare than Daniel and Shakespeare's Henry is more blunt than Daniel's in recommending 'foreign quarrels' (l. 343) to his heir in order to establish the line. Yet the two sides of Henry's mind, his recognition of political guilt, and his determination to found a new line, join formally in his concluding couplet:

> How I came by the crown, O God forgive,
> And grant it may with thee in true peace live!

> (ll. 347–8)

Like Elizabeth, Henry recognizes guilt but still sees his crime as part of a necessity of state he cannot repudiate. Hal assents to his own part in this vision. He does not use the *politique* language accorded him by Daniel ('Time will appease them well that now complaine, | And ratifie our interest in the end'),[20] but the more ringing and knightly:

---

[16] *2 Henry IV*, ed. Humphreys, 210–11.   [17] Ibid. 210, st. 122.
[18] Ibid. 242.   [19] Ibid. 211.   [20] Ibid.

You won it, wore it, kept it, gave it me;
Then plain and right must my possession be,
Which I with more than with a common pain
'Gainst all the world will rightfully maintain.

(ll. 350–3)

It is an argument of title which has been quite refuted by York and
Warwick in *Richard Duke of York*, I. i, but at this point in the later
and more mature play it is made to sound convincing.

III

Shakespeare's purpose in dramatizing, not only the education of a
new prince, but the establishment of a new line whose hereditary
title is not of the best, is still more evident in *Henry V*. This is seen
in a series of significant inclusions and exclusions in pointed relation
with one another. It is first of all notable in the Archbishop's 'Salic
land' speech in I. ii. This is at once familiar as another of Shakes-
peare's long and involved genealogical expositions similar to those
in *1 Henry VI*, II. v, and *The Contention*, II. ii. It is further notable
that, like the title of Richard of York in the first tetralogy, it derives
an hereditary royal right through the female line: that is of course
the issue at stake and the heart of the Archbishop's long explana-
tion. Like York's claim this one is in itself likely to have been
acceptable to loyal subjects of Elizabeth in that any 'female bar'
(such as Knox might have acclaimed against Mary, Queen of Scots)
would have deprived England of its reigning queen (*Henry V*,
Taylor I. ii. 42). The speech, as Shakespeare derives it from his
chronicle sources, is an argument from human and positive
law rather than natural law and metaphysics: the Archbishop does
not choose to dispute Pharamond's right to decree a 'female bar',
but simply to show that it had neither been intended nor since
interpreted to apply to France (ll. 40–95). This happens to accord
with Bodin's *politique* recognition that the states of the world
displayed a variety of different forms of equally legitimate (though
not necessarily equally effective) government. In itself the Arch-
bishop's argument is of a modern, orthodox, and convincing kind.
How it comes across in Shakespeare's scene depends on several
other factors.

The Archbishop's exposition, overladen perhaps with telling precedent, contrasts with the vigorous moral realism (ll. 13–21) and more terse expression of King Henry. That yields quite effective drama if at the cost of some impatience at the learned cleric. Then again, audience and readers alike cannot but remember the conversation of the two clergymen in the opening scene of the play: however good the argument of title now produced, we know that the Archbishop also favours the proposed war for the French crown because the Church might otherwise lose all its lands. Supporters of the Protestant settlement under Henry VIII, Edward VI, and Elizabeth would presumably think ill of this motive unless, like some of the measures of King John, the matter could be regarded as a reform whose time had not yet come. *Henry V*, I. ii, with its debate about the launching of a foreign war, inevitably also recalls Henry IV's dying advice to his son 'to busy giddy minds | With foreign quarrels' (2 *Henry IV*, IV, v. 342–3): that scene and the first scene of this play may well be regarded as the shady and cynical underside of the political enterprise now afoot. Not only Henry IV's words about 'foreign quarrels' are recalled but those about the 'by-paths and indirect crook'd ways' by which he had met the crown. Henry V's warning to the Archbishop not to 'fashion, wrest, or bow your reading' (l. 14) shows, by contrast, his determination that any move against France shall be backed by a clear title. Whatever the new king thinks of his title to his English crown—and it is not until the eve of the Battle of Agincourt that this is revealed—he is not prepared to bid for a further crown on the basis of a weak title. We are shown the example of a prince whose title to his native crown is open to challenge demanding a strong title before he makes war for a second crown. This at least demonstrates some respect in the new monarch for law and right. The final comparison of *Henry V*, I. ii, with the earlier Histories must be with Richard of York when, backed by a similarly well-derived but involved title through the female line, he set out to wrest the crown of England from Henry VI. The implications of this comparison are revealed as the drama of *Henry V* unfolds.

The second scene of *Henry V* to reveal Shakespeare's concern with succession is the conspiracy at Southampton (II. ii). What we have here is a significant exclusion. For this conspiracy is blamed in the most conspicuous and authoritative possible way—by the voice of the Chorus—upon bribery by 'fearful France' and corruption by the three conspirators (II. ii. 20–30). One of the conspirators, however, is Richard, Earl of Cambridge, who, in Mortimer's speech to Richard of York in *1 Henry VI*, II. v, figured as one who met his death attempting to assert the *de jure* title of Mortimer against *Henry V*. This Earl of Cambridge is in fact the father of *Henry VI*'s Richard of York. The motive for Cambridge's involvement in the Southampton conspiracy is mentioned in the Chronicle sources for the Henry VI plays but not for *Henry V*. While Shakespeare's audience, or readers, may be unaware of the scene from the earlier play, it is improbable that Shakespeare himself had forgotten what he had written before about this episode. Indeed two details in the present scene hint at civil disaffection stemming from other than mercenary motives: the conspirator Grey flatteringly assures Henry that 'Those that were your father's enemies | Have steeped their galls in honey, and do serve you | With hearts create of duty and of zeal' (ll. 29–31), while Cambridge adds, after the discovery of their treachery, 'For me, the gold of France did not seduce, | Although I did admit it as a motive | The sooner to effect what I intended' (ll. 151–3). Gary Taylor notes the veiled allusion of these last lines to the Yorkist cause.[21]

The present scene is thus not an example of Shakespeare simply following his major source and forgetting all else: it is the deliberate withholding of material and explanation which would have shown King Henry in an equivocal situation still at home, and which would have mitigated the guilt of the traitors. As Shakespeare handles the episode the audience, privileged with early information from the Chorus, is able to appreciate the courage and skill with which the King bides his time, gives the traitors more rope to hang themselves with, and directs the intensity of his indignation and rebuke against Scrope, his intimate and political confidant. This is the climax of a scene in which the management of suspense has been brilliant; it is a sustained denunciation of something of which Elizabethan Londoners had seen examples: treacherous assassination attempts on the part of those who had been trusted and favoured by the monarch. No dynastic theme is allowed to intrude into this simple and powerful scene.

But it is not the case that *Henry V* forgets about dynastic questions, as a lesser play on the same reign might have done. The theme

---

[21] *Henry V*, ed. Gary Taylor, New Oxford Series (Oxford, 1982), 138 n.

is introduced again in the final reach of that dramatized examin-
ation of the responsibility of the ruler which opens Act IV with the
King's acknowledgement to Gloucester 'that we are in great danger'.
The sequence of scenes opens the question of the relation of king
and people with Pistol's boastful tribute to Henry ('I love the lovely
bully' (l. 49)) and moves through Fluellen's learned rebuke to
Gower for making too much noise of the encounter between the
King and the three soldiers, Bates, Court, and Williams. The King's
testing summary of their bad situation ('Even as men wrecked upon
a sand, that look to be washed off the next tide' (ll. 97–8)) provokes
resentment first from Bates, who wishes Henry were alone in their
apparent trap ('So should he be sure to be ransomed, and a many
poor men's lives saved' (ll. 120–2)), and provokes from the dis-
guised monarch the affirmation that his cause is just and 'his quarrel
honourable' (ll. 126–7). This is then roundly challenged by Williams
as being 'more than we know' (l. 128) and there develops that
memorable discussion of how much responsibility rests 'Upon the
King' when it is his subjects' responsibility to obey his call to arms.
The parts of Bates and Williams as chief challenger are skilfully
changed: at the end of the long and serious dialogue between
Williams and the King it is agreed to Bates's satisfaction that,
contrary to what he originally implied, the personal sins of his
subjects do not rest with the King when his subjects die for him in
arms ('Every subject's duty is the King's, but every subject's soul is
his own' (ll. 175–6)). It may be seen that this does not fully answer
all the questions Williams raised, but these are for the moment
sidetracked by Henry's reassertion that the King will not be ran-
somed. This leads to his near-quarrel with Williams, their exchange
of gloves, and the departure of the soldiers.

   As the soldiers leave, and the King begins, with the words 'Upon
the King', the soliloquy they have prompted, we remember that the
justice of Henry's cause against France has been questioned, and
that a soldier dying on the battlefield when blood has been his
argument cannot be thought to have died well if the cause has not
been good. As Gary Taylor has observed, this takes the drama back
in no uncertain terms to I. ii, the Archbishop's speech, and the
King's warnings.[22] How important it now seems that the King
should have explicitly warned the Archbishop not to bend his

---

[22] *Henry V*, 39–40.

argument to what he might suppose the monarch wished to hear! In this regard the soldiers' comments need not arouse a guilty conscience in him. What impresses him, therefore, is the terrible breadth of the human responsibility borne by the monarch, as the serious and unflattering judgements of the soldiers have revealed it to him, in what both King and soldiers think may be the last night of their lives. The very general meditation on the nature of kingship in relation to ordinary life therefore follows: as the reflections of Henry, this speech seems not quite without self-pity; as the reflections of the dramatist, it reveals sympathy for the responsible monarch. Paradoxically, perhaps, its accusations against the 'idol ceremony' (l. 237) display an even greater gulf between the King and the common humanity he now so envies than appearances might suggest. It is the burden of responsibility that, alone, beneath ceremonial distinction, marks out the King from the 'wretched slave' who 'follows so the ever-running year | With profitable labour to his grave' (ll. 265, 273–4). The long soliloquy is broken by Sir Thomas Erpingham, 'A good old commander and a most kind gentleman' in Williams's view (ll. 95–6), who recalls Henry to the immediate demands of military leadership: the urgency of the situation most naturally turns his soliloquy into prayer. And here indeed we see the full import of what the common soldiers said about the justness or otherwise of the English cause. For however sound the reasoning of the Archbishop may have been concerning the applicability of the Salic Law to France and the English claim, it would not have been for Henry of Monmouth to assert this title if he had not had good right to his *English* title.

> O God of battles, steel my soldiers' hearts.
> Possess them not with fear. Take from them now
> The sense of reck'ning, ere th'opposèd numbers
> Pluck their hearts from them. Not today, O Lord,
> O not today, think not upon the fault
> My father made in compassing the crown.
> I Richard's body have interrèd new,
> And on it have bestowed more contrite tears
> Than from it issued forcèd drops of blood.
> Five hundred poor have I in yearly pay
> Who twice a day their withered hands hold up
> Toward heaven to pardon blood. And I have built
> Two chantries, where the sad and solemn priests

Sing still for Richard's soul. More will I do,
Though all that I can do is nothing worth,
Since that my penitence comes after all,
Imploring pardon.

(IV. i. 286–302)

The brilliance of Shakespeare's dramatic strategy is to be seen from its being at this moment of intense political, military, and human stress that the dynastic issue of England is for the first time in this play openly confronted. If the scene with the soldiers recalls the Archbishop's speech on title in I. ii, it is even more significant and interesting that what Henry speaks of now should have been mentioned in 'veiled allusion'[23] by the Earl of Cambridge in II. ii ('For me, the gold of France did not seduce, | Although I did admit it as a motive | The sooner to effect what I intended' (ll. 151–3): a typically Yorkist piece of *realpolitik*). What was hinted at then is fulfilled now. And now Henry himself is given the human virtue and greatest dramatic advantage to reveal the wound beneath the tissue, which Sidney saw as one of the roles of tragedy. The effect is to bring forward the concept of indefeasible hereditary right (which we must again remind ourselves was the claim to the crown which, however dubious in her case, Elizabeth herself never for a moment abandoned) in the way least damaging to Henry V. Also significant is the way Henry speaks of the matter. His words do not have the ringing confidence of his declaration in 2 *Henry IV*, 'Then plain and right must my possession be' (III. iii. 351), an affirmation perhaps meant to comfort his dying and anxious father. Notable too is that even Henry IV in that deathbed confessional speech did not call his appropriation of the crown 'a fault', though a matter for God's forgiveness. He did not recommend contrition, charities, or prayers for King Richard's soul: all these are developments in Henry V's own religious awareness and life.

What is the attitude of Shakespeare's text to the dynastic issue reintroduced in this way? It does not encourage us to think of the reign of Richard as an old, unhappy, far off thing, or battle long ago. Rather it is the virtue of Henry himself to see its present importance. In this crisis, and looking afresh at his royal burden in the light of his talk with the common soldiers, Henry is not satisfied with the

[23] *Henry V*, 138 n.

adequacy of his 'penitence' (l. 301) for his father's deposition and killing of Richard. Protagonist in a providential universe, he very naturally fears that God has inexorably worked towards this very time as the time to avenge the death of 'The deputy elected by the Lord'. For Henry, having followed his father's advice to seek 'foreign quarrels' albeit with moral scrupulousness over his French claim, now finds himself in a military trap. It is natural that at a time of such danger he should promise God in his prayer: 'More will I do.' His next three lines, however, are of crucial further interest to the political interpretation of Shakespeare's History Plays. Unfortunately, since the advent of the Oxford Shakespeare, they include a textual crux and now run (in that text):[24]

> Though all that I can do is nothing worth,
> Since that my penitence comes after ill,
> Imploring pardon.
>
> (ll. 300–2)

To the New Oxford editor's complex arguments for emending the Folio reading: 'all' to 'ill' (he is the only editor to suggest this so far as I know), it may be simply answered that the emendation turns l. 301 into a tautology: penitence *can* only come after ill, if it comes at all. (Nor do we need to know that the killing of Richard was an ill in Henry's view, since the word 'fault' has already been used.) Penitence is, of course, often difficult, especially when advantage appears to have accrued from the fault. This is the case here. 'Ill' makes no sense of the first tetralogy in which the active pursuit of Mortimer's and his successors' *de jure* title results in Richard III. It makes no sense of the earlier parts of the second tetralogy, in which the opponents of the admittedly flawed and illegal Henry IV evidently act chiefly out of personal and factional resentment rather than from political principle. Slowly some good has come out of Bolingbroke's usurpation, good to which simple penitence for a fault committed would be an inadequate response, for it would involve desiring undone all that had been done. Shakespeare, with characteristic circumspection and understanding of the complexities

---

[24] The case for emendment is made at length by Gary Taylor in his one-volume edition of *Henry V*, 295–300. There is no strictly *textual* evidence for the case: Q and F both give 'all'. Taylor wishes to change the line because 'all' is ambiguous and, in his view, does not make sense. However, his third postulated interpretation of 'all' draws close to the one I urge, which appears quite straightforward if the speech is read in a political as well as a theological context.

of historical process, used a more comprehensive word: 'all', which encompassed the good as well as the ill which had come of Richard's death. If adequate penitence meant wishing to turn the clock back to, for example, the point where Mortimer, Glendower, and Hotspur planned to divide England and Wales into three, how can Henry be wholly penitent? He is as penitent for the sin of his father as he can be, 'after all' that has followed.

This reading accommodates the Bodinian concept of kingship according to which a Lordly Monarchy may grow into a Royal Monarchy. It is not suggested here that at this crisis in his reign Henry makes an academic or theoretical remark: rather that his situation falls into one of the chief categories of political development that the encyclopaedic Bodin surveys. Shakespeare is pursuing his theme of the instauration of new dynasties, and at Agincourt it is put to the touch.

Much might be said at this point about Henry's famous speech before the battle. It is the heroic face of a war of which the politic, brutal, and sordid features have also been, and will be, displayed. It is a speech which subtly and appropriately remembers the tavern scenes of *1* and *2 Henry IV* (for example, 'he'll remember with advantages' just, and poignantly, recalls Falstaff's multiplication of his foes allegedly slain at Gadshill). This is part of the King's appeal to the human experience of his whole army at the time of danger, which seeks to make them a 'band of brothers' (l. 60). His speech also holds up the purgative ideal of a wound of honour. The original wounding of the kingdom in the killing of Richard, a wound which many sought to conceal, has now been opened up to God in prayer by the new King, and can be replaced by wounds that in future men will be proud to expose:

> Then will he strip his sleeve and show his scars . . .
>
> (l. 47)

This and much more lies behind the term twice used by Mountjoy the herald to Henry after the battle: 'great King' (IV. vii. 68, 79). Twice in his *Annals* Camden marvels at the great numbers of England's enemies slain, and small numbers of English: once on the defeat of the Armada, once on the Sack of Cadiz by the Earl of Essex.[25] Shakespeare takes his opportunity here to display the same

---

[25] *Annals*, 371, 463.

apparently providential pattern after Agincourt. Henry's conclusion seems to set the seal on the new dynasty which has arisen, originally, out of crime:

> O God thy arm was here,
> And not to us, but to thy arm alone
> Ascribe we all.
>
> (IV. viii. 106–8)

Transposed to the England of the later 1590s, with the succession to Elizabeth still unsettled (whatever the Queen and Sir Robert Cecil privately favoured), *Henry V* completes two sequences of history plays which, in different ways, encourage the idea of the founding of a new dynasty by a brave, charismatic, and politic leader. This is in many respects Parsons's solution to the succession question, however different his motives. The first tetralogy implicated indefeasible hereditary right, when pursued by practical political means, in the emergence of a tyrant. The second patiently and fully showed how usurpation could lead to the greater common good. It is thus of great significance that one of the very few contemporary allusions in Shakespeare traditionally acknowledged should occur in the Chorus between Acts IV and V of *Henry V*, and that it should refer, almost certainly, to the Earl of Essex.[26] As Londoners welcome Henry back from his victory:

> The Mayor and all his brethren, in best sort,
> Like to the senators of th'antique Rome
> With the plebeians swarming at their heels,
> Go forth and fetch their conqu'ring Caesar in—
> As, by a lower but high-loving likelihood,
> Were now the General of our gracious Empress—
> As in good time he may—from Ireland coming,
> Bringing rebellion broachèd on his sword,
> How many would the peaceful city quit
> To welcome him!
>
> (V, Chorus, 25–34)

A general not a king, Caesar had such an impact on the government of Rome that it changed from republic to monarchy in all but name

[26] I am grateful to Dr David Womersley, of Jesus College, Oxford, for discussion of this passage, and for allowing me to read in draft his paper, 'The Politics of King John', *RES* NS 40 (1989), 497–515, and other work bearing on the politics of the Essex circle, now published in *RES* NS 42 (1991), 313–42.

under the Julian House. Despite Shakespeare's very circumspect phrasing, audience and reader are invited to associate Julius Caesar, Henry V, and the Earl of Essex. The implication is as clear as it could be within the bounds of loyalty and safety. A triumphant Essex, or somebody like him, is what the kingdom will need.

The choric sonnet which concludes the play is a reminder both of what lay ahead in chronicle time—the reign of Henry VI and all that followed—and of what lay behind in order of composition—the first tetralogy. It holds together for us the two orders in which we can imagine, read, and see the Histories: chronicle order and composition order. My view is that the composition order, first tetralogy, second tetralogy, is the order which yields most fully the direction of Shakespeare's political thought, pointing to the need for a new Lordly Monarch and new dynasty. (This requires, however, a reading in chronicle order *within* the tetralogies, and care to remember that tellingly more explicit drama, *King John*.) To think of the tetralogies in chronicle order does not reverse the general direction of their political thought, though it shifts the later focus from something like ideal, to warning. It allows the true but superficial Tillyardian reading (civil wars brought to an end by a Tudor), but even here we notice how little is made of the deliverer's title to the crown. The weight of Shakespeare's dramatic and poetic exposition is still behind the view that the pursuit of *de jure* title, far from averting national evil, as York had argued in his speech to Parliament in Hall, may produce it.[27] The late Elizabethan Shakespeare thus emerges as the author of plays which address themselves to the chief issues in Camden and implicitly question one major feature of Elizabethan political orthodoxy: indefeasible hereditary right. Such questioning appears particularly relevant at times of national crisis. This does not make Shakespeare any less royalist; indeed it might be said to emphasize the need for a leader-like monarch who knows his subjects. Nor does it make Shakespeare a constitutional monarchist or a radical ahead of his time. (The debate about whether Shakes-

---

[27] I am glad to notice a similar argument to the one here proposed, in Sherman Hawkins, 'Structural pattern in Shakespeare's Histories', *Studies in Philology*, 88 (1991), 16–45. In addition, if Shakespeare positively wished the two tetralogies to be read in chronicle order he omitted, when changing Oldcastle to Falstaff in *1 Henry IV* and after, to rename Sir John Fastolfe in *1 Henry VI*, so that as things stand the fat knight who dies in *Henry V* has risen again in the next play. A Shakespeare who revised, and for whom chronicle order greatly mattered, would probably have set this right.

peare was conservative or radical in the modern sense of these terms seems misdirected.) In terms of chronicle discourse it makes him a Lancastrian; in terms of the real politics of the 1590s it aligns him with those who sought a king in a great man who would be greater, an Essex or someone like him, against the unspoken resolve of the Queen and Robert Cecil to bring in James VI.

IV

It would be unnatural to conclude this chapter without a brief look forward to the three royal tragedies of Shakespeare which dramatize issues of succession, and which bridge the gap between Tudor and Stuart Shakespeare: *Hamlet*, *Lear*, and *Macbeth*. *Hamlet*, most problematic of Shakespeare's plays, seems more complex even than is acknowledged by its three recent editors, all of whom ignore the possibility of political allusion in the play. For *Hamlet* is based on a variant of the Clytemnestra plot used thirty-five years earlier in Sir John Pikeryng's *Horestes* and elsewhere to allude to the sensational Scottish events which began the long imprisonment of the Scottish Queen. At its simplest, a queen connives or seems to connive with her lover to murder her royal husband and, after the killing, marries the murderer with shocking haste. The murderer becomes king. A son from the first marriage is left to contemplate revenge.

The view that there is a connection between the plot of *Hamlet* and the Darnley murder, 'the tragedie of umquhile king Henrie Stewart of gude memorie' (as a poem roughly contemporary with the murder put it) was proposed by Lilian Winstanley in her forgotten book *Hamlet and the Scottish Succession* (1920).[28] That the early features of the drama should resemble any situation of sixteenth-century high politics, let alone one with a clear bearing on the succession of the English crown, is striking enough. That the Darnley tragedy should have prompted one of the earliest English revenge dramas, possibly the earliest, is additionally remarkable. That there is some mysterious link between Shakespeare's *Hamlet* and the Scottish events of 1567 is a possibility worth consideration, and it

---

[28] Lilian Winstanley, *Hamlet and the Scottish Succession, Being an Examination of the Relations of the Play of* Hamlet *to the Scottish Succession and the Essex Conspiracy* (Cambridge, 1920; repr. New York, 1970), chs. 2–5. For further discussion see Appendix I.

will appear that the tragedy sits at the centre of a web of allusion, some quite marked, some of the most delicate and glancing kind.

The source, running back through François de Belleforest's *Histories tragiques* (1570, with many later editions)[29] to the *Historiae Danicae* of Saxo Grammaticus, is no bar to contemporary allusion in the light of the examination of Sir John Hayward. Further, Belleforest himself, as a writer on a dim margin of the Pléiade, an admirer of Ronsard who had praised the young Mary Stuart in his poetry, sometime historiographer to King Charles IX, and a contemporary pamphleteer with pronounced royalist and Catholic views, is an intriguing figure in the present connection. In his *Histoire des neuf roys Charles de France* (1568) he had already included an account of the murder of 'Henry Roy d'Escosse' and of the conduct of Queen Mary; in 1572 he would publish his French translation of John Leslie's *Defence* (1569). Did he turn from Bandello to Saxo Grammaticus in 1570 because, among other reasons, the story of Hamlet in some of its salient features was a reminder of a very recent and sensational modern tragedy?[30] Did his choice of narratives for translation sometimes afford him the opportunity of reflecting on contemporary affairs, as was to be the case with a collection of narratives by a later *conteur*, Dryden's *Fables Ancient and Modern*, at the end of the next century? Some of the major changes made by Belleforest to his Latin original concern Geruth (Gertrude). In Belleforest but not in Saxo Grammaticus she is implicitly supposed, but not explicitly stated, to have committed adultery with the murderer before the murder, as Mary, Queen of Scots, had allegedly done. In the bedchamber scene, however, Geruth is now given a long defence of her conduct, in which she claims to have been forced into her latest marriage, and repudiates complicity in the murder. She now encourages her son to take revenge and secure his succession to the

---

[29] The bibliographical complexities of Belleforest's *Histoires tragiques* are surveyed by Donald Stone, in 'Belleforest's Bandello: A Bibliographical Study', *Bibliothèque d'humanisme et renaissance*, 34 (1972), 489–99.

[30] Ibid. 492–3. Belleforest discusses the Darnley murder in Book XIX of his *Histoire des neuf roys Charles de France: contenant la fortune, vertu, & heurs fatal des roys, qui sous ce nom Charles ont mis a fin des choses merueilleuses* ... (Paris, 1568), 673–3. The latest work explicitly to deal with Mary, Queen of Scots, and the Darnley murder is *L'Innocence de la tresillustre treschast, et debonnaire Princesse, Madame Marie Royne D'Escosse* ... (1572). It is a translation of John Leslie's *Defence* of the Queen (see Chapter 1 above), and of *A Treatise of Treasons*, prefaced by a long harangue 'Au Lecteur'.

crown. These changes may be thought to point to the situation of
Mary, real or alleged, and perhaps have the effect of a partial
vindication. Belleforest's long moralizing reflections on the whole
story have, on this hypothesis, a contemporary stimulus.

Among the changes introduced by Shakespeare, and almost cer-
tainly in the old play of *Hamlet*, is the Ghost who is there to reveal
a hitherto secret murder and demand revenge. The notion of a
Senecan ghost after so terrible a murder could hardly fail to occur to
an Elizabethan dramatist, but it is worth noting that the idea of such
a ghost ('les ombres de Horvvendille indigné' and 'son ombre
s'apaise parmy les esprits bien heureux')[31] is implied in the words of
Belleforest's narrative. As one would expect several poems in which
the ghost of the murdered Darnley either demanded or discussed
revenge have survived, some popular, some learned. One was writ-
ten in Latin in 1587 by John Gordon, a Scot at the court of Henry
III of France, and entitled: *Henrici Scotorum Regis Manes ad Jaco-
bum VIum filium*. Both popular and learned poems see Darnley not
as an assassinated English aristocrat married to the Queen, but as
the murdered Henry, King of Scots. In Gordon's poem the ghost of
the royal father addresses his son, James VI:

> Believe no crime of me, unless 'tis wrong
> When any husband loves his wife too much.
> And thou my wife, dearer to me than breath,
> Whose heart so changed against me on behalf
> Of a vile rascal pardoned in despite
> Of Lord's just anger and the People's wrongs!
> To thee the evil life of such a boor
> Was aphrodisiac until, forgot
> Both royal fame and queen's decorum, thou,
> First trying me with poison, drov'st out fear
> Soon from thy mind, then murdered'st me with flames!
>   Nor rested here the wickedness. That Bothwell,
> Chief foe to the gods, author of thy great crime,
> Who after he the secrets of our couch
> Had violated, taught the erring wife
> Her hands to sprinkle with her husband's blood,
> That vile adulterer trod our marriage-bed.

---

[31] A. P. Stabler, 'The Histoires Tragiques de François de Belleforest', Ph.D. Diss.
(University of Virginia, 1959), 275, 278. His case is published in id., 'King Hamlet's
Ghost in Belleforest', *PMLA* 77 (Mar. 1962), 18–20.

FIG. 2. James VI, King of Scots, as a youth, anonymous engraving *c.* 1600. Apparently based on the 1578 £20 piece bearing this image and legend.

He recounts to his son the full historical outcome down to the execution of Mary, Queen of Scots. Finally he turns to the subject of revenge:

> But Heaven's Moderator has not let
> Me wander long a Shade still unavenged;
> He sent this cleansing feast of sacrifice
> Unto my ashes. Seek no other cause
> For this late punishment. But thou who scaped
> That bitter shipwreck in a little trough,
> Thou whom thy angry mother hardly spared,
> My son, sole hope of Scotland's royal house,
> If thou art mine, and if thou hear'st me right,
> Learn thou from me thy Master, aye to seek
> Justice o'er all . . .[32]

Prior to presenting this poem Bullough observes that, although 'the parallel between Amleth's situation and James's appears distant to us, the latter appears as a potential avenger of his father Lord Darnley . . .'.[33] Ever since the murder of the King of Scotland in 1567, the ghost of a murdered king, speaking to his son of revenge but counselling forbearance to his possibly guilty queen, a ghost such as the Ghost of Hamlet, was likely to be a reminder of one situation before all others.

Hamlet spins a wider web of approximate but in historical context suggestive allusion. Much of this hangs on the fact that Shakespeare, and probably the old play of *Hamlet*, boldly transpose Belleforest's story from the Middle Ages to Renaissance northern Europe—with a modern connection between Denmark and the Protestant University of Wittenberg. The Danish setting, unique in Shakespeare and rare enough in Elizabethan drama save for the old *Hamlet*, was a reminder of four things. First, after military defeat in Scotland James Hepburn, Earl of Bothwell, Duke of Orkney, briefly presumed King James VI of Scotland, took refuge in Norway and Denmark, where he made play with a hereditarily claimed title to give the Orkney and Shetland Islands back to Denmark. Secondly, James Stuart, James VI of Scotland, when a young man sailed through stormy seas to Denmark to bring back the Danish bride who became his Queen.

---

[32] Geoffrey Bullough, *Narrative and Dramatic Sources of Shakespeare*, vii. (1973), 125–7. The Latin text is printed by G. Lambin in 'Une première ebauche d'Hamlet (mars 1587)', in *Les Langues modernes*, 49 (1955), pp. 37–8; see Appendix I.

[33] Bullough, *Narrative and Dramatic Sources*, vii. 19.

Thirdly, Danish maritime and mercantile claims, and charges of piracy, had brought England into a state of restrained hostility with its northern Protestant neighbour by 1599.[34] Finally, and most significant of all, Denmark was known to be an elective kingdom, a point recognized in the text of *Hamlet*, in significantly and designedly belated fashion (v. ii. 66, 307–8). Shakespeare thus plays to the natural English assumption that the eldest son of a murdered king must be his rightful successor, against the eventual *politique* recognition that different states had different constitutions, as Bodin had shown, and that strictly Claudius and the young Fortinbras had as good a claim as the young Hamlet. This was obviously timely and relevant in the years of Elizabeth's perceived old age, when, in effect, the kingdom or some acting on behalf of the kingdom (Robert Cecil?) would 'elect' a successor and new dynasty. The strict principle of indefeasible hereditary right being questionable (and having been questioned by Shakespeare) the end of a dynasty in pragmatic terms certainly meant an election in some sense.[35] This above all makes *Hamlet* a drama of its historical and political moment.

This inclines me to the view that, if *Hamlet* reminds one of the Darnley tragedy, it is not merely an inert deposit from the old play of *Hamlet*. In the two parts of his *Faerie Queene* (I–III in 1590 and IV–VI in 1596) Spenser had brought the Scottish Queen to the fore so clearly in his myth of England that James VI, that circumspect and equivocal Orestes, had instructed his envoy to protest to Elizabeth at the Mercilla/Duessa episode in Book V, on the grounds that its treatment of his royal mother, in a poem dedicated to Elizabeth herself, seemed to reject his title to the English succession.[36] As the 1590s drew on, a myth to understand the experience of King James VI, the might-have-been Orestes, and possible successor to Elizabeth, was increasingly required, especially during and after that steady decline from grace of the Earl of Essex which ended in his disastrous uprising.

It is in the long narrative of the Ghost that the text of *Hamlet* approaches the flashpoint of connection with the historical events

[34] Bullough, *Narrative and Dramatic Sources*, 41–3.

[35] For an interesting discussion of electoral kingship in *Hamlet* see E. A. J. Honigmann, 'The Politics in "Hamlet" and "The World of the Play" ', in John Russell Brown and Bernard Harris (eds.), *Shakespeare Institute Studies* (1963), 129–47.

[36] See Richard A. McCabe, 'The Masks of Duessa: Spenser, Mary Queen of Scots, and James VI', *ELH* 17 (1987), 224–42.

alluded to above. His accusation that Claudius, 'that adulterate beast' 'won to his shameful lust | The will of my most seeming-virtuous queen' (I. v. 42, 45–6), his account of how he was murdered 'sleeping within mine orchard' (l. 59), and especially his description of the dreadful effect of the poison on his skin:

> . . . a most instant tetter barked about,
> Most lazar-like, with vile and loathsome crust,
> All my smooth body . . .
>
> (I. v. 71–3)

all this seems to remind one of the murder of the Scottish king. Holinshed has Darnley killed in an orchard (though not by poison),[37] while Buchanan saw the chief conspiracy to murder as the attempt to kill the King by poison, causing black pustules to break out on his body. Everything was done by Buchanan and his masters to suggest that Mary committed adultery with Bothwell while her first husband was alive, and great stress was laid on the speed of the marriage to Bothwell and the inadequate period of mourning for the former king (cf. *Hamlet*, I. ii. 147–58, 175–81).[38] The unfavourable appearance and character of Bothwell by comparison with Darnley was a further point much dwelt on in anti-Marian propaganda. These are details mainly deriving from sources other than Belleforest, above all from Buchanan.

Here, if anywhere, it is right to repeat that it is the argument neither of this chapter, nor of this book as a whole, that the poetry under discussion affords us complete and detailed portrayals of contemporary historical situations. It is obvious that much in *Hamlet* does not resemble the Darnley tragedy, notably, perhaps, that here the murderer is brother of the King, that James did not grow up to slay Bothwell personally, and so forth.[39] The development of the action is obviously the more fictive part of the play, more

---

[37] Raphael Holinshed, *The Chronicles of England, Scotland and Ireland* (1587), ii. 384.

[38] George Buchanan, *Ane Dectection* (1571), sig. C iii–F iiii.

[39] A final point concerning the Darnley murder is the identity of the culprit according to defenders of the Queen. According to Leslie, this was James Moray, the Queen's illegitimate brother, and brother-in-law of the murdered king. Belleforest, in his *Histoire des neufs Roys Charles*, touches on 'le seigneur Bastard' in the same connection (673), and one wonders whether the jealousy and inferiority of Fengon to Horvendile in the Hamlet story did not fit this aspect of the Scottish events as seen by those who opposed Buchanan.

independent of any of the sources used, and constituting a reflection, as it were, on the implications of the situation presented. If it be accepted that Act I of *Hamlet* alludes in some of its more striking features to the Darnley tragedy, what follows? Hamlet appears a prince with a strong natural right by primogeniture to the crown of his native kingdom. He seems unnaturally dispossessed, something which Claudius attempts to put a favourable gloss upon by his promise at I. ii. 109. The audience's feeling that Claudius has no right to rule is obviously fortified by a growing knowledge that he is guilty of fratricide, and growing indignation at the behaviour of Gertrude, not here queen *suo jure* like Mary Stuart but consort to two royal brothers, and thus contaminated by incest. This experience dominates the tragedy, giving Hamlet himself unique power as the drama's centre of moral and religious consciousness. Here Hamlet has two features relevant to a consideration of James, each of which keys in to well-known and major debates about the play. Hamlet like James appears a Protestant raised out of a Catholic and crypto-Catholic parental milieu. He has been at Wittenberg and has some Protestant doubts as to the existence of ghosts of the departed, as opposed to evil spirits; while his father's Ghost, if he can be believed, assumes a Catholic cosmology and doctrine of purgatory (I. v. 9–13). This was obviously a widespread experience in early Reformation countries, where the filial bond might necessitate a bridging of the religious divide. Secondly, Hamlet is a new kind of prince in Shakespeare: not wild, not warlike, but, if ambitious and passionate, predominantly contemplative and intellectual. By the late 1590s James was known to be that unusual thing, a prince who was also a poet and controversialist. He was not, as Essex or Leicester might have been, and as Young Fortinbras is, a martial prince. Hamlet's intellectual life, however, can no more save him than his right-seeming title to the crown. In the end the horrors of the original murder reach up to entangle and claim him, more dramatically by far than Richard II's early crime incapacitated him in his later, fatal, crisis. Despite his modern, late sixteenth-century consciousness, Hamlet cannot master the energies released by the bloody and faithless tragedy of his parents. This is a historical recognition on Shakespeare's part, not one into individual moral psychology.

As King Henry in *1 Henry IV*, III. ii implicitly instructed the audience in the ways in which chronicle material in drama might diagnose the present and predict the future, so the play within the play of *Hamlet* alerts the audience as to how a drama might communicate a dangerous state secret, and how players and authors might defend themselves against accusation. The murder of Gonzago unmistakably recalls the murder of Hamlet the King to all in the play who have heard anything of the latter murder. Yet both the Ghost's narrative and the play within the play recall the murder of Francesco della Rovere, warlike Duke of Urbino, allegedly killed by his nephew in 1538 by having poison poured into his ears.[40] And, after all, Hamlet the King had not sickened before he died (III. ii. 153–8), his name was not Gonzago, he was not an Italian, and he was not murdered by his nephew. Hamlet the Prince hints at the 'offence' in the play (Claudius's word at III. ii. 221) up to the moment when the nephew Lucianus pours the poison. Then he states what must have been the classical defence:

A poisons him i'th' garden for's estate. His name's Gonzago. The story is extant, and writ in choice Italian.

(ll. 249–51)

finally promising a further contemporary allusion. There is as much difference and resemblance between the murder of Hamlet the King and the Darnley tragedy, as between the murder of Gonzago and the murder of Hamlet the King.

In so far as the plot of the play was a reminder of the Darnley tragedy—and only our modern tendency to separate drama from its historical context allows us to be sure it was not—then Shakespeare in *Hamlet* seems to have dramatized the position of King James VI, partly known, partly imagined, as the tragically incapacitated inheritor of the unnatural scene into which he had been born. The drama's understanding of its modern, intellectual prince in his predicament is here Shakespeare's supreme achievement, but it is equally clear that this is no pro-Stuart play. Rather it seeks to write James VI and his claims out of history, with more compassion, but no less decisiveness, than had Spenser in *Faerie Queene*, Book V; and in a not dissimilar way, as we shall see in a later chapter, to that of Dryden with King James II in *Don Sebastian* (1689). Gertrude as Mary Stuart does, however, win exoneration for the worst crime

[40] Bullough, *Narrative and Dramatic Sources*, vii. 30–4.

with which she had been charged: complicity in the murder. This is the convincing conclusion of G. R. Hibbard on Gertrude's words 'As kill a king' (III. iv. 29) in the bedchamber scene.[41] As in Belleforest, Gertrude becomes Hamlet's ally at the very end. If we can use *Hamlet* hypothetically to construe Shakespeare's attitude to the succession at the near end of Elizabeth I's reign, he doubted the value of King James's *de jure* claim, fearing that it would only open the way to some young Fortinbras, a straightforward martial king from abroad, with some pretensions to a title (V. ii. 342–4). This seems to me the balance of political implication at the end of *Hamlet*, but, by focusing more on character and less on position, it would be possible to argue that Young Fortinbras alludes to the Essexes of the political world.[42]

In more than one sense, *Hamlet* was to be Shakespeare's last Tudor drama of state. Never narrowly partisan, Shakespeare's dramatic explorations of relevant political issues and situations had, nevertheless, a certain Lancastrian or Tudor (but not Elizabethan) political inclination, up to this point. The marks of this inclination are his treatment, within the larger dramatic structure, of genealogical derivation, claims of *de jure* title, and, especially in *John*, issues of illegitimacy and legitimacy. It is in these respects that we now notice a change. Stuart Shakespeare shows not less, but in even greater measure, that almost unparalleled capacity to understand and explore opposing experience and views through drama. Yet the focus of interest in kingship shifts, and it is hard not to see some connection between this and the fact that, in the end, it was the unwarriorlike and unleaderlike prince, the reluctant Orestes with the best *de jure* claim by primogeniture, who succeeded Elizabeth on her throne. Yorkist ideology (and the statecraft of Elizabeth and the Cecils) seemed to have triumphed when James VI became James VI and I.

Shakespeare appears to have responded. His change can be seen by comparing his treatment of bastardy in *John*, his most politically explicit play of the 1590s, with bastardy in *The History of King*

---

[41] *Hamlet*, ed. G. R. Hibbard (Oxford, 1987), 59.

[42] If Harold Jenkins and G. R. Hibbard are right to say that Shakespeare's *Hamlet* was performed in 1599, then Fortinbras might allude to Essex himself. But this theory would need to confront the implications of the soliloquy 'How all occasions do inform against me', in Act IV, considered by Hibbard and the other Oxford editors to have been eliminated by Shakespeare in late revision. (*Hamlet*, ed. Hibbard, 104–10, 362; *Textual Companion*, 399–402.)

Lear which was written in 1605–6 and published in 1608. In *John* the dispute over seniority and legitimacy was resolved by Philip Falconbridge embracing bastardy to become Sir Richard Plantagenet, the valiant if initially sceptical supporter of a *de facto* king, and the best patriot in the drama. His legitimate brother Robert Falconbridge fades from the action. In *Lear* Edmund the bastard, with all the energies and ambition of the Bastard in *John*, grows swiftly into a predator, while 'legitimate Edgar' (I. ii. 16), far from fading from the action, endures to become with Cordelia one of the two consistently loyal, compassionate, and redeeming figures of the play. The claims of the two brothers are finally decided by Edgar's victory in the duel in Act V. In the Folio text, *The Tragedie of King Lear*, 'legitimate Edgar' assumes still greater prominence. In *Macbeth* (perhaps composed in 1606) the long genealogical derivation common in the Histories becomes an epiphanic vision of the future, the line of Banquo's posterity in IV. i culminating with some kings 'That twofold balls and treble sceptres carry' (l. 137), a pageant in which hereditary kingship displays its power to triumph over usurpation and murder. The line of true kings does indeed stretch out 'to the crack of doom' (l. 133). 'Tempest-tossed' though the ship of royalty may be, as the witches chant, it never can be lost (I. ii. 23–4).[43]

Many features of *Lear* and *Macbeth* link them with Jacobean allusion and Stuart ideology, itself a major strand in Elizabethan political awareness. For example, the warning against the division of the realm, delivered by *Gorboduc* (1561; reprinted in 1590) and by the division scene in *1 Henry IV*, was taken up by James VI himself in his *Basilikon Doron* (1603), addressed to his eldest son Prince Henry, whom he hoped would inherit three kingdoms. This is of course a great part of the warning of *Lear*—and in other and smaller ways *Basilikon Doron* is an important text for this tragedy.[44] In a profound sense, *Macbeth* is well understood as an occasional and Stuart tragedy, responding to a sensational attempt to subvert the new dynasty and its government by violence: the Gunpowder Plot. The argument of H. N. Paul's *The Royal Play of*

[43] H. N. Paul, *The Royal Play of Macbeth* (New York, 1950). See also J. M. Nosworthy, *Shakespeare's Occasional Plays* (1965), 8–9.
[44] See C. H. McIlwain (ed.), *The Political Works of King James I* (Cambridge, Mass., 1918; repr. New York, 1965), and Glynne Wickham, 'From Tragedy to Tragi-Comedy: *King Lear* as Prologue', *Shakespeare Survey*, 26 (Cambridge, 1973), 35–43.

Macbeth remains (if not in every detail) substantially convincing, and the book remains one of the best contextual studies of a Shakespeare play we have.[45] Generally, Stuart Shakespeare turns to the imagining of new roles of kingship: even Duncan lacks the royal charisma of Richard II. Decisive, patriarchal, unwarlike, less ceremonious, and more natural, he is offered as the cynosure of fidelity and love. Lear is the royal patriarch whose patriarchal spirit fatally fails; so, in different ways, are Cymbeline and Leontes,[46] who deviate from the patriarchal path to be restored to it, through tragicomic structure and romantic evolution, at the end. In Prospero Shakespeare imagines the king as magus, the faithful patriarch even in exile, aggrandizing this role with his special magic. Those conceptions of kingship crucial for the Histories, the new prince and the warrior king, no longer dominate Shakespeare's dramas of state. We do not now see how royalty is made; an eternal feature of human society, it can now only be recognized or, if lost, rediscovered. Perdita the lost princess attracts the love of a prince though her lineage is unknown to him. The natural love of Ferdinand and Miranda has a similar royal magic. This particular mystique of royalty is a response to the character, roles, doctrine, and situation of James himself, scholar, patriarch, and father of children whose life at once protected his throne and empowered his dynastic diplomacy. Needless to say, it is not claimed that this is the full truth about James, nor about the Jacobean Shakespeare.

But, with the coming of James, the succession question had, after all, been settled. Some of the sharp political questions and *politique* recognitions which it had raised could be laid to rest. After the

---

[45] David Norbrook, in his essay 'Macbeth and the Politics of Historiography', in Kevin Sharpe and Steven N. Zwicker (eds.), *Politics of Discourse: The Literature and History of Contemporary England* (1987), 78–116, 313–21, offers an interesting and learned reading against the grain. It is valuable to see *Macbeth* in relation to Buchanan's and Boece's histories of Scotland; and it is common ground between us that to do so is 'to call in question Shakespeare's alleged independence from political ideology' (115). Norbrook agrees with Paul that 'the most plausible suggestions for topical allusions link the play with the Gunpowder Plot' but is right to add that 'its concerns are not only so immediately topical' (314–15). Since he has the integrity not to attempt to incorporate the drama into 'democratic' theory (78) he is reduced to the claim that *Macbeth* and plays like it 'retain elements of the attitudes they are rejecting' (116). Yet something more might be claimed of MacDuff's response to a self-proclaimingly monstrous Malcolm in the English scene (IV. iii. 103–14): 'Fit to govern? | No, not to live.'

[46] Emrys Jones, 'Stuart Cymbeline', *EC* 2 (1961), repr. D. J. Palmer (ed.), *Shakespeare's Later Comedies* (Harmondsworth, 1971), 248–62.

Gunpowder Plot, for some years at least, England was in a happier and more secure position than in the last years of the Queen. Some wrongs could be righted. Some reputations restored, at least in ceremony, art, and historiography. Thus the remains of Mary Stuart, Queen of Scots, were, by order of King James, exhumed from their resting place in Peterborough Cathedral, and brought for reinterment to Westminster Abbey, where a statuary monument to her was erected. The beautiful, tragic, guilty, vulnerable, dangerous Queen, Clytemnestra to Pikeryng, to Spenser Duessa, despite all an emblem of *de jure* royalty, imaged by Shakespeare, through the Elizabethan idiom of allusion to precedent, as imprisoned Mortimer, as Prince Arthur, as Richard II, as Gertrude, finally appears (as Glynne Wickham convincingly suggests[47]) as the wronged Hermione vindicated, the statue that comes to life at the end of *The Winter's Tale* (1611). The terrible charges of murder and adultery being even then repudiated by Camden in his *Annals*, the statue would release the reputation of the Catholic Mary into affection and fame. It is appropriately to Perdita that the appropriate words are given:

> And give me leave,
> And do not say 'tis superstition, that
> I kneel and then implore her blessing. Lady,
> Dear Queen, that ended when I but began,
> Give me that hand of yours to kiss.
>
> (*The Winter's Tale*, v. iii. 42–6)

[47] Wickham, 'From Tragedy to Tragi-Comedy', 48.

PART II

The Republican Tide

4

The Charisma of Italy

ON 23 July 1553 Mr John Lock, on his voyage to Jerusalem, glimpsed 'the white walles' of the fortified city of Ragusa, on the coast of Dalmatia or, by its ancient name, Illyria.[1] Ragusa was, however, more than a fortified city. It was an ancient sovereign republic, with a system of government that differed from, though it somewhat resembled, that of Genoa, and which was maintaining itself as an important maritime and trading city on the fringe of the Ottoman Empire. When finally destroyed by the armies of Napoleon, it would have subsisted for a thousand years. Nothing might seem more remote from English political awareness than the longevity and constitution of the little republic of Ragusa, and at the time of Lock's voyage that was perhaps the case. Yet such were the historical changes to take place in England that, just over a century later, in 1659, a tract entitled *Government Described . . .*, setting forth the constitution of Ragusa, was one of several in the debate conducted by James Harrington, Matthew Wren, and others, concerning the merits and resilience of the republican form of government.[2]

I

The title of Part II, 'The Republican Tide', alludes to a period of English history which ended with the establishment of a republican

---

[1] 'The Uoyage of M. Iohn Lok to Ierusalem, Anno 1553'; *The Principal Navigations . . . of the English Nation*, collected by Richard Hakluyt (1598–1600), ii. 102.

[2] J. S., *Government Described . . . Together with a Brief Model of the Government of . . .* (1659). It is in the British Library's Thomason Collection, and was endorsed by Thomason 'June 1'. It is noted in Veselin Kostić, *Cultural Relations Between Yugoslavia and England before 1700* (Belgrade, 1972), 516. I am indebted to Blair Worden for the suggestion that the author may have been John Streater, one of the publishers of *Oceana* in 1656, on whom see J. G. A. Pocock (ed.), *The Political Works of James Harrington* (Cambridge, 1977), 9–12. *Government Described* is partly reprinted in my article 'The Image of the Adriatic Republics in English Writing from the Sixteenth to the Eighteenth Century', in Rudolf Filipović and Monica Partridge (eds.), *Dubrovnik's Relations with England: A Symposium* (Zagreb, 1977). Some sections of this article are incorporated, in revised form, into the present chapter.

polity in London, when the wide sense of the word 'republic', body politic, commonwealth, became narrowed by practice to indicate a commonwealth without a king. It survived various crises, becoming a quasi-monarchy *de facto* in Oliver Cromwell's last years, but finally collapsed before the enigmatic power of General Monck, and the popular desire to restore the ancient monarchical constitution and the old royal house of Stuart. The tide came in during the civil war and was, perhaps, ebbing in the late 1650s. The metaphor indicates a sequence of events in high politics but should not suggest a necessary natural pattern. This tide would not, in Wordsworth's words, 'return again'[3] in the period discussed by this book, not to the full, not in Britain; but it returned eventually with redoubled force to the European continent.

If there were no inexorable forces leading to civil war and regicide, how does the Renaissance interest in modern and ancient republics (commonwealths without kings) relate to political developments in England? It is surely plausible to suppose that these practical and intellectual interests had some bearing, if no decisive influence, on the outcome of events. As we shall see, Hobbes would argue that study of classical republicanism had helped produce rebellion in the civil war period, while Aubrey considered that Thomas May's interest in the republican poet Lucan had turned him from the royalist to the parliamentary cause. But some caveats must be conveyed. It may be that what most interested English intellectuals in, for example, ancient Rome or modern Venice, was the possibility of mixed government: of the one, the few, and the many. Again, the kind of retrospective knowledge available to us was not available to a Ben Jonson writing under James I, or a Milton writing when Charles I was still alive and at large. What seem to us pointers in a now known direction may have been seen by their authors at the time as works quite compatible with the presumed continuance of monarchy. The question of Milton warrants a moment's further consideration. At first sight it seems quite obvious that Milton became a republican. Did he not publicly defend the people of England for trying and executing him who had been, and in royalist eyes remained, their legal, hereditary king? On the eve of the widely predicted Restoration did not Milton oppose the return of Charles II and imply criticism of the Cromwellian protectorate? Does not his

---

[3] *The Prelude* (1805), x. 72.

presentation of monarchy in the last books of *Paradise Lost* convey his aversion from this form of rule? This evidence can hardly be set aside. Yet Milton nowhere expresses specific support for republican political forms, as does James Harrington, whose proposals Milton mocks. Is not Milton a metaphysical monarchist, also seeing Christ as 'Israel's true King'?[4] Milton, we may suppose, was chiefly concerned with Godly rule.

These reflections on Milton modify but hardly supplant our earlier description of a markedly anti-monarchical writer. In addition, in *Areopagitica* (1644), Milton seems close to that Machiavelli who thought that monarchies enervated or suppressed political energy, while republican polities opened the opportunity of choice and the competitive development of talent. In the case of the earlier Milton there may well be some connection between his development of an Arminian doctrine of individual choice and his readiness to abandon monarchy for what he may have hoped would prove a more free political structure, such as parts of Italy had earlier enjoyed in modern times.

This should alert us to the importance of modern as well as ancient republics in the political awareness of Renaissance England. Republican polities, though exceptional, were not the irrevocable property of the past. The situation was volatile in several areas of Europe. Louis Le Roy's *Aristotle's Politiques, Or Discourses of Government ... Translated out of French into English* cited the modern examples of Venice, Genoa, and Berne.[5] Camden, commenting on the unstable situation in France in 1589, reported that some French sought to change the form of their state,[6] and in a vituperative later passage accused the Netherlands of lapsing into a democracy in which all the nobility were cast out 'save one or two that are useful unto them in the warres',[7] a judgement which points to issues raised in Shakespeare's *Coriolanus*. Machiavelli in his *Discorsi* and at the margins of his military discourse in his *Arte della Guerra* supported republican government in principle and opposed the monarchical superstate such as Rome became under Augustus and after. It was chiefly to Italy, of course, that men looked for modern republican polities in action. Perhaps the earliest account of

---

[4] *Paradise Regained*, iii. 441.
[5] Louis Le Roy, *Aristotle's Politiques, Or Discourses of Government ... Translated out of French into English* (1596), 2.
[6] *Annals*, 386.   [7] *Annals*, 490.

them in English is to be found in William Thomas's *The History of Italy, A Book Exceeding Profitable to be Read Because it Entreateth of the State of Many and Divers Commonwealths, How They Have Been and Now Be Governed* (1549). A copious chronicler of the past as well as describer of the present, Thomas allows his reader to see some of the vicissitudes through which the states of Italy had passed.

Commenting on papal Rome he remarks that 'the Romans have in their hearts unto this day a certain memory of their ancient liberty, which they have attempted many times to recover, yet doth the Bishop [the Protestant Thomas's invariable term for the Pope] keep them in such subjection that they dare not once stir for their lives . . .'.[8] He notes how the ascendency over Florence gained by Lorenzo de Medici was lost by his son Piero, 'so that the state of Florence returned unto the common rule of the magistrates and citizens', gives a blow by blow narrative of how through influence, arms, determination, and opportunism Florence swayed between being a self-governing republic and a *de facto* duchy under one or other of the Medici, and describes how the young Cosimo de' Medici, originally elected duke in a military crisis, finally consolidated his power 'and is now absolute lord and king within himself'.[9] Thomas offers no generalizations on his narrative of Florentine history. Contingency appears to rule, though the odds may seem against republican survival. A similar pattern of forces is found in Thomas's description of the much smaller republic of Genoa. Once again republican institutions are overshadowed by the power of a great man, in this case Andrea Doria, 'the Emperor's admiral for the middle seas', who, among many naval victories, ended the threat to Genoa from France 'and the city restored to her ancient liberty, notwithstanding that many thought Andrea Doria would have taken the rule of it unto himself'. Thus Genoa came to be ruled by 'a duke, eight governors, and proctors chosen according to the order that yet remaineth', the duke being 'changeable every two year'. Nevertheless, Thomas notes, Andrea Doria 'useth all at his will in matters of peace or war, and almost in every other thing'.[10] From Thomas's account we may infer that this small republic survived through the confrontation of the two great powers of France and the Empire,

[8] William Thomas, *History of Italy* (1549), ed. George B. Parks (Ithaca, NY, 1963), 46–7.
[9] *History of Italy*, 99–104. [10] *History of Italy*, 109–11.

and the prudence of Andrea Doria who chose to wield a powerful practical influence without seeking formal authority.

Of course it is the Venetian Republic which most attracts Thomas's interest; he seems to have been both fascinated and repelled. He gives his fullest account here of the government of an Italian state, the Doge, or duke, elected for life; the Council of Six, the Council of Ten, the Signoria; and finally the Great Council which 'may be likened to our Parliament, for unto it many matters of importance are appealed, and that it doth is unreformable. By it all offices are given and into it entereth the Duke and all the other offices'.[11] Thomas stresses the small power of the Duke, 'I have heard some of the Venetians themselves call him an honorable slave',[12] in decisions of state, patronage, and even apparel. He praises the regular termination of office (with the exception of the Duke), balloting to fill vacant offices, and the fact that the ballot is secret. Though he does not discuss the point formally it is clear that Thomas recognizes the government of Venice to be an aristocracy in effect.[13] It certainly is not a democracy; and while the Duke looks at first sight like a monarch, he is far more circumscribed than an ordinary prince.

Beyond these precisely political points, Thomas gives a broad survey of the life and customs of the Republic. He is notable for giving a much worse picture of Venice than he does of the other states of Italy. In a full survey he makes observations on the site of the city, its buildings, its dominions on mainland Italy and in the eastern Mediterranean, its revenue, its public officers, its government, its wealth, its laws, its warfare, its welfare and charities, its customs of life, and the liberties it accorded to resident foreigners. He dwells memorably upon certain paradoxes: magnificence of building in 'the unwholesomest place to build upon . . . throughout an whole world';[14] a high rate of taxation raised, 'not upon lands but upon customs';[15] an admirable system of justice, 'if it were duly observed', yet 'corruption (by the advocates' means) . . . crept in amongst the judges';[16] the employment of Venetians as captains of its warships, but, an important point this, of 'strangers, both for general, for captains, and for all other men of war' by land, out of

[11] *History of Italy*, 73.   [12] *History of Italy*, 70.
[13] *History of Italy*, 72–5.   [14] *History of Italy*, 63–83.
[15] *History of Italy*, 69.   [16] *History of Italy*, 77.

fear of Caesar's example;[17] the remarkable freedom and prosperity of 'strangers' in the state, and especially Jews,

For in every city the Jews keep open shops of usury, taking gages of ordinary for fifteen in the hundred by the year, and if at the year's end the gage be not redeemed it is forfeit, or at the least done away to a great disadvantage, by reason whereof the Jews are out of measure wealthy in those parts.[18]

Finally, he brings out the remarkable blend of avarice and luxury in the manners of the Venetians, 'spare of living', yet their wives and courtesans 'sumptuously appareled', and the latter in particular, on whom they beget bastards lest the number of gentlemen increase and their commonwealth 'wax vile', 'are so rich that in a mask . . . you shall see them decked with jewels as they were queens'.[19] This strange duality of Venetian manners, public parsimony yet, behind the mask, a fantasy world of wealth and luxuriousness, was to be fully conveyed in the Venice of Jonson's *Volpone*, fifty-six years later.

The influence of Thomas's unenchanted description of Venice must have been countered, in some measure, by the popular victory of the allied Venetian and Spanish fleet over the Ottoman Turks at the Battle of Lepanto in 1571. *Letters sent from Venice. Anno 1571. Containing the certaine and true news of the most noble victorie of the Christians ouer the armie of the great Turke . . .* (1571) recounted how, as Don John came to Corfu, the Christians of Greece 'began to ryse', 'offring to follow what part soeuer shall please him to go, saying, to haue very wel knowne that the *Venetians* are chiefe lords of the sea, but neuer so wel tried as at that present'. These pages of news lay great stress on the small numbers of Christians slain by comparison with those of the Turkish fleet. This providential victory of the Christians which James VI of Scotland, in what must have been a well-known poem, *Lepanto*, celebrated, undoubtedly threw the Venetian Republic into a more heroic light. So, perhaps, for those who read it, did Gasparo Contarini's panegyrical *De Magistratibus et Republica Venetorum* (1543), which was to be translated into English, with a number of highly significant commendatory poems, by Lewis Lewkenor in 1599. These poems, while offering a series of more or less admiring variations on Contarini's

---

[17] *History of Italy*, 78.   [18] *History of Italy*, 69.   [19] *History of Italy*, 82.

praise of his native republic, also suggest a specifically English viewpoint.

The offering of Edmund Spenser, in the manner of his imitations of Du Bellay's *Antiquitez de Rome*, recalls two ancient empires, 'Babel, Empresse of the East . . . And second *Babell*, tyrant of the West [Rome]', each fallen through its pride, now replaced by a third:

> Fayre *Venice*, flower of the last worlds delight,
> And next to them in beauty draweth neare,
> But farre exceeds in policie of right.

> (ll. 10–12)

Venice is not blamed as a Babel, but the parallel is appropriate, no doubt, because Venice, like Babel and Rome, could be seen as an international empire that drew in 'strangers', and as Contarini argued, a market to the whole world.[20] Spenser also appears to echo Contarini's view that the growth of Venice has been due to providence and to her having always aimed at the 'preseruation of Ciuill concorde and agreement'.[21] John Harington also deploys the comparison between Venice and Rome, at a time when the notion of an emulous parallel between Britain and Rome was beginning to spread:

> Fair *Venice*, like a spouse in *Neptunes* armes,
> For freedome *Emulous* to ancient *Rome*,
> Famous for councell much, & much for armes . . .

For Harington, evidently, it is not of the Augustan empire of Rome, but the aristocratic republic, that Venice was emulous. Another poem stresses chiefly the civil achievement of Venice:

> *Venice*, inuincible, the Adriatique wonder,
> Admired of all the world for power and glorie,
> Whom no ambitious force could yet bring vnder,

---

[20] Gasparo Contarini, *De Magistratibus et Republica Venetorum* (Venice, 1543), trans. Lewes Lewkenor (1599), 1. A useful account of Contarini in context is W. J. Bouwsma, *Venice and The Defence of Republican Liberty: Renaissance Values in the Age of the Counter Reformation* (Berkeley and Los Angeles, 1968), 123–53. Zera S. Fink, *The Classical Republicans: An Essay in the Recovery of a Pattern of Thought in Seventeenth Century England* (Evanston, Ill., 1945) inaugurated the study of republican ideas in the early modern period.

[21] *Edmund Spenser Works, A Variorum Edition*, ed. Edwin Greenlaw, Charles G. Osgood, and Frederick M. Padelford (Baltimore, 1932–57), *Minor Poems*, II. 266, 507–8.

Is here presented in her States rare storye,
Where all corrupt meanes to aspire are curbd,
And Officers for vertues worth elected.
The conrarie whereof hath much disturbed
All states where the like course is not respected,
A document that Justice fortifies
Each gouernment (although in some things faultie)
And makes it dreadful to the enuying eyes
Of ill affecting foes, and tyrants haulty . . .

Already, here, a commentator upon Venice is hinting at the durability of its constitutional forms. How far, then, could the subjects of the English monarchy admire the republican constitution of Venice? Lewkenor himself, in his preface, suggests that Venice comprehends 'the fruite of all whatsoeuer other gouernments', for the Doge is royal, the Senate aristocratic, and the Great Council democratic. Contarini had argued the same, and analysed the Venetian constitution as an 'equal' and therefore lasting mixture, unequal political balances tending to dissolution, as in music an excessively loud chord destroys harmony.[22] Those who wished to argue that England too possessed a balanced constitution could find a pattern in the state of Venice as expounded by Contarini. This and other comparisons may have been in the mind of J. Ashley, the author of the most politically interesting of the prefatory sonnets to this volume:

Fayer mayden towne that in rich *Thetis* armes,
  Hast still been fostered since thy first foundacion.
  Whose glorious beauty cals vnnumbred swarmes
Of rarest spirits from each forein nation,
And yet (sole wonder to all *Europes* eares,
  Most louely Nimph, that euer Neptune got)
  In all this space of thirteene hundred yeares,
  Thy virgins state ambition nere could blot.
Now I prognosticate thy ruinous case,
  When thou shalt from thy Adriatique seas,
  View in this Ocean Isle thy painted face,

<hr>

[22] Contarini, *De Magistratibus*, trans. Lewkenor, preface and 67. A similar argument concerning the relevance of Venice can be found in Thomas Starkey's *Dialogue Between Cardinal Pole and Thomas Lupset* (c.1538), in S. J. Heritage (ed.), *England in the Reign of Henry VIII* (1878). I am indebted to Professor Dominic Baker-Smith for this reference.

In these pure colours coyest eyes to please,
Then gazing in thy shadows peereless eye,
Enamour'd like *Narcissus* thou shalt dye.

This poet goes well beyond the echoing with variations of the sentiments of Contarini. Nor does he merely wish to express a patriotic preference for his own state. He can see the virgin condition of the maritime republic of Venice, unstained by ambition and unraped by conquest, as in a twinned relation with his own 'Ocean Isle', ruled unconquered by its Virgin Queen. England is the natural mirror to Venice; in the 'Ocean Isle' Venice will see the natural counterpart of her own 'painted' face, and will die from love of this reflection. Venice will recognize England as her natural successor, and defer to the rise of a greater international maritime power. So much is implied by the ingenious conceitedness of this sonnet. Ashley's poem is prophetic of that moment, fifty-five years later, when his 'Ocean Isle' would be transformed into the idealized 'Oceana' of James Harrington, with the republic of Venice proposed as its chief political model.

Two different but connected questions arise from a consideration of the prefatory sonnets to Lewkenor's translation of Contarini, one political, and one literary. William Thomas had likened the Great Council of Venice in certain important respects to the English Parliament, and Ashley's sonnet proposes his 'Ocean Isle' as the natural reflection or counterpart of Venice. How far was there serious political content in such brief comparison? Did anyone regard the polity of England as a combination of the three chief Aristotelian forms of government as Contarini held Venice to be? There is a sixteenth-century English political work, Sir Thomas Smith's well-known *De Republica Anglorum* (begun in 1565 and first published in 1583), which at first sight seems to present England as a mixed and balanced polity. Though the difference between the lucid, consistent, but probably misleading formulation of Contarini and Smith's less easily unified account of England will perhaps suggest a negative answer, *De Republica Anglorum* is relevant to several phases of the argument of this chapter. The first question arising thus concerns Sir Thomas Smith's description of England.

Having warned that 'seldome or never shall you find common wealthes or government which is absolutely and sincerely made' of

one form 'but alwayes mixed with an other',[23] Smith defines 'a com-
mon wealth' as 'a society or common doing of a multitude of free
men collected together and united by common accord and cove-
nauntes among themselves as well in peace as in warre'. Slaves or
bondmen cannot be members of a commonwealth.[24] Those 'which
be participant of the common wealth' may be divided between men
who bear office, and men who bear none, between 'magistrates' and
'private men'. They may also be divided by rank, as 'among the
Romanes of *Patritii* and *plebei*', in France '*les nobles* and *la popu-
lare*, or *gentils homes* and *villaines*': but 'we in England divide our
men commonly into foure sortes, gentlemen, citizens, yeomen artifi-
cers, and laborers', gentlemen including king and aristocracy.[25] The
word 'participant' appears to include labourers even though, in the
later chapter devoted to them, they are designated as 'the fourth sort
of men which doe not rule'.[26] These last distinctions may be re-
garded as Smith's inclusive description of the many.

He might be thought to treat rule by the few, and by one, as he
turns to the subjects of Parliament and the Crown. Parliament is
described as 'The most high and absolute power of the realme of
Englande. . . . everie Englishman is entended to bee there present,
either in person or by procuration and attornies. . . . And the con-
sent of the Parliament is taken to be everie mans consent'.[27] The
remarkably modern sound of these sentences, and of Book II, ch. 1,
from which they are drawn, must immediately be set against Smith's
comments on the Crown in Book II, ch. 3. Here 'the Monarch of
Englande, King or Queene, hath absolutelie in his power the auth-
oritie of warre and peace, to defie what Prince it shall please him.
. . . His privie counsell be chosen also at the Princes pleasure. . . . So
that heerein the kingdome of Englande is farre more absolute than
either the dukedome of Venice is, or the kingdome of the Lacedo-
monians was'.[28] In war the king has absolute judicial power; he has
absolute power over the currency, over the dispensing from laws,

[23] Bk. I, ch. 6; Sir Thomas Smith, *De Republica Anglorum: A Discourse on the
Commonwealth of England*, ed. L. Alston (Cambridge, 1906), 14.
[24] Smith, *De Republica Anglorum*, 20–1.
[25] Smith, *De Republica Anglorum*, 30–1.
[26] Smith, *De Republica Anglorum*, 46–7. This account of the participants in the
polity of England and the ranks of English society occurs in chs. 16–24 of Bk. I, and
is based on William Harrison's *Description of England* as found by Smith in the 1577
Holinshed (*De Republica Anglorum*, pp. xvi–xxiv).
[27] Smith, *De Republica Anglorum*, 48–9.
[28] Smith, *De Republica Anglorum*, 58–9.

over appointments to the highest office, and 'To be short the prince is the life, the head, and the authoritie of all things that be doone in the realme of England'.[29] Finally, as Smith has already pointed out in Book I, ch. 9, 'our nation' never used 'any other generall authoritie . . . neither *Aristocraticall*, nor *Democraticall*, but onely the royall and kingly majestie'.[30]

It is now clear that while in Smith's view the commonwealth of England is in one sense mixed, it is not really a harmony of different powers. Powers are not seen to be sufficiently distinct to generate conflict or point to the need for a dynamic equilibrium. The king is more powerful—'more absolute'—than the Doge of Venice, and Smith sees no conflict between Crown and Parliament, even though some things are specifically the responsibilities of Parliament, others the prerogative of the king. There is no conflict because Parliament is a court rather than a sovereign legislative body, and a court whose acts speak for the whole commonwealth including the king.[31] Just as Venice, despite Contarini, was regarded as an aristocratic republic rather than a polity of mixed powers, so England was a monarchy before all else. Yet in each case that appearance of a mixture of the three basic Aristotelian forms of government remains. Smith's account could be regarded as an outline of a polity containing potential controversy and conflict between one and another part, apparent in retrospect though not to the eye of the author himself. At all events he is aware that forms of government change, just as states rise and fall, and as the human body grows, suffers sickness, and decays.[32]

The second question arising from the prefatory sonnets to Contarini concerns the evolution of the public and political sonnet. Spenser, the best known of the contributors, had a kind of model for the public sonnet in Du Bellay's *Antiquitez de Rome*, which the English poet had imitated in part in his *Ruines of Rome: by Bellay*. To be sure, Du Bellay's response to Rome is chiefly to its physical remains: Rome is the prime emblem of the mutability of man's most supreme public effort, and thus of the vanity of human wishes. These sonnets are contemplations, or complaints, but a careful

---

[29] Smith, *De Republica Anglorum*, 62.
[30] Smith, *De Republica Anglorum*, 19.
[31] Geoffrey Elton (ed.), *The Tudor Constitutions: Documents and Commentary* (Cambridge, 1962); id., *The Parliament of England, 1559–1581* (Cambridge, 1986).
[32] Smith, *De Republica Anglorum*, 12–13.

reading does reveal different explanations of the fall of Rome. It was the chastisement of hubris, the course of nature, or the doom of the very world itself to come to nothing. Sometimes the two poets seem to allude to the Machiavellian explanation (conveyed in his *Art of War*) that Rome quenched the freedom and *virtú* of the world through drawing it all into one mighty domination. This perhaps is the case with Spenser's Sonnet 8. Sonnet 18 registers Rome's evolution from kingdom to republic, and thence to empire. Other sonnets (27 and 30) are less single and final in their vision, holding out some hope of renewal (Sonnets 27 and 30 of *Ruines of Rome*). What is common to all these sonnets is their long overview of history and time. Spenser's Contarini sonnet shares this feature, though the term 'policy of right' in praise of Venice briefly shows his awareness of the role of law and statecraft in Venetian political practice. It is an interesting moment because the virtue of a balanced polity—such as Contarini considered Venice to be—was that it was supposed, in principle, to last for ever. There is a sense in which the very dynamism of a republican constitution could be seen as a creative answer to the *ubi sunt* emblem of Rome in its ruins. At all events the salient development from this tradition of the public sonnet, in the next century, would be the political sonnets of Milton. There the lofty overview of history would frequently be exchanged for the strife and controversy of a republic in the making. In the meantime a nearer view of the image of the modern republic in late Elizabethan and early Jacobean England can readily be found in those plays of Shakespeare and Jonson which were set in Venice.

II

Probably nobody now thinks that all Shakespeare's plays, behind the mere *name* of their setting, display Renaissance England. I would not suggest that the named setting is the heart of the play; I certainly would not suggest that Shakespeare laboured to produce detailed historical accuracy, as Jonson (with a few deliberate and significant exceptions) seems to have done with his two tragedies set in ancient Rome. It does, however, seem that Shakespeare makes broad recognizable distinctions between one place and another, one time and another, and that these differentiated settings are not static backdrops, as it were, to the moving action, but that there is a dynamic relation between foreground action and the dramatized community in which the action takes place, whether it be modern Venice, early republican Rome—or the England of Richard II. At other times Shakespeare chooses to suggest place and polity without specification; at other times still his settings are the realms of fiction and countries of the mind. In the case of his two Venetian plays, *The Merchant of Venice* (?1586–8) and *Othello* (?1604), Shakespeare dramatizes a place recognizably different from any to be found elsewhere in the canon. Shakespeare's main sources (Ser Giovanni's *Il Pecarone* in the case of *The Merchant of Venice*, and Cinthio's *Gli Hecatommithi* in the case of *Othello*) gave him his usurous Jew of Venice, and his Moorish captain in the service of the state; Thomas's account and these Italian sources convey what were doubtless widespread ideas of Venice, which Shakespeare appears to accept. In these, as in most other plays of Shakespeare, the setting is important, not because it can be shown to have detailed historical accuracy, but because the dramatist himself uses current material and ideas to dramatize different conflicts and states of mind.

Both Shylock and Othello are 'strangers' in the Venetian state, in the sense in which Thomas used the term, and each is cast in one or other of the roles which, according to Thomas, 'strangers' played: Jewish residents who were professional moneylenders, and military commanders appointed to serve the state in the field lest a native Venetian general should be tempted to usurp the republic. This having been said, the Venice in which 'strangers' have such importance plays a different role in each of these two plays. The Venice of *The Merchant* is a commonwealth of laws, while that of *Othello* is a martial republic in its long struggle with Turkish power. Thus Antonio, replying to Solanio's suggestion that 'the duke | Will never grant this forfeiture to hold', predicts that Shylock will have his bond since

> The Duke cannot deny the course of law,
> For the commodity that strangers have
> With us in Venice, if it be denied,
> Will much impeach the justice of the state,
> Since that the trade and profit of the city
> Consisteth of all nations.
>
> (III. iii. 26–31)

Shakespeare may remember a specific passage from Thomas here,[33] but what is of most interest is the way the lines balance between recognition of strict and impartial law—a good—and 'commodity'—a word certainly charged with associations of cynical materialism in the Bastard's great soliloquy in *King John* (II. i. 561 *et seq.*). The argument, however, is one that Shylock certainly puts to the Duke and the Magnificoes at the Court of Justice, 'If you deny me, fie upon your law! | There is no force in the decrees of Venice' (IV. i. 100–1), but in the romance-like heightening of Ser Giovanni's tale and Shakespeare's drama the law is vindicated in its very strictness, threatening Shylock's life if he spills one 'jot of Blood' or takes anything beyond his pound of flesh (IV. i. 302–9). The Venice of *Othello*, on the other hand, is the Venice of the naval wars with the Ottoman Turks, and, while the civil structure of the state and its judical function are not insignificant, it is in the framing of the domestic tragedy with the 'services which I [Othello] have done the signiory'[34] that the Republic is most conspicuous in the drama. The unexpected wrecking of the Turkish fleet in the storm deprives Othello of the martial role everyone expects him to play, leaving him to a struggle of a very different kind, and for which he is to prove ill-equipped. His final speech recalls in its carefully understated claim to have 'done the state some service' all the martial glory he has elsewhere more fully and passionately expressed (III. iii. 350–9).[35] In the acted simile of his closing lines he becomes as a 'malignant and a turbaned Turk' who 'Beat a Venetian and traduced the state', in that each is smitten 'thus': it is a way of concealing his intended suicide to the last, but also a way of saying that he has betrayed the state, betrayed the best (Desdemona) that the state has entrusted to him, and indeed that he 'Like the base Indian, threw a pearl away | Richer than all his tribe' (V. ii. 347–65).

Venice is, on balance, favourably portrayed in both these plays of Shakespeare, and it is possible (though not I think demonstrable) that Lewkenor's translation of Contarini had some influence on the writing of *Othello*. Ben Jonson certainly knew Contarini, for his Sir

---

[33] *The Merchant of Venice*, ed. J. R. Brown, New Arden Series (1955; rev. edn. 1959), 93.

[34] See G. R. Hibbard, '*Othello* and the Pattern of Shakespearean Tragedy', and Emrys Jones, '*Othello*, *Lepanto* and the Cyprus Wars', *Shakespeare Survey*, 21 (Cambridge, 1968), 39–46 and 47–52 respectively.

[35] Hibbard, '*Othello* and the Pattern of Shakespearean Tragedy', 45, makes this point.

Politick Would-Be, boasting how within the first week of his landing 'All tooke me for a citizen of *Venice* . . .', goes on to explain that 'I had read CONTARENE, tooke me a house, | Dealt with my *Jewes* . . .' and later in the same scene discourses knowingly of the 'great councell', 'the forty', and 'the ten'. He too wishes 'to serve the state | Of *Venice*,—with read herrings, for three years, | . . . and at a certain rate, from Rotterdam.'[36] Through the naïvely 'knowing' eyes of Sir Politick, something of the thoroughly secular reputation of Venice—or of its strangers—is conveyed:

> . . . beware,
> You neuer speake a truth—*Per* How! *Pol.* Not to strangers,
> For those be they you must conuerse with, most;
> Others I would not know, sir . . .
> And then, for your religion, professe none;
> But wonder, at the diuersity of all;
> And, for your part, protest, were there no other
> But simply the lawes o'th' land, you could content you.

> (IV. i. 16–25)

Jonson, in fact, despite his knowledge of Contarini's panegyrical account, is thoroughly sceptical of Venetian society, and much closer to William Thomas's description than any other play discussed here. It may be argued that Jonson is equally sceptical of English society. This is in great measure true, but Venice is none the less explicitly characterized, in its manners and institutions, and the contrast between a mean everyday life and a luxurious fantasy fulfilment is given a distinct local colour. The judges of Jonson's Venice, however, are ultimately just and ṣtrict, though Jonson has managed to intimate in passing their vulnerability to corruption (v. xii. 50–1).[37]

It may fairly be objected that the attitude of the Venetian state to 'strangers' is hardly an essential feature of Renaissance republican thought. That may be the case, despite the propensity for assemblies deciding policies by vote to rest on a severely limited franchise. But Venice dominated the Renaissance picture of the modern republic, and in that respect its treatment of 'strangers' is of importance. Even the views of a stranger such as Sir Politick Would-Be help to sharpen

[36] C. H. Herford and Percy and Evelyn Simpson (eds.), *Ben Jonson* (Oxford, 1925–52), v. 90–1; ix. 722 (140 n.).
[37] Ibid., v. 132.

our sense of how utterly different from England Venice is. His confidence that within a week 'All took me for a citizen of *Venice*' is palpably absurd, and we see that for Sir Politick to serve the state among its strangers is only to bring off a ridiculous business deal. For him the situation of 'strangers' in Venice is a kind of irresponsible secular opportunity: a release from allegiance, in favour of red herrings. For Shylock and Othello, on the other hand, their very sense of self is bound up with their relation, as 'strangers' to the state. The Venetians are not Shylock's tribe but their law matters to him intensely: it is the secular contract granted by Christians which can vindicate him against Christians. The law shows how he needs the state, and, as he holds to it, marks him out as bitterly alienated from it. His tenacious insistence on the laws of Venice betrays, on Shakespeare's part no doubt, a Christian view then general of the blind adherence of the Jews to the old law, but the fact remains that the law here in question is the Venetian law governing men of different religions. In a play which can be seen as a parable of the pilgrim's voyage to salvation, imperilled by storms, rocks, and treacherous sands, the Venetian law is seen to be as inadequate as any other, when not fulfilled by mercy. Such mercy it was the prerogative of the monarch (in Smith's *De Republica Anglorum*) to exercise. In this drama a brilliant lawyer from the Venetian university city of Padua comes to foil Shylock with a stricter legalism even than his.

Unlike Shylock, Othello takes no stand on the letter of the law. As a 'stranger' he takes pride in his service to the state at the pitch of its maritime crisis with the Turkish Empire. Cyprus itself is under formidable threat, that same Cyprus, now in the play a possession of Venice, which 'not long agone . . . hath had a king alone'.[38] To Othello Venice gives more than rights under its laws; it gives the responsibility of military leadership, and, in recognition of its hour of supreme need, it breaches its own barrier between senatorial families and military command to deny Brabantio's suit and sanction the marriage of his daughter to the Moor. This, I think, underlines the appropriateness of Othello's invocation of the state of Venice in his suicide speech when his command has been 'taken off'. It does indeed recall a sphere of activity in which the Moor was always bravely and honourably in command, unlike the heartbreak-

[38] Thomas, *History of Italy*, 68.

ing domestic tragedy into which he has been lured and betrayed himself. But at the same time he esteems Venice for all that the state gave him: his wife as well as his command, and it is notable that the speech which has at its centre the hand still carrying the pearl that, like a base Indian, it is to cast away, begins and ends with Venice and its state affairs.

An example of where Shakespeare chooses to suggest place and polity without specification (as proposed earlier in this chapter) is the comedy of *Twelfth Night* (1601). The argument that *Twelfth Night* is set in Ragusa, hardly known in England, is familiar in south slav studies of Shakespearian comedy.[39] Since Shakespeare does not specify, as he does, for example, with Navarre in *Love's Labours Lost*, and Verona in *Romeo and Juliet*, not to mention the two Venetian plays discussed above, the elaborate detail of the older controversies on the point seems misconceived. Yet there is a general idea concerning setting and polity worth rescuing from these disputes for brief consideration. 'Illyria' (I. ii. i) was for Shakespeare, in all probability, not merely associated with a world of late Greek romance,[40] but a classical place-name with a well-understood modern equivalent: Dalmatia. This is not an unreasonable supposition; George Sandys could write in 1632 of '*Dalmatia*, which lyeth between *Istria* and *Epirus*: called anciently *Illyria*',[41] and the existence of a Ragusan merchant community in London in the late sixteenth century means that knowledge of the cities of the Dalmation coast would not have been inaccessible to Shakespeare.[42] Furthermore, it is clear enough when a play by Shakespeare has been given a classical or pre-Christian setting (he may not be historically accurate but he does make recognizable distinctions) and the society of *Twelfth Night* is recognizably Christian. This should mean that Orsino rules over a modern state on the coast of what was anciently called Illyria. If so, Ragusa is the only plausible possibility; the other cities of the coast were Venetian, and Shakespeare elsewhere makes it quite plain when he is depicting either Venice or a Venetian

---

[39] Kostić, *Cultural Relations*, 182.
[40] *Twelfth Night*, ed. J. M. Lothian and T. W. Craik, New Arden Series (1975), 8 (l. 1 n.); Kostić, *Cultural Relations*, 498–9.
[41] George Sandys, *A Relation of a Journey . . . 1610 . . .* (1632), 2–3.
[42] For this community, see Kostić, *Cultural Relations*, 498–9. He points out that the young Ragusan merchant Paule Gundulić used to meet Englishmen and Italians at the Elephant and the Dolphin Taverns, in the parish of St Helen Bishopsgate, in which Shakespeare had been living in 1597. Cf. *Twelfth Night*, III. iii. 39.

dependency such as Cyprus. On the other hand it may be urged that 'Illyria' is either England nominally disguised, or indeed nowhere in particular. It goes without saying that much that is Renaissance England is to be found in all Shakespeare's plays but, once again, *Twelfth Night* has its significant distinguishing features. In I. ii, II. i, III. iii, and, above all, v. i. 47–88, there is established, despite the incorporation of an intriguing English reference (to the Elephant Tavern, a resort of the Ragusan community in London) the specific nature of Orsino's Illyria: a state ruled by a duke, familiarly called a count; one which, to a newcomer at least (I. ii. 51–8), has associations with oriental or eastern Mediterranean courts; and one to which the maintenance of mercantile trade with the eastern Mediterranean was of the first importance, and the menace of piracy the more serious (v. i). There are many other arguments against the dismissal of the proposed connection between 'Illyria' and Ragusa,[43] but, falling short of demonstration, they display the delicacy with which Shakespeare lightly sketched a setting and a city geographically between those of his two main sources.[44]

[43] See Appendix II.
[44] *Gl'Ingannati* for Modena; *Riche His Farewell* for Constantinople.

5
Rome and English Republican Poetry

IN his notes on the life of Thomas May, royalist poet but later parliamentarian historiographer, Aubrey notes: 'That of Lucan is true, scil., that it made him incline to a republic',[1] and after the Restoration it was one of the great charges of Hobbes in his *Behemoth* that the study of the classical republics of Greece and Rome eroded men's loyalty to monarchy.[2] When in 1627 May published his translation of *Lucan's Pharsalia: or the Ciuill Warres of Rome, betweene Pompey the great, and Iulius Caesar*, Ben Jonson wrote in praise both of Lucan and his translator:

> . . . when againe I view the parts so peiz'd,
> And those in number so, and measure rais'd,
> As neither *Pompey*'s popularitie,
> *Caesar*'s ambition, *Cato*'s libertie,
> Calme *Brutus* tenor start; but all along
> Keepe due proportion and the ample song. . . .[3]

The different forces of the commonwealth of Rome are here seen to have been transformed into the 'dynamic equilibrium' of Lucan's poem, 'arts and eloquence' giving each figure or force its due. The poem suggests the 'ample' range of Jonson's ideas and judgement, and raises a question about him and others that is also prompted by Hobbes and Aubrey. Did Jonson's elaborate study of the Roman Republic, especially perhaps for *Catiline His Conspiracy* (1610) incline him in any degree towards republicanism? Or was it the case that men like Jonson had no trouble in equating ancient republics with the royal *republica anglorum* of England? What significance for the political thought of Shakespeare

---

[1] John Aubrey, *'Brief Lives', Chiefly of Contemporaries . . . between 1669 & 1696*, ed. Andrew Clark (Oxford, 1898), ii. 56.
[2] Thomas Hobbes, *Behemoth: Or an Epitome of the Civil Wars of England* (1679); *The English Works of Thomas Hobbes*, ed. W. Molesworth, 11 vols. (1839–45), VI. 168.
[3] ll. 7–12; *Ben Jonson* [*Works*], ed. C. H. Herford and Percy and Evelyn Simpson, 11 vols. (Oxford, 1925–52), viii. 395.

has *Coriolanus* (?1608), his tragedy set in early republican Rome—or *Julius Caesar* (1599) set in the very late republic? What relations, if any, do these republican dramas have to current affairs of state?

I

In dramatizing the Roman Republic in *Coriolanus* and *Catiline* Shakespeare and Jonson sought a political mode which would more clearly display contemporary tensions and dangers than a British chronicle source, a modern republican setting, or even the recent French world of Chapman's Bussy and Biron plays. Shakespeare wished to explore, among other things, the question of military leadership in a non-deferential and precariously hierarchical society. Another way of putting this is to say that he wished to dramatize the fraught relations between different ranks of men: aristocrats habituated to political and military leadership on the one hand, urban artisans (perhaps, if we remember the current anti-enclosure riots, rural labourers) on the other.[4] Jonson wished to take a recent crisis, the desperate papist Gunpowder Plot, seen by Protestant and Catholic as of intense religious significance, and transpose it into the pagan world of the late Roman Republic. This contrasts markedly with Shakespeare's play in response to the same crisis, *Macbeth*, which invoked patriarchal kingship at its most powerful. Given that the allusions to the gods of Rome in Jonson's tragedy reveal little significant religious conflict, his choice of subject has the final effect of secularizing a religious crisis, and setting all on the basis of cruel ambition on the one hand, wise and effective loyalty to the state on the other. Like Shakespeare, Jonson is concerned with rank, though in a different and less comprehensive way. One of the salient points in *Catiline* is that Cicero is not one of the ancient nobility, but a new man. Nevertheless Cicero, contrary to Sempronia's very confident prediction, 'It will be cross'd, by the nobilitie' (II. 113),[5] is elected Consul. But *Catiline* shows no concern with the plebeians comparable to that of *Coriolanus*. We may note, finally, that each play draws in a people other than

---

[4] *Coriolanus*, ed. G. R. Hibbard, New Penguin Series (Harmondsworth, 1967), 10–12.
[5] *Ben Jonson*, v. 458.

the Romans, *Coriolanus* most strongly the Volscians, rivals of Rome, *Catiline* the Allobroges, potential allies either of Catiline or Cicero.

I think there can be no doubt that each drama displays serious republican thought. Republican Rome is not just a setting—or a disguise—for an English action, though in Jonson's case a historical English action, and in Shakespeare's case an English problem, were at the forefront of the dramatists' minds. Because *Catiline* is politically the simpler case, and also more closely allied to recent historical events, it will be best to consider it first.

Catiline is Jonson's third Roman drama but his only republican one. *Sejanus His Fall* (1604), as a tragedy of state which dramatizes the rise and fall of a favourite, alludes in all probability to the recent fall of Essex.[6] Its general remarks on princes are uncomplimentary in the extreme, and in one case Jonson toned down his censure for the folio version. It is a matter of record that he was in trouble with the Privy Council over the play,[7] and possible that he wrongly supposed a drama on a late Elizabethan episode would not offend James. Perhaps the recent historical focus was insufficiently clear. *Catiline* has in common with Jonson's first Roman play, *The Poetaster* (1601), the fact that it brings on stage figures of fame and authority from Latin antiquity: in the earlier drama Horace and Augustus; in the later Cicero and Cato. The effect is to activate a Roman standard, judging more recent time in the light of their wisdom and their deeds. It has always been accepted that *The Poetaster* deals among other things with the contemporary English literary scene;[8] Barbara De Luna in her book *Jonson's Romish Plot* succeeds, to my mind, in showing the allusion of *Catiline* to the Gunpowder Plot in certain major central features at least, though not perhaps in all she sets out to demonstrate. In both plays, therefore, seventeenth-century London and Roman antiquity are brought together on the stage. In *Catiline* there is once again a measure of personal involvement on Jonson's own part, as De Luna establishes. For the spectator, or reader, of *Catiline* the fiddled Roman date, coming out as 'thy purpose | Was, on the fifth (the kalends of November) | T' have slaughtered this whole order' (IV. ii.

---

[6] B. N. De Luna, *Jonson's Romish Plot: A Study of Catiline and its Historical Context* (Oxford, 1967), 6–7.

[7] *Ben Jonson*, ix. 587–91.

[8] Howard Erskine-Hill, *The Augustan Idea in English Literature* (1983), 112–15.

245–7),[9] and Cicero's suggestive remark, 'no religion binds men to be traitors' (III. ii. 369),[10] are clear references to the date and circumstances of the Catholic conspiracy, with the current dispute, about whether papists could be loyal to Protestant princes, lying behind it. The issue of character identification then arises, and if the points just made are accepted the allusion of Catiline to Catesby is virtually entailed. 'Catiline' was of course a stock name for a violent conspirator; Catesby had been called a 'Catiline' often enough; his conspiracy was the recent example all would remember; the two names even happened to resonate. Beyond this, a little hesitation is in order. It used to be supposed that Horace simply spoke for Jonson in *The Poetaster*, but a closer inspection suggests that Jonson's views are more widely distributed among the characters, at least between Horace and Augustus.[11] Augustus himself was represented as the ideal prince in relation to poetry, morality, and religion, though he may have been what Jonson hoped Elizabeth's unannounced successor would be. There seems to have been no further contemporary allusion in Augustus. For this and other reasons De Luna's argument for *Catiline* as a 'parallelograph' in which almost every character points to an English historical original,[12] and in which, for example, Cicero is Robert Cecil, Quintus Curius Jonson, and so forth, seems to me doubtful though it is certainly not absurd.

It does, however, touch on a major issue for the question of republicanism. It was King James's government which discovered the plot in time to avert catastrophe. Most central in the discovery was the king's Secretary of State Robert Cecil, Earl of Salisbury, though James himself, target of plots enough in the past, added significantly to the recognition of imminent danger. If Jonson's Cicero is, for example, an exemplary figure of a ruler loyal to the commonwealth, then the relevant transposition of Roman republic to English kingdom has been effected: we are asked to think about the public interest in each case. But if the Consul Cicero here alludes to Robert Cecil alone, then the royal aspect of England's polity may be thought to be occluded by Jonson's choice of Catiline's conspiracy as the ostensible subject of his play. This possibility links with Jonson's treatment of two other figures in the drama: Lentulus and

9 De Luna, *Jonson's Romish Plot*, 37–9.
10 De Luna, *Jonson's Romish Plot*, 39–45.
11 Erskine-Hill, *The Augustan Idea*, 113–21.
12 De Luna, *Jonson's Romish Plot*, 179.

Caesar. It is in Lentulus that Jonson allows the subject of kingship to be raised explicitly, for it is Lentulus whom Catiline flatters and fools into thinking he 'Should be a king in *Rome*' (I. 138), by virtue of his ancestry and a Sibylline prophecy. This is not an isolated moment in the play; the royal aspirations of Lentulus are a minor motif through the whole work. There is ferocious irony in the way Catiline and the bloodthirsty Cethegus, sharks of the common-wealth, play upon Lentulus:

CATILINE. All that can say the sunne is ris'n, must thinke it.
LENTULUS. Men marke me more, of late, as I come forth!
CATILINE. Why, what can they doe lesse? CINNA, and SVLLA
  Are set, and gone: and we must turne our eyes
  On him that is, and shines. Noble CETHEGVS,
  But view him with me, here! He lookes, already,
  As if he shooke a sceptre, o're the *Senate*,
  And the aw'd purple dropt their rods, and axes.

(I. 270–7)[13]

At the end of the play Cicero, contemplating what might have been, sees Lentulus as a kind of puppet-ruler, reigning over the slaughter of Rome (v. 261–70). De Luna's proposed parallel of Lentulus with Garnet the Jesuit does not carry conviction (ambitious as this priest may have been) but Catholics in England and abroad always had their own candidate for the throne. It was of course a historical commonplace that the name of king was hated in Rome after the Tarquins, but Jonson's choice of Roman material could easily have been managed so as to play down or omit this feature in the original conspiracy. It may seem that Jonson only raises the idea of kingship to scoff at it, though perhaps it is nearer the mark to see in Jonson's Lentulus one in what was to be a long line of papist pretenders to a throne.

The issue of kingship in *Catiline* does not end here. A more significant figure than Lentulus is Caius Caesar. This is he who in popular wisdom became monarch of Rome as the first Caesar, a kingly example if not a king by name; and who, together with his adopted son Augustus in Bodin's more sophisticated analysis, in-itiated Rome's slow change of government from republic to mon-archy under the Julian House. A part of this historical transition was dramatized by Shakespeare in *Julius Caesar*, where, though the

---

[13] *Ben Jonson*, v. 443.

republicans Brutus and Cassius are accorded deeply sympathetic treatment, their political desisions are hardly endorsed, and Caesar is clearly the figure of kings to be.[14] Jonson's Caesar is very different. He is sympathetic, perhaps complicit, with the plotters. 'Be resolute, | And put your enterprise in act', he tells Catiline (III. 491-2),[15] and at the end, having pleaded in the Senate for mitigation of the conspirators' punishment and been denied by the advice of that last-ditch republican Cato, Caesar barely evades discovery (V. 447-97, 571-82).[16] Jonson's treatment of Lentulus and Caesar gives his republican hero Cicero a more specific political significance than he might otherwise have had. The transference of value from Roman republic to English kingdom is made less easy; and, while I would not suggest that *Catiline* is a complete statement of faith by an author so overtly royalist in other works, the tragedy does seem to be specifically republican in spirit. Within the range and proportion of Jonson's mind the public spirit of republican Rome, articulated by Cicero and Cato, is held up as an example to the seventeenth-century English kingdom.

The circumstances meant to be illuminated by the example were of a kind that Jonson had had a good opportunity to observe. A Catholic from 1598 to the murder of Henry IV of France in 1610, he knew something of the Catholic party and was acquainted, apparently as a spy, with the chief plotters.[17] Barred as recusants from office and emolument, the committed Catholics might, so long as Elizabeth lived and failed to declare a successor, hope for some favourable change at her death. The succession of James, with its confirmation that they had little enough advantage to expect from him, made some of them desperate to a degree out of proportion to their power and numbers in the kingdom. Sallust's account of the discontents of the Catilinarians, from which Jonson builds Catiline's first speech to his supporters (I. 325-420), constitutes a fair parallel. Jonson's invocation of the Rome of Cicero and Catiline to dramatize the desperate action of his recent co-religionists, recognized religion as a bond of the plotters but not their motive. While, as already noted, the world of Catiline displays no conflict between gods and religions, the conspirators, as they vow to achieve their purpose, partake in a ghastly sacrament in which human blood is

---

[14] Erskine-Hill, *The Augustan Idea*, 134-8.   [15] *Ben Jonson*, v. 484.
[16] *Ben Jonson*, v. 541-5.   [17] De Luna, *Jonson's Romish Plot*, 115-43.

mingled with wine. This is in Sallust, where 'sacramentum' means
an oath-taking;[18] Jonson's retention of the word 'sacrament' (I. 423;
IV. 449)[19] and of the story of the human blood constitutes a clear
and crude allusion to the Catholic concept of the Eucharist. It was
widely alleged that the Catholic plotters of 1606 had taken a solemn
sacrament and oath.[20] It may be seen that Jonson effectively margi-
nalizes religion in his tragedy by concentrating it into the lurid oath,
and contrasting it with the secular ideal of the good of the common-
wealth. Or more precisely, perhaps, this is a way of affirming the
author's new Protestant conviction 'that no religion binds men to be
traitors' (III. 369).[21]

Though introduced by the Ghost of Sulla as a man epitomizing
'mischief', 'guilt', 'furie', 'crime', and 'impietie' (I. 43–60),[22] Catiline
is initially a less simple and more human figure. Denied the military
command he desired in the Pontic war, he is animated by disap-
pointment and rejection: 'I will, hereafter, call her step-dame, euer',
he says of Rome, 'If shee can loose her nature, I can loose | My
pietie' (I. 87–93).[23] His first speech to his supporters has consider-
able force as a sermon against the power, wealth, and greed of
Rome, but its rhetorical drive is towards a challenge to Rome's
rulers for the monopolizing of all this wealth, power, and glory (I.
325–73).[24] His concluding keynote is that of freedom, eagerly taken
up by his followers. To these motives must be added the resentment
of rank, so often voiced by the Catilinarians when Cicero is men-
tioned. The election of Cicero rather than Catiline to the Consul-
ship, despite aristocratic support for the latter, is the final blow that
triggers off his rebellion. From then on the resentment of the ex-
cluded Catiline is simplified, through the events and discoveries of
the action, to the point before the final battle when, in his oration to
his troops, he speaks first of the desperateness of their military
situation, then of 'glorie' and 'libertie', finally of sustenance and self
(V. 378–410).[25] At this point his cause appears to be emptied of any
ideology it once contained, and becomes sheer political evil, desper-
ate and pure. Catiline has become all that the choric Ghost of Sulla
announced. The wisdom of Cicero, Cato, and their supporters, in

---

[18] Ibid. 173–5; Ben Jonson, x. 130.   [19] Ben Jonson, v. 448, 512.
[20] De Luna, Jonson's Romish Plot, 173–5.   [21] Ben Jonson, v. 480.
[22] Ben Jonson, 436–7.   [23] Ben Jonson, v. 437.
[24] Ben Jonson, 445–6.   [25] Ben Jonson, 539–40.

taking the decisive action they do, is abundantly and perhaps rather uninterestingly demonstrated.

This conclusion obscures the first-sight similarity between Catiline and Coriolanus. Catiline like Coriolanus seeks and is denied the Consulship. Like him he feels powerful resentment against the commonwealth, part of his sense of the rejection of the right of rank. Banished from Rome (IV. 503),[26] Catiline, like Coriolanus, returns against it with an army. Like Coriolanus, Catiline draws another people against Rome, here the Allobroges, whom he seeks to use for his own purposes. This similarity between two tragedies firmly based on two different sets of classical sources need not surprise. Sources are chosen for what they contain; they do not impose completed works on later authors. However, the conflict between the ambitious military leader and the commonwealth which it is his duty only to serve, and not to usurp, was endemic in the polities of the ancient world and in their modern republican successors, as we have seen in the cases of Genoa and Venice. It is not remarkable that Shakespeare, drawing on Plutarch and Livy, and Jonson, drawing on Cicero and Sallust, should within a few years focus on this conflict. It is also possible that Shakespeare's treatment prompted Jonson to deal with it in a different way. For authors who were subjects of King James, and writing in the light of Bodin's discussion of Rome's transition from republic to monarchy, the conflict must have seemed hard to resolve. Might it not be for the best for the figure of military might to found a monarchy? Jonson's answer in *Catiline* is an unambiguous negative. The state, its civilian leaders, and loyal armies, take precedence equally over individual military virtù and subversive religion. *Coriolanus*, a far deeper exploration into political relations and political psychology, returns a more open reply.

The question of monarchy hangs over *Coriolanus*. Lacking the direction in this regard afforded by Jonson's Lentulus and Caesar, *Coriolanus* remains a drama more delicately poised between opposing answers. It is notable that Plutarch specified the war in which Caius Martius first won glory, though 'but a stripling': it was against Tarquin the Proud and a 'great and mightie armie' assembled to 'put him into his Kingdome againe'.[27] This opportunity to

---

[26] *Ben Jonson*, 514.
[27] Geoffrey Bullough (ed.), *Narrative and Dramatic Sources of Shakespeare*, 7 vols. (1957-75), v. 507.

present Coriolanus as a youthful republican hero is not taken by
Shakespeare when it first arises, with Volumnia's 'To a cruel war I
sent him, from whence he returned his brows bound with oak' (I. iii.
13–14)—indeed it is never fully taken at all. However, the point is
not unnoticed or neglected. It is when the question of Coriolanus's
office comes up that his mother says: 'He received in the repulse of
Tarquin seven hurts i th' body' (II. i. 146–7), and Cominius uses the
point in his panegyric on him in II. ii. The effect is to play down any
republican fervour in the young Martius but to note the relevance of
service against Tarquin when it comes to running for Consul. A
similar deferral is seen in the charge of the Tribunes against Corio-
lanus that he sought to make himself king. This, the major formal
accusation against him in Plutarch, arises in the Greek narrative
when he seeks the Consulship, and is effectively refuted. In Shakes-
peare the issue of affecting the tyrannical power is briefly mentioned
at that point in the action but, much later, in the short spell of false
security that Rome enjoys after Coriolanus has been expelled and
before the news breaks of his invasion, the Tribunes make the full
charge:

BRUTUS. Caius Martius was
　A worthy officer i'th' war, but insolent,
　O'ercome with pride, ambitious past all thinking,
　Self-loving—
SICINIUS. And affecting one sole throne
　Without assistance.
MENENIUS. I think not so.

(IV. vi. 30–5)

Shakespeare's delicacy in reducing the salience of an idea without
erasing it is again notable. The train of thought continues as Menenius
says of an apparently implacable Coriolanus in v. iv: 'He sits in his state
as a thing made for Alexander' (ll. 21–2); and continued, with great
irony, when a messenger to the reprieved Rome can announce:

A merrier day did never yet greet Rome,
No, not th' expulsion of the Tarquins.

(v. iv. 43–4)

Was Coriolanus a potential Tarquin the Proud? Perhaps; but he
finally saved his city, despite his expulsion. Or did he save Rome
from another potential monarch, Tullus Aufidius, whom North's

Plutarch notes to have been 'honoured emong the Volsces as a King',[28] an observation just registered in Shakespeare's text when, in the ominous scene of the meeting of the two spies, the Volscian describes the gathering Volscian army as 'A most royal one' (IV. iii. 41). These are possibilities to which the text gives rise. More obvious, perhaps, is the reflection that Rome had expelled Tarquin the Proud by its own resolution and strength. On this occasion it is militarily helpless and internally divided: it is saved only because 'the ladies have prevailed' (V. iv. 41).

A final point should be remembered. Just as Venice could be seen as a harmonious mixed polity combining the three chief Aristotelian forms of government, by the one, the few, and the many, Rome could be seen as a discordant mixed polity. In his *Observations Touching Forms of Government* (1652), Sir Robert Filmer, to whom a mixed state seemed simply impractical, was to declare that Rome was 'broken and distracted into two shows of Government', the 'popular' at home and the 'regal' (consular) abroad. In the same spirit Sir Thomas Elyot, in his *Boke Named the Governour* (1531), probably known to Shakespeare, had written of republican Rome's repeated dependence on '*Dictators*' who had 'the pristinate authoritie and maiestie of a kyng'.[29]

Shakespeare's purpose in his delicate handling of the matter of kingship in *Coriolanus* can be detected only in the light of the fuller action of the drama. *Coriolanus* seems Shakespeare's most Aristotelian play—Aristotelian not only in its use of a tradition of moral psychology concerning temperance and extremes which stemmed from the *Nicomachean Ethics*,[30] but in its clear dramatization of a polity divided between the three kinds of men that corresponded to Aristotle's three true forms of government: plebeians, patricians, and the kinglike individual leader. (Aristotle defined one form of royalty as 'a generalship of life', another as a dictatorship, 'legal' and sometimes held only for 'a term of years' (*Politics*, III. xiv. 1–12). To the retrospective eye the consulships of Rome seemed to approach this category.) Plutarch's narrative yields a political example, dynamic and discordant, many sided and problematic, not

[28] Bullough, (ed.), *Narrative and Dramatic Sources*, v. 526.

[29] Sir Robert Filmer, *Patriarcha and Other Political Works*, ed. Peter Laslett (Oxford, 1949), 209; Sir Thomas Elyot, *The Boke Named the Governour*, ed. H. H. S. Croft (1880), i. 19–20.

[30] Erskine-Hill, *The Augustan Idea*, 153–5.

a demonstration like *Catiline*, but a parable from which various lessons may be learned. It displays Rome at that juncture when the Tribunate had just been established, but its powers not yet clearly defined. Shakespeare's Coriolanus rails against this innovation in the first scene of the play (I. i. 203–19), and it is interesting that Sir Thomas Smith had seen the first consuls of Rome as having provided 'the rule of the best men' but found a case of the usurpation by the few in the Senators 'after the death of *Tarquinius* and before the succession of the Tribunate'.[31] For Smith the Tribunate re-established the balance of the Roman polity, rather than threatened the 'insurrections' predicted by Shakespeare's Coriolanus. Smith's *De Republica* is of further interest because its chapters in Book I on 'the sundrie degrees of estates in the commonwealth of England' incorporated with minor revision William Harrison's chapters on the same subject from the first edition of Holinshed (1577), these then being expanded to include part of Thomas's account of Parliament before inclusion in that 1587 Holinshed so frequently drawn on by Shakespeare himself. Thus the military and political contribution of yeomen to the commonwealth, and the 'participation' in it of those men 'which doe not rule', but who are not slaves, could well have been known to Shakespeare. It may also seem that Shakespeare's tragedy probes those difficult areas of relation between rank and rank where Smith lacked a sufficiently clear analysis and formulation.

If the relation of *Catiline* to its time lies, through Jonson's recent conversion, in its allusion to the Catholic conspiracy of 1605, the occasion of *Coriolanus* was clearly the dearth of 1604–8 and the food rebellion of the Midlands in 1607.[32] The story of Coriolanus, in part also a story of dearth, bore·upon the problems of its time, both pressing and underlying. Shakespeare here dramatizes the common people in a somewhat new way, not as named and particularized figures such as Cade, or Francis the Drawer, nor as the crowd as such, as in *Julius Caesar* or the draft for *Sir Thomas More* (1603–4). Here he displays the estate of the common people: not only as a crowd, on a specific occasion, but also on the battlefield, and at the choosing of a consul. Further, there is a distinction between unnamed voices. Some of the most effective, and most wise

---

[31] Sir Thomas Smith, *De Republica Anglorum*, ed. L. Alston (Cambridge, 1906), 12.

[32] Bullough (ed.), *Narrative and Dramatic Sources*, v. 455–9.

things said in the entire play are uttered by certain of these voices. What could better in irony the First Citizen's response to Coriolanus's opening address to the crowd with its talk of dissension, itches, and scabs:

FIRST CITIZEN. We have ever your good word.

(I. i. 164)

What more profound comment on the play's fraught relations between rank and rank could there be than the First Citizen's reply in the consulship scene:

CORIOLANUS. Well then, I pray, your price o'th' consulship?
FIRST CITIZEN. The price is to ask it kindly.

(II. iii. 73–4)

(The First Citizen would not seem to be the same man in these two scenes.) Not perhaps models of behaviour, and easily manipulated by their Tribunes, the common people in *Coriolanus* are intelligent commentators. They are not a blindly destructive mob as in *Julius Caesar*, but their lack of development in named characterization enables the onlooker to continue to think of them as the common people, the plebeians, one of the social ranks which constitute the state. In keeping with this interest of Shakespeare, the Fable of the Belly is moved from its place in Plutarch's narrative to the opening of the play which thus poses the problem of the relation of rank and rank from the start. The action of the Midlands insurgents, who tore down enclosures and called themselves Levellers, is thus at first presented only as an articulate discontent at hunger. If Shakespeare was well informed about the Midlands rebellion, as he is likely to have been since it was near his own home, he did not allow the courage and determination of the English common people to pass into his Roman parable. That their demands may have been for more than immediate relief, however, is implicitly recognized by the Roman story Shakespeare chose, where the Senate not only distributes free grain, but makes a substantial political concession in the establishment of the Tribunate. Coriolanus himself, perhaps like some of the English nobility who put down the Midlands revolt, sees a fundamental political danger in this appeasement. He has a vision of war between the lower and higher ranks of Roman society,

which will in time
Break ope the locks o'th' senate and bring in
The crows to peck the eagles.

(III. i. 140–2)

Coriolanus's attitude to the common people appears almost a datum of the drama. He is contemptuous of them in the opening scene, before he knows what is the occasion of their gathering, or the tactic of Menenius's presence. The first exchange of the two tribunes in that scene is about his unparalleled pride (I. i. 251–2) and it is an irony that (as we subsequently learn) he had helped, as a young soldier, to repel Tarquin the Proud. There is a structural and moral simplicity that is more than eloquent in the way the early scenes, the first and then those on the battlefield, lead to and are balanced by the great central sequence of scenes concerning the choice of Coriolanus for the Consulship (II. ii–III. iii) and present him, incongruously enough, in 'the gown of humility' (II. iii. 41). During the course of this sequence a great deal is learned. The dilemma of choice, first recognized in the important exchange between the two officers (II. ii. 1–35), is that Coriolanus deserved well of the state by his martial deeds but hated the common people. The common people who speak recognize this quite clearly. Despite the priming of the tribunes (II. ii. 156–61) he does actually get a majority of voices for the consulship before Sicinius and Brutus urge a reconsideration, and up to this point the majority of voices we actually hear seem to be in favour. To this extent, despite the obvious dilemma, borne out by Coriolanus's behaviour to the plebeians, the state composed of the one, the few, and the many has just about managed to work coherently. However we also learn that it is scarcely enough to go through the motions of humility, and that if there *have* been 'great men that have flattered the people who ne'er loved them' (II. ii. 7–8), still, if you need the support of the common people, it is no good treating them like dirt or with blatant sarcasm. We also discover, however, that Coriolanus simply does not have it in him to treat the common people with courtesy, and that the reason for this is, at least in part, that his mother Volumnia taught him to despise them when it came to debate about peace or war (III. ii. 6–12). The issue of peace or war raises the most important lesson of all. Here it is worth remembering that the issue of war and peace and the conduct of war were, in the *republica*

Anglorum set forth by Sir Thomas Smith, the responsibility of the king.

From the opening scene, with its exposition of the social conflicts of Rome, the threat of external military attack has been ever present. Towards the end of I. i (l. 224) and at the start of III. i, at crises of civil conflict, the news breaks that the Volscians have made new headway. We see Coriolanus in action on the field of battle, in Act I, in both unsurprising and surprising ways. In the earlier conflict between the plebeians and the Senate he had imagined himself taking control of the situation as a swordsman:

> Would the nobility lay aside their ruth
> And let me use my sword, I'd make a quarry
> With thousands of these quartered slaves as high
> As I could pitch my lance.

(I. i. 195–8)

This is still the introduction of Coriolanus: we note his image of himself as a ruthless man of action in sole control of his weapons, and we see how political frustration seeks release in desire for physical combat. We note too the words he uses to express his anger at the plebeians. The word 'slaves' might be thought a contemptuous term that merely came readily to the mouth, and indeed he often uses it (e.g. I. v. 2–7; I. vi. 6). But it is given its precise meaning here by its association with the quarry of dead deer, piled up and quartered, after the hunt. In each case Coriolanus is thinking of creatures that are possessions (as Smith had described slaves or bondmen) rather than members of the body politic.[33] This makes all the more remarkable and significant that moment when Coriolanus appeals on the battlefield to his fellow patricians and to the common soldiers to follow him in a further attack, and they wave their swords, cast up their caps, and shout their support. And as in the prayer before Agincourt in *Henry V*, so here, there is a textual crux that affects the meaning of the entire play. Folio gives to Coriolanus the line:

> Oh me alone, make you a sword of me

(I. vii. 76)[34]

[33] It may be remembered that game was conserved for the hunt, and was thus a form of property, from an early time in England, as we may note, for example, from *Sir Gawain and the Green Knight*.

[34] Amended in the New Arden edition, but retained in the one-volume Oxford Shakespeare.

denoting both a unique moment when he is at one with his fellow Romans including the commonalty, and a reversal of the customary way in which he and others think about his swordsmanship (e.g. IV. ii. 27). Here Rome holds the sword by the hilt and Coriolanus himself, he alone, is the blade.[35] In this image the body politic commands, and its warrior,

> Nor yet grown stiffer with command
> But still in the *Republick*'s hand,

is its weapon to do the state some service. If, however, the New Arden editor, and several predecessors, are right to give this line to the soldiers who thus answer Coriolanus's appeal, the meaning is reversed. Then the cheering soldiers will be the cutting edge of the weapon: Coriolanus will as usual hold the hilt. I shall come to the political implications of this, but, for the moment, it is necessary to return to the defence of Rome. Just as there is a structurally striking simplicity in the spectacle of the proud Coriolanus in his garb of humility, so there is a similarly striking, massively simple, and significant reversal when, the tribunes and plebeians having banished their proud and contemptuous military leader, Rome finds itself defenceless before the advancing enemy armies of the Volscians led by him. It is a dramatized political lesson of dreadful power. And we may recall Camden accusing the Netherlanders of becoming a democracy, and relegating the aristocrats, 'save one or

---

[35] The line is a well-known crux in the text of *Coriolanus*, affecting the meaning of the play as fundamentally as the 'all'/'ill' crux in King Henry's prayer before Agincourt. Philip Brockbank, in his New Arden edition (1976), 138, reviews the evidence on the side of those who have amended the text so as to give the line to the soldiers: 'The response O *me alone*! is invited by *Let him alone* (l. 73), and *Make you a sword of me*! by *Wave thus* (l. 74); both are cued by the stage direction, in a way recognized by the present division of the direction. . . . The producer who follows F must find other words for the soldiers to shout—perhaps the mere name of Martius.' He thus comes down against the Folio reading. Yet perhaps the attribution of such a line to Coriolanus himself is so unexpected that it should be trusted and retained? It yields a more republican interpretation of this scene, and accords better with Coriolanus's '*Alone* I did it' [my Italics] in v. vi. 117. But critical considerations of this kind cannot much affect the textual decision. The New Oxford Shakespeare's *Textual Companion*, 595, offers no discussion of the point. For other political readings of the tragedy, see C. C. Huffman, *Coriolanus in Context* (Lewisburg, NS, 1971); and Anne Barton, 'Livy, Machiavelli, and Shakespeare's *Coriolanus*', *Shakespeare Survey*, 38 (1985), 115–29. Barton argues that Livy is a historian of political evolution. So was Bodin. Livy sees an evolution away from kingship; Bodin from it and back to it. Each provides a valuable view of history against which to read Shakespeare's delicately balanced drama.

two that are useful unto them in the warres' (p. 117 above). Had Coriolanus been made consul Rome would have had its sword and shield against the enemy, and the Volscians been denied their sudden access of strength in a formidable new general. Military leaders may be arrogant, their motives egoistic, but in military crises the state will need them.

Rome can now hope to save itself only by persuasion: a forlorn hope. Cominius, who for the first time feels Coriolanus's pride turned against him, is coldly rejected. Menenius is humiliatingly received and as humiliatingly sent back, his emotional appeal rebuffed (though significantly he is offered some minor concessions in v. iii. 12–15). Finally Volumnia, Virgilia, Valeria, and Coriolanus's little son Martius, making a powerful appeal by their very presence and posture, attempt the persuasion, evidently subjecting Coriolanus to wellnigh intolerable pressure. It is at this point that Volumnia, whose strong influence on her son has hitherto been devoted to urging him on in the field of battle and the theatre of public office, draws on a deeper resource than these great vocational goals of patrician rank. Naturally she now needs a concept that will bind up rather than sever: since she pleads for Rome as a whole she grounds her appeal in the family and nature. Coriolanus foresees the basis for her oratory—

> But out, affection!
> All bond and privilege of nature break;
> Let it be virtuous to be obstinate.
>
> (v. iii. 24–6)

—but can hardly withstand (as North's Plutarch puts it) 'the affection of his bloode, as if he had bene violently caried with the furie of a most swift running streame'.[36] Volumnia's speech opens and closes with emphasis on her own motherhood, and the concept of parenthood, but adroitly grafts on to this appeal the notion, neither of the state, the city, nor the commonweal, but of 'country':

> Making the mother, wife, and child to see
> The son, the husband, and the father tearing
> His country's bowels out.
>
> . . . .
>
> Alack, or we must lose
> The country, our dear nurse, or else thy person,

[36] Bullough (ed.), *Narrative and Dramatic Sources*, v. 539.

> Our comfort in the country.
>
> (V. iii. 102–4, 110–12)

Volumnia's motherhood of Coriolanus is thus developed into 'the country, our dear nurse': it is as if she herself now personifies Rome, a name which on this occasion she has not so far used, but does so in the last part of her great speech, ll. 138, 143, and 173:

> So we will home to Rome,
> And die among our neighbours.

All that the roles of warrior and avenger denied in Coriolanus now breaks out: the family bond and martial heroism which originally flowed together, and were afterwards at odds, now suffer violent revolution in his soul as the experience of nurture overturns the policy of his alliance and its military goals. In a moment of rare prescience he foresees the consequence of his having yielded to his mother's appeal. The parenthood of Rome itself has been vindicated, but she has killed her son in effect. Her last words in the drama have been uttered and they consummate its tragedy.

It is now clear that Shakespeare passes lightly over Coriolanus the youthful republican hero because he is to be presented as probable consul and potential king, with the pride of the expelled Tarquin. The dramatist plays down the formal issue of republic versus kingdom, not only in order to explore through drama the forces in society making for rule by the one, the few, and the many, but, more important, to display what may in the end be a ground of loyalty firmer than the vocations of rank. The play has in this way many implications for the republican theme of the present chapter. Rome is presented formally and historically as a republic that has recently thrown off its kings, but the traits of *Tarquinius Superbus* continue to appear amidst its senatorial leadership. The office of consul is the kingly element in its polity, and one way of reading *Coriolanus*, rare but not implausible, is to see Rome entangled in difficulty because its kinglike man cannot be accorded the royal power and responsibility which the protection of the state requires. The Senate, for its part, cannot as a whole be accused of arrogance or rigidity; whether or not the food shortage is the fault of the Senate we never learn, but corn is soon distributed *gratis*, and a substantial political concession to the plebeians made in the establishment of the Tribunate. This measure, though approved by Sir Thomas Smith in his treatise, proves disastrous in Shakespeare's play. Government by the few emerges from the drama pragmatic but helpless. As for the many, they are defiant yet readily persuadable, and even more easily manipulated. Not treacherous, not stupid, not contemptible, they do not deserve Coriolanus's scathing contempt save perhaps for their early behaviour on the field of battle, but his scorn for them goes back earlier still. They are no less tragically divided over the issue of the consulship than Coriolanus himself. Despite their mobility, indeed perhaps because of it, they constitute the touchstone by which Coriolanus's dangerous pride is recognized and judged. If, as it appears, a leader is needed, they need a leader with fellow feeling like Antony or Henry V, and it is interesting that Cominius, when he pleads before Coriolanus for Rome, should invoke the notion of unexpected pardon proper to royalty (v. i. 18–19). To forgive is a capacity that Coriolanus, despite his eventual vulnerability to the appeal of nurture and nature, never shows. Each rank of Roman society falls short of the standard which could turn a mixed polity, deeply divided by conflict of interest and resentment of rank, into the dynamic equilibrium of a serene republic. More attentive than *Catiline* to the needs and character of the common people, and thus the potentialities for democracy, *Coriolanus* is not really republican in spirit as Jonson's tragedy is. It displays the problems of a mixed polity, and may rather demonstrate the need for kings than their dispensibility. In its purpose 'Of government the properties to unfold' (*Measure for Measure*, i. i. 1) *Coriolanus* finally shows forms of government as secondary though necessary to the nurturing 'country' or *patria* in which men and women find themselves born, but do not choose, and cannot desert without dividing their very selves.

II

In Shakespeare's earlier Roman tragedy *Julius Caesar* the republican Cassius describes how in his swimming contest with Caesar in the Tiber

> The torrent roared, and we did buffet it
> With lusty sinews, throwing it aside,

And stemming it with hearts of controversy.

(I. ii. 109–11)

This appears to be a narrative invented by Shakespeare and, like the Temple Garden scene in *1 Henry VI*, is exceptionally important in revealing his guiding hand on his source material. The story is of wide significance,[37] but for our purpose it is the phrase 'hearts of controversy' that points the way to a republican poetry in mid-seventeenth-century England. The appropriateness of the word 'controversy' in the speech of Cassius lies in its exact meaning: 'contentious (as to ones rights)', and in the slightly broader sense that the swimmers are contending with the waves and with one another.[38] Cassius is contentious, a combatant of controversy, throughout the play, his rights residing in the republican polity of which Caesar now contemplates the subversion into a monarchy. Cassius also buffets it with a tide in the affairs of state which does not flow his way. Behind this narrative, and indeed Cassius's whole outlook, lies that tradition of republican thought of which Tacitus was an ancient and Machiavelli a modern spokesman. It holds that free republican institutions spur men on to virtù through contest and opportunity, while monarchies subdue and constrain the energies of their subjects. In this view republican government creates both the desired dynamism and the necessary equilibrium of the successful state.

The example of 'the noble Brutus and Cassius' is noted by Milton in his Commonplace Book, probably during the period 1640–2: it occasions the Thomas Smith-like reflection (the Commonplace Book refers elsewhere to Smith's treatise) that some forms of government suit one people and time, some another:

the form of state to be fitted to the peoples disposition some live best under monarchy others otherwise. so that the conversions of commonwealths happen not always through ambition or malice. as amoung the Romans who after thire infancy were ripe for a more free government then monarchy, beeing in a manner all fit to be Ks. afterward growne unruly, and impotent with overmuch prosperity were either for thire profit, or thire punishment fit to be curb'd with a lordly and dreadfull monarchy; wch was

---

[37] Erskine-Hill, *The Augustan Idea*, 135–8.

[38] *Julius Caesar*, ed. Martin Spevack, New Cambridge Series (Cambridge, 1988), 59; ed. A. R. Humphreys, New Oxford Shakespeare (Oxford, 1984), 108.

the error of the noble Brutus and Cassius who felt themselves of spirit to free an nation but consider'd not that the nation was not fit to be free, whilst forgetting thire old justice and fortitude which was made to rule, they became slaves to thire owne ambition and luxurie.[39]

Milton does not yet seem a principled republican; but Brutus and Cassius were protagonists on behalf of the republic in the theatre of civil war. Their energy and independence, their virtù, having been dynamic within the old republic, are dynamic also against the rising figure of Caesar, once weaker than Cassius in the turbulent waters of the Tiber, and against the apparently closing constraints of the monarchical form coming to be imposed on the old freedoms and privileges.

It is in these senses of republican that, if there is a republican poetry to be found in the period of England's experiment with republicanism, it is in the public sonnets of Milton. They are sonnets of the civil war against the king as well as, later, of the virtù of the English Commonwealth. In suggesting this I am not thinking only of the content of these sonnets, salient and rare as that is in the political poetry of the seventeenth century, but also of something pertaining more closely to literary structure and practice. There is a certain aptness in the fact that Petrarch, great practiser of the energetic yet artificial, structured, and harmonious sonnet form, should, in however politically impractical a way, have admired the political forms of ancient republican Rome, hailed the extraordinary bid by Cola di Rienzi, as 'tribune' to revive them in 1347, and been crowned poet laureate in the Capitol by a Roman 'senator'. Giovanni Della Casa evolved the energetic counterpoint of syntax against the subdivisions of the sonnet form—an evolution of which Milton would take full advantage. There is a certain aptness, too, in that the English translation of Contarini's praise of the Venetian constitution should have been prefaced by sonnets. Milton's sonnets, however, are an evolution of a line of sonneteering begun by Petrarch in an amatory mode, transformed into poems of public and historic vision by Tasso and du Bellay's *Antiquitez*, but only receiving political dynamic and republican 'controversy' at the hands of the servant of the English Commonwealth. The Petrarchan origins of the Milton sonnets are clear in his first seven, especially of course the Italian

---

[39] John Milton, *Complete Prose Works*, ed. Douglas Bush *et al.* (New Haven, 1953–82), i. 420.

ones, and Sonnet VI, 'Giovane piano', shows that these poems are
not merely meditative and mellifluous imitations as Sonnet I, 'O
nightingale', might suggest, but can also sound a note of challenge
and crisis:

> Quando rugge il gran mondo, e scocca il tuono,
> S'arma di se, d'intero diamante,
> Tanto del forse, e d'invidia sicuro,
> Di timori, e speranze al popol use
> Quanto d'ingegno, e d'alto valo vago,
> E di cetra sonora, e delle muse:
>
> (ll. 7–12)[40]

Nevertheless Sonnet VIII, 'When the assault was intended to the
City', in its drama of civil crisis, and confrontation in verse of
the voice of the muse and the expected military attack on London
by the royal army, unmistakably shows the new impact of war and
public affairs:

> Captain or colonel, or knight in arms,
>   Whose chance on these defenceless doors may seize
>
>   .   .   .   .
>
> Lift not thy spear against the muses' bower,
>   The great Emathian conqueror bid spare
>   The house of Pindarus, when temple and tower
> Went to the ground: and the repeated air
>   Of sad Electra's poet had the power
>   To save the Athenian walls from ruin bare.
>
> (ll. 1–2, 9–14)[41]

Behind the spear and the song stand the king and the republic,
Alexander and Athens, whose different kinds of power, so separate-
ly present when the crashing *caesura* 'Went to the ground' is suc-
ceeded by the sung words of Euripides sounding from ruin, engage
with each other: and the city is spared. But note how the Petrarchan
rhyme scheme denies close concluding harmony to the relatively
happy end of that story, and the final phrase 'ruin bare' goes
echoing back to the proffered example of mercy at l. 10. Notable

---

[40] John Milton, *Poems*, ed. John Carey and Alastair Fowler (1968), 96: 'When the
whole world roars and the lightning flashes my heart arms itself in itself, in perfect
adamnant, as safe from chance and envy and from hopes and fears as it is eager for
distinctions of mind and real worth, for the sounding lyre and for the Muses.'
[41] *Poems*, 285.

too when, on arrival at 'ruin bare' the lyrical drama has worked its catharsis on us, is the propagandist effect of the poem. Alexander spared the house of Pindar but razed Thebes to the ground; at the song from Euripides Lysander and his Spartan officers are said to have spared Athens. But who thinks that Charles I was bent on the destruction of London, in November 1642 or (less likely) May 1641?[42] To have secured his capital would have been advantage enough. Rumour, of course, must have been rife on each occasion. But the military attack of the MS title has become intended punitive destruction by the end. Sonnet X, 'To the Lady Margaret Ley' (?1642), continues the theme of classical freedom. A panegyrical presentation of 'that good Earl, once President | Of England's Council' (ll. 1–2) which, as the mode allows, overlooks some of his notorious corruptions, leads on to that dissolution of Parliament in March 1629 which began King Charles's eleven years of single rule. Once again an English and a Greek event are linked, 'the sad breaking of that Parliament' with 'that dishonest victory | At Chaeronea, fatal to liberty': once again the rise of the Macedonian kings over the Greek republican cities is invoked as a myth for England which both encourages and warns. Milton affords a vision in which kingship is the innovation, republican liberty a freedom originally established. This casts an interesting light on the English historical situation at the outbreak of the civil war, and while a republican slanting may well be observed, it was certainly the case that for Charles I to rule without a parliament for eleven years was sufficiently unusual in Tudor and Stuart practice to afford some basis for Milton's vision.

This committed and classicizing vision of the early 1640s, with its republican implications, may be recognized the more clearly when contrasted with a popular political song of the time, which came to be known by its refrain: 'When the King enjoys his own again' (and variations), and which the late eighteenth-century radical and collector Joseph Ritson termed 'the most famous and popular air ever heard in this country':

> What *Booker* doth prognosticate
> Concerning Kings and Kingdoms' state,
> I think myself to be as wise

---

[42] John Milton, *Sonnets*, ed. E. A. Honigmann, (1966), 101–3. Honigmann favours the earlier date.

As some that gazeth on the skyes:
My skill goes beyond, the depth of a *Pond*,
Or Rivers in the greatest rain,
  Whereby I can tell, all things will be well,
  When the King enjoys his own again.

There's neither *Swallow*, *Dove*, nor *Dade*,
Can soar more high, or deeper wade;
Nor shew a reason from the stars,
What causeth peace, or Civil wars:
The man in the Moon, may wear out his shoo'n,
By running after *Charles* his Wain;
  But all's to no end, for the times will not mend
  Till the King enjoys his own again.

Full forty years this Royal Throne
Hath been his father's and his own:
And is there any one but He,
That in the same should sharer be?
For who better may, the Sceptre sway,
Than he that hath such right to reign:
  Then let's hope for a peace, for the Wars will not cease
  Till the King enjoys his own again.

Though for a time we see *White-hall*
With Cobwebs hanging on the wall,
Instead of gold and silver brave
Which formerly it used to have,
With rich perfume in every room,
Delightful to that Princely Train;
  Which again shall be, when the time you see
  When the King enjoys his own again.[43]

Martin Parker, the ballad-writer, who wrote this song perhaps in
1643 (see ll. 21–2) and certainly before 1647 when it is attributed to
him in *The Gossip's Feast*, cast his poem in the idiom of the
common man which he may have shared and which he certainly
understood. The singer seems a man on the margins, involved but
not combative, bewildered but sure of one or two fundamental
things, who unaggressively asserts that he is at least as wise as the
almanac makers (Booker) and astrologers. His language is homely

[43] David Norbrook and H. R. Woudhuysen, (eds.), *The Penguin Book of Renaiss-*
ance Verse (Harmondsworth, 1992), 163–5. James Hogg, *The Jacobite Relics of*
Scotland . . . (Edinburgh, 1819–21), i. 1–3. For Martin Parker, see *DNB*, and H. E.
Robbins, *MP* 15 (1919).

but not without wit (*The Man in the Moon* was a royalist journal;
the constellation 'Charles's Wain', or The Plough, is a heavenly sign,
but in a play on words Charles's wane is figured in the drift of stars);
his royalism is affirmed in each refrain and more fully in the third
stanza. He shows neither resentment nor awe at the splendour of
court life; it is what was fit and will return. From his choric
viewpoint the civil war is envisioned at first as a natural disaster, a
flood which must abate, but in the end the biblical story of the Flood
is invoked to fortify faith in the return of the king and the old order.
Milton's two sonnets were published in his *Poems* (1645); Parker's
song, with its popular royalism, evidently became one of the two or
three best-known political poems for the next century and more.

A year later, in *Areopagitica*, Milton expressed contest and con-
troversy in a series of famous metaphors of physical and athletic
force. The virtue that Milton can there praise is not 'unexercis'd &
unbreath'd' but one which 'sallies out' against its adversary into 'the
race, where that immortall garland is to be run for, not without dust
and heat'.[44] The renewed nation he there sees is 'of a quick, inge-
nious, and piercing spirit, acute to invent, suttle and sinewy to
discours, not beneath the reach of any point the highest that hu-
manity can soar to'.[45] Its capital, 'this vast City' is 'a City of refuge,
the mansion house of liberty. . . . the shop of warre hath not there
more anvils and hammers waking . . . in defence of beleaguer'd
Truth, then there be pens and heads there'.[46]

And now the time in speciall is, by priviledge to write and speak what may
help to the furder discussing of matters in agitation. The Temple of *Janus*
with his two *controversal* faces might now not unsignificantly be set open.
And though all the windes of doctrin were let loose to play upon the earth,
so Truth be in the field, we do injuriously by licencing and prohibiting to
misdoubt her strength. Let her and Falsehood grapple; who ever knew
Truth put to the wors, in a free and open encounter.[47]

Milton's treatment of the Temple of Janus is a striking reversal of its
more common use, in which Augustus and later rulers were praised
for making peace and *shutting* the doors of the famous Roman
temple. Milton welcomes controversy in metaphors of war; 'calls
out his adversary into the plain, offers him the advantage of wind
and sun, if he please; only that he may try the matter by dint of

[44] *Prose Works*, ii. 515.   [45] *Prose works*, ii. 551.
[46] *Prose Works*, ii. 553–4.   [47] *Prose Works*, ii. 561.

argument'.[48] Indeed, with a commonwealth in arms and in the midst of the struggle to throw off its royal and prelate lords, warfare and argument seem to grow together, nurtured by the city of refuge and liberty in their race, wrestling, and reach. If the poetry of republican spirit in England is in Milton's sonnets, the prose is in his *Areopagitica* above all. In the three controversial sonnets of 1646–7, XII, 'On the detraction', XI, 'A book was writ of late . . .', and 'On the new forcers of conscience under the Long Parliament' (not numbered in Milton's sequence) a different voice from that of the earlier sonnets can be heard: strong, scathing, combative in the rude lists of detraction and insult. In 'On the detraction' the phrase 'ancient liberty' in l. 2 is contrasted with a salient series of examples of low diction: 'clogs', 'cuckoos, asses, apes and dogs', 'frogs', and 'hogs':

> I did but prompt the age to quit their clogs
> By the known rules of ancient liberty. . . .

The first line of the sestet, 'That bawl for freedom in their senseless mood', brings high and low together in sharp contrast and manages to associate 'Licence' (l. 11) with low and senseless life, though some might have felt that Milton in his divorce tracts urged licence himself, in one sense of the term. What might have made a compressed, sententious conclusion to the sonnet, 'Licence they mean when they cry liberty', (l. 11) is in this Petrarchan rhyme scheme kept from the end which instead is spent, like the controversy itself perhaps, in 'all this waste of wealth, and loss of blood'. 'A book was writ of late called *Tetrachordon*', though not next chronologically, addresses the controversy more explicitly, and more comically. Milton's contrived rhymes, pre-*Whistlecraft* and pre-*Don Juan* though with precedent in the Italian, mark the harsh ridicule: '. . . now seldom pored on. | Cries the stall-reader, Bless us! what a word on | A title-page is this! And some in file | Stand spelling false, while one might walk to Mile- | End Green' (ll. 4–8). The forced rhyme ('pored on') and the enjambed place-name farcically mime the problem of reading Milton's learned but graceful title. In this sonnet the apes and dogs and hogs are replaced by the bearers of Scottish names (political and theological enemies of the poet): 'Colkitto, or Macdonnel, or Galasp?', an easy laugh for the metropolitan English

[48] *Prose Works*, ii. 562.

poet. But the imagined reaction of Quintilian softens the invective. The great Latin authority on rhetoric is not hostile, only dumb-founded. The sonnet rises from the babble of dispute and names, at the end, to invoke a value from early Protestant and humanist England:

> Thy age, like ours, O soul of Sir John Cheke,
>   Hated not learning worse than toad or asp;
>   When thou taught'st Cambridge, and King Edward Greek
>
> (ll. 12–14)

However the most turbulent and scathing of Milton's sonnets of controversy is the 20-line *sonetto caudato* 'On the New Forcers of Conscience under the Long Parliament', whose enactment of contest happens to use the same word, 'dare', employed by Caesar to Cassius ('Dar'st thou, Cassius, now I Leap in with me . . .') in the swimming narrative of *Julius Caesar* (I. ii. 102–3):

> Because you have thrown off your prelate lord. . . .
> . . . .
> Dare ye for this adjure the civil sword
>   To force our consciences that Christ set free.
>
> (ll. 1, 5–6)

This form of sonnet, unique in Milton and unusual in English, has the capacity here of outrunning the hostile competitor who is its subject. Indeed, as Honigmann observes,[49] the form has the mocking ability both to 'clip' and cut short, and run long and write large:

> But we do hope to find out all your tricks,
> Your plots and packing worse than those of Trent,
>   That so the Parliament
> May with their wholesome and preventive shears
> Clip your phylacteries, though baulk your ears,
>   And succour our just fears
> When they shall read this clearly in your charge
> New *Presbyter* is but old *Priest* writ large.
>
> (ll. 13–20)

This is one of the few notable occasions when Milton concludes his sonnet with a strong sententious statement, the trophy, as it were, in the race. This enactment of victory in sonnet form is abetted by

---

[49] *Sonnets*, ed. Honigmann, 199.

modes of allusion as calculatedly insulating as Milton ever used in a poem. The comedy of the 'rugged names' in 'A book was writ of late' is quite gone here: 'mere A. S. and Rutherford' is merely belittling, 'shallow Edwards and Scotch what d'ye call' (l. 12) worse still. But this contemptuous spirit is here in the cause of liberty—liberty not as an easy positive abstraction, but negative freedom from specific, named, historical, and ecclesiastical forcers. The poet has no doubt about whom his sonnet confronts: mental despotism here has a pronounced Scottish accent and Presbyterian form. Again we may note a slanting rhetorical effect: the Presbyterian interest was a larger party than that of the Independents, and by no means merely a Scottish movement, supported by the Scots though it was.

The metaphor of warfare informs Milton's writing about controversy and controversial writing; by August 1648 when he wrote his sonnet 'On the Lord General Fairfax' the new republic had been astonishingly successful in the field. The sonnets to Fairfax, Cromwell, and Vane, unpublished in Milton's lifetime, seem likely to have been an attempt to exemplify and celebrate republican virtù at moments of triumph which were also, by the highest standards, moments of crisis too. They dramatize a totally new ethos, and create a bold new sense of citizenship and of participation in history.

> Fairfax, whose name in arms through Europe rings
> Filling each mouth with envy, or with praise,
> And all her jealous monarchs with amaze,
> And rumours loud, that daunt remotest kings,
> Thy firm unshaken virtue ever brings
> Victory home . . .

(ll. 1–6)

After the Restoration someone (perhaps Edward Phillips) described to the avid Aubrey this and the sonnet to Cromwell as 'two admirable panegyricks, as to sublimitie of wit', though he hesitated then to show them, obviously for political reasons.[50] Panegyric which in the hands of Pindar celebrated the values shared by victor and *polis* is an appropriate term here in some measure, but its post-Pindaric appropriation into a more courtly mode renders it less than apt for the bold plain voice of warning that is heard after the turn of the sonnet:

[50] Aubrey, '*Brief Lives*', ed. Clark, ii. 70.

> . . . what can war, but endless war still breed,
> Till truth, and right from violence be freed,
> And public faith cleared from the shameful brand
> Of public fraud. In vain doth valour bleed
> While avarice, and rapine share the land.

(ll. 10–14)

Between the years of the sonnets on Fairfax and Cromwell, in 1650, Andrew Marvell's 'Horatian Ode' was composed. How does it compare with the republicanism of Milton's sonnets on Fairfax, Cromwell, and Vane? The attention paid in it to 'antient Rights', and to the drama and moral victory of the king at his execution, often persuades readers to see Marvell's Ode as a balanced poem that endorses neither the 'Kingdome old' nor the new state of which Cromwell would shortly be (if he were not already) captain-general and commander-in-chief of the military forces. The Ode is certainly more comprehensive, circumspect, and subtle than the bold commitment of Milton's sonnets, yet its third and final movement,

> This was that memorable Hour
> Which first assur'd the forced Pow'r. . . .
>
> . . . .
>
> And yet in that the State
> Foresaw its happy Fate. . . .
>
> . . . .
>
> But thou, the Wars and Fortun's Son
> March indefatigably on. . . .

shows clear commitment to Cromwell and the new order.[51] Perhaps its formal balance has suggested political reserve; perhaps by pure republican standards Marvell's sense of what Cromwell might become—a new Augustus, if echoes and parallels with various odes of Horace are politically significant—appears like a reservation as to Cromwell himself. For the moment, however, and perhaps so far as the Ode knows for ever, Cromwell is

> still in the *Republick*'s hand:
> How fit he is to sway

---

[51] Andrew Marvell, *Poems and Letters*, ed. H. M. Margoliouth and Pierre Legouis with the collaboration of E. E. Duncan-Jones (Oxford, 1927–69), i. 93–4. It is hard to see why a tradition concerning the Ode's poised neutrality should have arisen, only to be demolished by later commentators who rediscover a Cromwellian stance well known before. See ibid., i. 296–7.

That can so well obey.
He to the *Commons* Feet presents
A *Kingdome*, for his first years rents.

(ll. 82–6)

Like Coriolanus when (and if) he cries: 'O me alone, make you a sword of me' Cromwell is 'still in the *Republick*'s hand', the weapon of the commonwealth. However, the word 'still', which alone might have meant 'obedient', 'fixed', has been lent a nuance of political awareness concerning political process by the words of line 81:

Nor yet grown stiffer with command. . . .

The way to monarchy is there hinted. The Ode is a predominantly republican and wholly Cromwellian poem, but with a Shakespearian awareness of the beauty of the 'Kingdome old' (recall *Richard II*) and an Augustan awareness that the model of Augustus is most truly understood as an enabling model for a new dynasty and, perhaps, change again in the form of the state.[52]

Unlike the Ode as managed by Marvell, Milton's sonnets on Fairfax and Cromwell are not three- but two-movement poems. Balancing judgement comes in the use of *volta* (not invariably present in Milton), as in 'O yet a nobler task awaits thy hand' in the Fairfax sonnet, and the dramatically deferred 'peace hath her victories' (l. 10) in the sonnet on Cromwell:

Cromwell, our chief of men, who through a cloud
  Not of war only, but detractions rude,
  Guided by faith and matchless fortitude
  To peace and truth thy glorious way hast ploughed,
And on the neck of crowned fortune proud
  Hast reared God's trophies and his work pursued,
  While Darwen's stream with blood of Scots imbrued,
  And Dunbar field resounds thy praises loud,
And Worcester's laureate wreath; yet much remains
  To conquer still; peace hath her victories
  No less renowned than war, new foes arise
  Threatening to bind our souls with secular chains:

(ll. 1–12)

Here the rise of the uncrowned and untitled 'chief of men' is summed up in classical images of political and religious import ('on

[52] See Howard Erskine-Hill, *The Augustan Idea*, 194–8.

FIG. 3. Oliver Cromwell as Lord General. The crowned and severed head of King Charles I is at the bottom right. Anonymous seventeenth-century engraving. By permission of the Ashmolean Museum, Oxford.

the neck of crowned fortune proud | Hast reared God's trophies') before the recitation of his fields of victory presses on into the sestet as though it cannot be confined by the form. With the example of Alexander longing for more worlds to conquer, 'yet much re-mains | To conquer still' does not yield its actual judgement until after the word 'peace' is uttered; and in this sonnet, unlike that on Fairfax, it is not just that peace is recommended after war, but the intensification of the struggle for God's cause in the civil arena. The sonnet defines freedom as republican, God is now set above *'crowned* fortune proud' (my italics) but other and 'new foes' than kings arise which threaten freedom too. As in the sonnet 'On the new forcers of conscience' and probably due to similar reasons and emotions, Milton concludes this sonnet with the rare force of a couplet:

> Help us to save free conscience from the paw
> Of hireling wolves whose gospel is their maw.
>
> (ll. 13–14)

The extraordinary military dynamic, enacted within harmonious form, in the sonnets on the two Lords General, is barely checked by the strength of the language with which the need for peace, or the continuing imperatives of freedom, are expressed. In a sense, the sonnet 'To Sir Henry Vane the Younger' is a more truly republican poem, in that it is more *politique.* Warfare is not here an energy released into effort required by God; it is rather a phenomenon that can be intellectually understood and advised on,

> how war may best, upheld,
> Move by her two main nerves, iron and gold
> In all her equipage . . .

—a Machiavellian problem—as 'spiritual power and civil' may also be understood and balanced. It is the power of political wisdom, 'counsel', senate, and gown, which grasps and controls these oppo-sitions as the helmsman steers the ship. The *volta,* '. . . besides to know | Both spiritual power and civil . . .' is much less pronounced than in the two previous sonnets, since political sagacity is invoked as Vane's special talent from the start. And though 'Religion' is scarcely scanted, it has its place in a civil harmony conveyed in the Petrarchan sonnet as inflected by Della Casa, an animated yet serene structure.

The primarily religious sonnet ('Avenge O Lord . . .'), the primarily personal ('When I consider . . .'), and the primarily social ('Lawrence of virtuous father . . .') fall outside the political scope of the present discussion but 'To Mr Cyriack Skinner upon his blindness', a sonnet both personal and political, affords the perfect final example in this exploration of republicanism in English Renaissance poetry. Here a dignified pathos, conveyed in the long, waning first sentence, is countered by pride in a series of more abrupt declarations:

> Cyriack, this three years' day these eyes, though clear
>   To outward view of blemish or of spot;
>   Bereft of light their seeing have forgot,
>   Nor to their idle orbs doth sight appear
> Of sun or moon or star throughout the year,
>   Or man or woman. Yet I argue not
>   Against heaven's hand or will, nor bate a jot
>   Of heart or hope; but still bear up and steer
> Right onward. What supports me dost thou ask?
>
> (ll. 1–9)

There is much physical energy in the short plain words of this later part of the sonnet ('nor bate a jot | Of heart or hope') and it might be thought that the poem has three decisive breaks in the area where a *volta*, if any, should be found: 'Yet I argue not . . .' (l. 6), 'But still bear up and steer' (l. 8), and 'What supports me dost thou ask?' (l. 9). Then is the moment when the political affirmation best comes, and the heroic causality which binds blindness to freedom best dramatized:

> The conscience, friend, to have lost them overplied
>   In liberty's defence, my noble task,
> Of which all Europe talks from side to side.
>
> (ll. 10–12)

The two final lines, which see the cause of freedom as a sufficient though not supreme guide through the appearances and deceptions of the world and perhaps discover in the mask of reality the form of Truth, might have been marked off by a couplet. But here, as in the majority of his sonnets, the Italianate Milton has no interest in that Shakespearian ascent from lower to higher levels of power, as the sonnet moves from octet, to quatrain, to couplet, from the many, as it were, through the few, to the one. Though ll. 13–14 are a separate thought and sentence, with that uncanny art, in which Milton seems pointedly to ignore the harmony of sound he has arranged, their very separateness chimes musically back into the sestet, and the proud declarations of ll. 6–9 fade into a relative diminuendo. Religious faith is partly masked, only half revealed ('had I no better guide'), and the complex harmony of the form perfected as its sentiments sink to rest.

III

That Marvell should not print his 'Horatian Ode' during the Interregnum is understandable, despite the Cromwellian commitment of its conclusion. That Milton should have been content with manuscript publication of his political sonnets is perhaps surprising. Possibly he expected to publish a further volume of shorter pieces in due course, and the revolution of 1660 forestalled the plan. After the Restoration it would of course have been sheer folly to publish (though the sonnet to Vane was printed by his biographer in 1662). However it may also be that Milton held back through disappointment with the two Lords General. Fairfax withdrew from the court set up to try the King on 8 January 1649, and may, with the other eighty-one reluctant commissioners, be reflected on in *The Tenure of Kings and Magistrates* (1649).[53] Cromwell, after the expulsion of the Rump, proved himself not to be the Tolerationist whose power Milton appealed to in his sonnet. In the great formal defence of England and himself, the *Defensio Secunda* (1654), Milton again praised both. Perhaps the public strategy of the occasion demanded no less. His more personal public tributes, poems not required by his office under the Commonwealth, were withheld from the widest circulation. And when Marvell published his *First Anniversary of the Government under O.C.* (1655), and Waller his *Panegyric on the Lord Protector*, Milton remained poetically silent. He wrote no poem on Cromwell's death. The 'chief of men' had become a monarch; republicanism reverted to the residual legitimacy of the

---

[53] David Masson, *The Life of John Milton: Narrated in Connexion with the Political, Ecclesiastical, and Literary History of His Time* (1859–94), iv (1877), 70; see *Prose Works*, ed. Bush *et al.*, iii. 194. See too the telling discussion of John S. Smart, *The Sonnets of Milton* (Glasgow, 1921), 89–92.

Rump, to be twice restored before the return of the Stuarts. The death of Cromwell may have been the public event which turned Milton back, with considerably deeper perceptions, to his long postponed project of 'Adam Unparadised'.

For Milton, as would become plain when he wrote *A Readie and Easie Way* (1660), the cause of 'a free commonwealth' had become separated from the Cromwellian cause. However the republican idealist Harrington still looked to Cromwell to establish a lasting republic in England when he published his *Commonwealth of Oceana* in 1656. It is in the writings of Harrington, his supporters, and some of his opponents, that the influence of Italian experience, both historical example and political theory, is at its most powerful in English political thought.[54] The period 1656–60 was, intellectually speaking, a high republican moment, contrasting lamentably with the actual political confusion and collapse during those years. To read this work, and to perceive this discrepancy, is to be reminded of a reason for republican idealism easy to overlook when we read Milton. Englishmen who admired Venice admired it for its longevity and stability. Republicanism for Milton meant godly energy and freedom; for Harrington it meant civil order and permanence. All Harrington's ingenuity and Italian learning were devoted to the devising of a polity both harmonious and lasting. The most original proposal of his republican theory, the Agrarian Law which would regularly readjust imbalances of property, was directed to this end. Yet he also seems to have indulged something of a republican mystique: the prosperous and powerful Venetian republic and the tiny republics of San Marino and Ragusa did seem to him to have survived the threat of their mighty neighbours so long by the sheer virtù of their form of government. That order of choice and rotation of office, a poetry of politics as it might seem, cast a spell on a certain kind of political thinker, even more after the civil wars than before. In his *Prerogative of Popular Government* (1658) Harrington wrote:

the world is *in faece Romuli*, ripe for great changes which must come. And look to it; whether it be Germany, Spain, France, Italy or England, that comes first to fix herself upon a firm foundation of policy, she shall give law unto and be obeyed by the rest. There never was so much fighting as of late

[54] See J. G. A. Pocock (ed.), *The Political Works of James Harrington* (Cambridge, 1977), 15–76.

days to so little purpose; arms, except they have a root in policy, are altogether fruitless. In the war between the king and parliament, not the nation only, but the policy of it was divided, and which part of it was upon the better foundation?

But, saith he, 'Ragusa and San Marino are commended for their upright and equal frame of government, and yet have hardly extended their dominion beyond the size of an handsome manor.'

Have Ragusa or San Marino been conquered by the arms of any monarch? For this (I take it) is the question . . .[55]

Policy and harmony had never been more needed. Harrington's antagonist quoted above, the staunch royalist and Laudian bishop, Matthew Wren, writing from his prison in the Tower, saw stability in a return of the country to its allegiance to its lawful king. For their part, the last significant republicans in England for a century or more cherished the more complex and *politique* vision of a balanced state, imaged if imperfectly in the miracle of Venice, and the white walls of far away Ragusa.

[55] Ibid. 456.

PART III

After the Revolution

6
Defeat and the Relevance of Epic

MILTON and Dryden, though conventionally considered to belong to different phases of English literary culture, inhabited the same historical world. They were part-contemporaries (Dryden living through the major crises of Milton's career) and each, towards the end of his life, survived a change of state, Milton the revolution of 1660, Dryden that of 1688, in which almost all his political hopes were dashed. Each poet was engaged to a fragile supremacy, for Milton the Commonwealth, for Dryden the Catholicizing regime of King James II, the collapse of which left him isolated and exposed. Each resumed his poetic vocation with a new spirit in the post-revolutionary era. The consequence in Milton's case was the achievement of three major classics of our literature, *Paradise Lost*, *Paradise Regained*, and *Samson Agonistes*, works the fame and monolithic strength of which make them seem, almost, incomparable. Dryden's post-revolutionary output, less famous, very much more varied, also displays the marks of a literary intelligence accustoming itself to navigating through new seas and among strange currents. Dryden's late writing is, of course, different in character from Milton's. Unlike Milton Dryden writes odes and songs, epistles and prologues, opera and comedy. Finally, Dryden devoted his latest years to the fable, a form which, in his hands, could encompass Chaucerian romance, Ovidian metamorphosis, and the *conte* of Boccaccio. This development seems quite contrary to the spirit of Milton's late, great poems.

Yet the post-revolutionary poems of the two writers are not so utterly different that there are no points of contact, rendering comparison a fruitless or a foolish task. Each of them produced an epic poem, Dryden's *Aeneis* being a sufficiently independent version of its original to sustain comparison with Milton's original Christian epic, *Paradise Lost*, which was sufficiently aware of the *Aeneid* to make comparison with Dryden's *Aeneis* a matter of interest. Again, each poet produces drama focusing on a warrior-hero in defeat and exile: *Samson Agonistes* may be seen in interesting relation with *Don Sebastian*—and *Cleomenes*. There is one further comparison, relevant to the purposes of this chapter, but which strictly falls just outside the bounds I have proposed. Before the forcing away of James II Dryden wrote, in support of that monarch and of the Catholic faith they now shared, his greatest and most mysterious long poem, *The Hind and the Panther* (1687). To some, perhaps, Catholicism seemed to be enjoying a triumph in that year; to the intelligent and politically sagacious Dryden the scene was lit as much by portents of disaster as of '*James* his late nocturnal victory' (II. 655) of Sedgemore. There could hardly be a less triumphalist poem, politically speaking, than *The Hind and the Panther*. Like certain of Milton's later writings to Oliver Cromwell it conveys anxiety about the future. Like *Paradise Regained* it is a poem of temptation and isolation, of argument, statement, and counter-statement. Utterly different in faith and form, each poem is at heart a vision of the Word in the wilderness and in each the dangers of the secular kingdom are never far from view. The poets have so much in common, but are yet so different, that they could be subjects of a parallel-life study, such as one finds in Plutarch.

I

Samuel Johnson was to write of Milton's praise of Cromwell in *Defensio Secunda* that 'Caesar when he assumed the perpetual dictatorship had not more servile or more elegant flattery'.[1] It is a memorable and valuable judgement in its recognition that Cromwell, proclaimed Protector of the Commonwealth in December 1653, had now gone beyond that point when he was, in Marvell's words, 'still in the *Republick*'s hand'. For Colonel John Hutchinson, in terms similar to Marvell's, Cromwell had 'quitted himselfe soone of his Triumvirs, and first thrust out Harrison, then tooke away Lambert's commission, and would have bene King but for feare of quitting his Generallship'.[2] Milton, in the great personal apologia which is the *Defensio Secunda*, is forced to treat him as if he were a

[1] *Lives of the Poets*, i. 118.
[2] Lucy Hutchinson, *Memoirs of the Life of Colonel Hutchinson with the fragment of an Autobiography of Mrs Hutchinson . . .*, ed. James Sutherland (Oxford, 1973), 208.

prince. There is flattery but, despite Johnson's plain speech, flattery is not the whole story. Milton's praise of Cromwell is of course panegyric: praise is there to recognize and keep favour but also to instruct and warn. Recounting Cromwell's military achievements and concluding that God is 'unmistakably at your side' Milton turns to his dismissal of the Rump, 'you put an end to the domination of these few men',[3] and persuasion of the Nominated Parliament to dissolve itself. Now all depends on one man alone. 'Deserimur, Cromuelle, tu solus superes':

there is nothing in human society more pleasing to God, or more agreeable to reason, nothing in the state more just, nothing more expedient, than the rule of the man most fit to rule. All know you to be that man, Cromwell![4]

When Milton comes to consider Cromwell's new title of 'Protector' (he spurned the name of king and adopted 'a title very like that of father of [his] country') his Yale editor says he becomes 'fidgety'.[5] He soon praises the Protector as 'author' and 'guardian' of liberty, and, after a sentence of quite hyperbolical praise, the theme of liberty becomes the *motif* of warning:

Consider again and again how precious a thing is this liberty which you hold. . . . If the republic should miscarry, so to speak, and as quickly vanish, surely no greater shame and disgrace could befall this country.[6]

These passages make the central point succinctly. Having resolved to offer total support to Cromwell in his new role, Milton can but rely on Cromwell alone not to betray it. It is the classic dilemma of the panegyrist to his prince. That Milton is not without fear for the future is quite plain. And, if we consider other revolutionary leaders praised in *Defensio Secunda*, and the way they are praised, more of Milton's mind emerges into clear implication. The first to receive glowing and prolonged tribute is John Bradshaw, 'a name which Liberty herself . . . has entrusted to eternal memory for celebration'.[7] Bradshaw had, of course, presided at the trial of Charles I. He had also defended John Lilburne at his first trial. More important, he had opposed Cromwell's assumption of sole power.[8] Bradshaw is not among those Milton praises to Cromwell in order to recom-

---

[3] John Milton, *Complete Prose Works*, ed. Douglas Bush *et al.* (New Haven, 1953–82), iv. part 1, 1650–55, ed. Don M. Wolfe (1966), 670–1.
[4] *Prose Works*, iv. 671–2.   [5] *Prose Works*, iv. 372 n. 509.
[6] *Prose Works*, iv. 673.   [7] *Prose Works*, iv. 637–8.
[8] *Prose Works*, iv. 261–2, 637–8.

mend them as advisers. Another opponent of Cromwell, Harrison, is not even mentioned. Among the recommended councillors is Robert Overton, Milton's friend, who had 'expressed doubts openly' about the Protectorate.[9] So too is Bulstrode Whitelocke who once or twice proposed the recall of the Stuarts to an unwilling Cromwell.[10]

Milton's anxious support for Cromwell in 1654 can be set in an interesting perspective by comparison with the opinions of another revolutionary leader, Colonel Hutchinson. An Independent in religion, a signatory to the King's execution, a staunch supporter of 'a free Republick', Hutchinson was the kind of conscientious idealist with whom one would expect Milton to agree. But Hutchinson had withdrawn from public affairs with the expulsion of the Rump, and his view of Cromwell himself, as later recounted by his wife, Lucy Hutchinson, rings with the truth of what many must have felt as they beheld from close quarters this inexorable rise:

But now had the poyson of ambition so ulcerated Cromwell's heart that the effects of it became more apparent than before, and while as yett Fairfax stood an empty name, he was molding the Army to his mind, weeding out the godly and upright-hearted men, both officers and souldiers, and filling up their roomes with rascally turnecoate Cavaliers, and pittiful sottish beasts of his owne alliances, and other such as would swallow all things and make no question for conscience' sake.[11]

The constant emphasis of Lucy Hutchinson's narrative is upon the dissimulation, the ambition, but also the imperious ruling spirit, of Cromwell.[12] That Hutchinson held such opinions, while seeming in so many other ways like Milton, does not mean that Milton must have shared them in his heart. It does, however, suggest that such opinions will have occurred to Milton, and must have been readily available to him in confidence from many of his friends, to go no

---

[9] *Prose Works*, iv. 676 n. 519.   [10] *Prose Works*, iv. 676 n. 520.
[11] *Memoirs*, ed. Sutherland, 193–4.
[12] It is not known exactly when Lucy Hutchinson wrote her *Memoirs* of her husband's life, but probably between his death in prison in 1664, and 1671. One must naturally ask how far her account of her husband's views was coloured by the Restoration of 1660. The answer would seem to be: hardly at all. She is unlikely to have planned publication; but in any case no royalist reading her narrative could have been gratified or felt that Hutchinson deserved compassion. Her material would have been likely to offend on all sides except, perhaps, that of die-hard, principled republicans. Of course a die-hard, principled, republican was what Milton, after Cromwell's death, might seem (ibid., pp. xviii–xix).

further than Bradshaw and Overton. It also underscores the risks
Milton might be thought to take when he offered such fulsome
support to the Lord Protector.

Behind the proclamation of the Commonwealth in 1643 and the
Protectorate in 1653 there yawned an ever more obvious and seri-
ous void. Cromwell had not achieved a stable parliamentary settle-
ment. He found no satisfactory replacement for the Rump he
had expelled, and ruled illegally, and ever more nearly absolutely,
far more so than had the executed King. To Milton all must
have seemed to hang on Cromwell's life, for what confidence can
the poet have had in the hereditary principle? As the Miltonic State
Letters go out, Oliver, Protector of the Commonwealth of England,
is at last succeeded, on 6 September 1658, by Richard, of the same
title, and Richard, Protector, on 15 May 1659, by the Parliament
of the Commonwealth of England,[13] with the name of William
Lenthall, Speaker of Parliament, at the end of the Letter. Richard
Cromwell had abdicated. The Rump was back in the saddle. Not
for long. Expelled again, this time by General Lambert, it reassem-
bled for the last time on 26 December 1659 and was in power, if
power it could be called, when Milton wrote his last, major, polit-
ically partisan tract, *A Readie and Easie Way to set up a Free
Commonwealth, And the Excellence thereof Compar'd with The
Inconveniences and Dangers of Readmitting Kingship in this
Nation. The author J.M.* (first version published by 3 March 1660).
This passionate and courageous republican plea is of interest in
many ways. Milton's bravery in defying kingship when the pros-
pects of a Stuart restoration seemed so strong sometimes eclipses the
clear implication that he cannot have been happy under Cromwell's
monarchy. Had he wished for a renewal of the monarchical formula—
might not Lambert or Monck have aspired to become Protector?—
he would not now have proposed government by perpetual council.
Further, in recounting England's achievement of a 'free Common-
wealth' Milton writes of 'our liberty thus successfully fought
for, gaind and many years possessed, except in those unhappie
interruptions, which God hath remov'd, and wonderfully now the
third time brought together our old Patriots, the first Assertours of
our religious and civil rights . . .' The phrase 'unhappie Interrup-
tions' recalls the remarkable words 'short but scandalous night of

[13] *Prose Works*, v, part II, 850, 871.

interruption' in *The Likeliest Means to Remove Hirelings* (August 1659) which on balance and after much controversy seem more probably to refer to the whole of the Protectorate than to the brief and recent military interruption of the Rump.[14] As if the revolution of stance between *Defensio Secunda* and *A Readie and Easie Way* were not striking enough, this reversal is astonishing. But then perhaps the praise of Cromwell in the former work had always been strategic.

Milton's vision is now of a permanent body, as though the advisers he had urged the Protector to consult in 1654 were to become the sovereign legislature, in which vacancies would only occur when one of its members retired or died. While this proposal is for a senate considerably larger than the Rump in power when Milton was writing this tract, it is clear that it is a rationalization and idealization of that tenaciously surviving body of men. This is evident from the awkward opening admission of the tract: Milton trusted the Rumpers alone, but after he had completed the body of the work he saw Monck readmit the secluded members, thus enlarging the parliament, preparing for new elections, and making a restoration the more likely. With difficulty Milton tries to link his proposals to the enlarged parliament. Roger L'Estrange recognized this awkwardness when in *Be Merry and Wise . . .* (13 March 1650) he derisively summarized Milton's position: 'he recommends the *Rumpers* to us . . . to perpetuate themselves *under the name of a Grand or Generall Counsell*, and to rule *us* and our *Heirs* for ever.'[15] The historical judgement on Milton's proposals is that they were quite impractical.[16] Yet when he composed the first version of the tract he might have supposed that, in contrast to the Harringtonian debate on model commonwealths, he was at least basing his recommendations on an existing and experienced body of men. Further, the survival of 'The Present Means', a summary of *A Readie and Easie Way* designed for Monck with additional advice,[17] shows that he thought something could be done, and that it was worth trying to manage the parliamentary elections to which he had been so opposed. The

[14] *Prose Works*, v. 356, 85–7.
[15] J. Milton French (ed.), *The Life Records of John Milton* (New Brunswick, 1949–58), iv. 1655–1669, 304.
[16] See the masterly Historical Introduction by Austin Woolrych in *Prose Works*, vii (revised edn.), 186–7.
[17] *Prose Works*, v. 389–92.

revision of the tract (pub. April 1660), though acutely addressed to the most current circumstances and concerns, and expanded in many important ways, may, it is conjectured, have been motivated at heart by the desire 'to distill more perfectly for posterity' his republican ideals of the last twenty years and to prophesy more powerfully the moral evils he foresaw in the return of kingship.[18] The heroism of his attempt and nobility of his ideals are notions which certainly command the mind when reading his text; equally important to weigh is the unmistakable oligarchic or aristocratic direction of his political thought, his confident rejection of parliamentary majorities in the name of minorities that know better, and equally confident rejection of popular opinion:

What I have spoken, is the language of that which is not call'd amiss *the good Old Cause*: if it seem strange to any, it will not seem more strange, I hope, then convincing to backsliders. Thus much I should perhaps have said though I were sure I should have spoken only to trees and stones; and had none to cry to, but with the Prophet, O *earth, earth, earth*! to tell the very soil it self, what her perverse inhabitants are deaf to. Nay though what I have spoke, should happ'n (which Thou suffer not, who didst create mankinde free; nor Thou next, who didst redeem us from being servants of men!) to be the last words of our expiring libertie. But I trust I shall have spoken perswasion to abundance of sensible and ingenuous men: to som perhaps whom God may raise of these stones to become children of reviving libertie; and may reclaim, though they seem now chusing them a captain back for *Egypt*, to bethink themselves a little and consider whether they are rushing; to exhort this torrent also of the people, not to be so impetuos, but to keep thir due channell; and at length recovering and uniting thir better resolutions, now that they see alreadie how open and unbounded the insolence and rage is of our common enemies, to stay these ruinous proceedings; justly and timely fearing to what a precipice of destruction the deluge of this epidemic madness would hurrie us through the general defection of a misguided and abus'd multitude.[19]

This eloquent self-dramatization sweeps us towards the Miltonic view, but concern with Milton also entails concern with what he dismissed or ignored. The 'misguided and abus'd multitude' are derided for their belief that kingship can restore a measure of prosperity, and it is the essential role of the historian to remind that 'two years of deepening economic depression' and 'the quarrels of the bankrupt claimants to the good old cause had brought trade to

[18] *Prose Works*, v. 207.   [19] *Prose Works*, vii. 462–3.

its lowest ebb'.[20] This un-Miltonic assessment found literary expression, among other places, in a popular poem with a chorus, apparently performed before Monck and the Council of State on 28 March 1660. It is *A Dialogue Betwixt Tom and Dick/The former a Country-Man, The Other a Citizen*, and runs partly as follows:

TOM   Why *Richard*, 'tis a *Devilish thing*,
   We're not left worth a groate
  My *Doll*, has sold her *wedding-ring*,
   And *Su* has pawned her Coate.
  The *sniv'ling Rogues* abus'd our *Squire*,
   And call'd our *Mistress Whore*.

DICK   *Yet—if* GEORGE *don't what we desire*,
  Ne're trust Good-fellow more.   CHORUS

  'Faith, *Tom*: our *Case* is much at one;
   We're *broke* for want of *Trade*;
  Our *City's baffled* and *undone*,
   Betwixt the *Rump* and *Blade*.
  We've emptied both our *Veines* and *Baggs*
   Upon a Factious Score
  If GEORGE *Compassion not our Raggs*,
  Ne're trust Good-fellow more.   CHORUS

TOM   But what doest think should be the *Cause*,
   Whence all these Mischiefs spring?

DICK   *Our damned breach of Oathes and Lawes*;
  Our Murther of the King.
  We have bin *Slaves* since CHARLES his *Reign*,
   We liv'd like Lords before.
  If GEORGE *don't set all right again*,
  Ne're trust Good-fellow more.   CHORUS

The Dialogue reaches its climax as Tom and Dick bow to 'GEORGE' [Monck] and beg him to do what he is '*bound to do*': '*Restore us to our Lawes agen*' and, in unmistakable implication, recall Charles II.[21] For just over ten days Monck had been secretly bound to do exactly this.[22]

---

[20] *Prose Works*, vii. 186.
[21] *A | Dialogue | Betwixt | Tom and Dick | The Former a Country-Man, The Other a Citizen, Presented to his Excellency and the Council of State, at the Drapers-Hall in London, March 28. 1660*, BL 669, fo. 24 (49).
[22] *Prose Works*, vii. 195.

De Hoogh gebooren Prince Carel. outste Soone en
Erfgenaem van Carolus den I. Coninck van
Engelandt, Scotlandt en Jrlandt. etc.

w. Dobson pinxit   C. Danckertz excudit.

FIG. 4. Charles II as a boy. Engraving by C. Danckertz after William Dobson,
c. 1645.

A Dialogue is a popular poem in sentiment and language. It is full of bawdy and country terms, vehemently anti-Puritan, and has its own skilful minor drama as Tom and Dick drink a health to 'GEORGE', grow merry, then, alarmed at themselves, quiet, serious, and bitter. They hint at a desired royal restoration but ostentatiously refuse to come out with it, even at the end. The poem was written by somebody in the know, unlikely to have been a simple citizen or countryman. It seems at the least the work of an accomplished ballad-writer, of the calibre of Martin Parker, but could possibly be a ventriloquistic *tour de force* by a royalist gentleman.[23]

A mere two more months accomplished what 'Tom' and 'Dick' desired and what Milton dreaded. Biography must dwell on the terrible days when he was within a hair's breadth of being excepted from the royal Indemnity, and when, believing himself safe, he was suddenly arrested and had to sue for pardon under the Act. Bargaining behind the scenes there must surely have been, but no sources descend to us on the point. The First Defence and *Eikonoklastes* were of course called in and condemned to be publicly burned. If some quiet deal were made between Milton's friends and those with influence on the scope of the Indemnity, it may have resembled the bargain considered by Dryden in 1699, that he would not write against the government currently established.[24] The development of Milton's work bears this out, and, while we cannot assume that this alone accounts for Milton's return to his earlier poetic projects, any more than that he got on with *Paradise Lost* merely because he now had time on his hands, it is the case that 1660 marks a much more radical disjunction in Milton's literary career than 1688 does for Dryden. Literary critics who weigh the influence of historical circumstance on literary production will draw their own conclusions from this.

[23] This is in Thomason Tracts, Thomason endorsing it 30 Mar. 1660. Cf. John Evelyn, *Diary*, ed. E. S. De Beer (Oxford, 1955), iii. 243 (17 Feb.–5 Apr. 1660). Note the line 'Drench me you slave' as the two drink. This sounds like a cavalier idiom to me, though perhaps the Toms and Dicks of that world might use such words?
[24] John Dryden, *Letters*, Charles E. Ward, ed. (Durham, NC, 1942), 123 (Dryden to Mrs Steward, 7 Nov. 1699). See also Dryden's 'Discourse of Satire', ll. 31–2, in *Works*, ed. E. N. Hooker, H. T. Swedenberg, *et al.* (Berkeley and Los Angeles, 1961–), iv. 23; and James Anderson Winn, *John Dryden and His World* (1987), 434.

II

On 5 January 1687 Evelyn records what he had never thought to see: the public celebration of Mass at Whitehall.[25] Milton, had he been living at that hour, could have asked no clearer vindication of his prophecies in *A Readie and Easie Way*: kingship had corrupted the nation and now perpetrated the unthinkable in actually bringing back popery to the English court. Many must have felt this. For those, on the other hand, whose knowledge of, and attraction to, the Catholic faith had been gradually growing, the emergence of what had long seemed an undercurrent of the Stuart court into public endorsement by the king must have seemed a remarkable conciliation of the personal and political. This was the case with Dryden, and the public events, the gathering and precarious religious revolution in favour of the Catholic minority, became the occasion not just for his conversion to Rome but, through that, to a more deeply devotional orientation.[26] This has long been noted in the two confessional passages in Parts I and III of *The Hind and the Panther* (1687). Each of these has a broad human and religious appeal while being unmistakably Roman Catholic. In the first the repudiation of youthful vanity and error addresses itself finally to the mystery of transubstantiation (i. 135–46),[27] while in the second the 'immortal' Hind, emblem of the Roman Catholic Church in the poem, speaks for a spell specifically to the repentant Dryden as he looks forward to 'those may-be years' he has to live before yielding himself, with nothing, to the redeeming blood of his Saviour. In dramatizing a personal conversion, however, Dryden never forgets the political future in which devotion and statecraft were likely to be closely and cruelly entangled. His vision of a prosperous future at the end of *Absalom and Achitophel* has always seemed rather provocatively absolute, involving a perceptibly unspoken doubt. The *Hind and the Panther*, on the other hand, offers in the two inset fables of its third part two contrasted versions of the future. In the first of these the Catholics, as swallows who now expect the summer of favour to last for ever, are benighted and trapped by winter:

> The joyless morning late arose, and found
> A dreadfull desolation reign a-round,

[25] Evelyn, *Diary*, ed. De Beer, iv. 535.
[26] Winn, *John Dryden*, 418–19.   [27] *Works*, iii. 127.

> Some buried in the Snow, some frozen to the ground:
> The rest were struggling still with death, and lay
> The *Crows* and *Ravens* rights, an undefended prey.
>
> (iii. 622–6)[28]

To this fable told by the Anglican Panther the Catholic Hind responds with her fable of the pigeons and the buzzard, a narrative based on the current, sensational, and true rumours that William of Orange was then preparing to invade England.[29] In this tale the Anglicans, as pigeons, plot to depose their farmer-patron (James II) by inviting a buzzard to rule over them. This buzzard, a composite creature suggesting the Whig Bishop Burnet, then in Holland, and possibly his patron the Prince of Orange, ends up as their tyrant:

> Nor can th'Usurper long abstain from Food,
> Already he has tasted *Pigeon*'s Blood:
>
> (iii. 199)[30]

While this monitory tale comes to a terrible ending for the Church by Law Established, thus contrasting with the end of the Panther's tale, its vision of a usurper supplanting King James II was hardly gratifying to the teller of the tale, the Hind. Dryden's commitment to his papist prince, strong as it is, yields only warning visions of overthrow and persecution. Dryden's strange poem goes considerably beyond *Defensio Secunda* in the expression of fear for the future. James himself, as the royal lion or the patient farmer, is endorsed without any of the hyperbolical praise bestowed by Milton on Cromwell.

 The Hind and the Panther was published, probably, on 27 May 1687.[31] While it was in the process of composition Dryden wrote to Etherege in Ratisbon: 'Oh that our Monarch wou'd encourage noble idleness by his own example. . . . for my minde misgives me, that he will not much advance his affaires by stirring' (16 Feb. 1686/7).[32] Though this well-known political remark may partly affect an aristocratic scepticism likely to commend itself to its recipient, its consistency with the fearful prophecies of *The Hind and the Panther*, Part III, underlines the same political diagnosis. Through that spring and summer King James's 'stirring', his use of

---

[28] *Works*, iii. 179. [29] *Works*, iii. 449. [30] *Works*, iii. 1279–80.
[31] *Works*, viii. 326. [32] *Letters*, ed. Ward, 27.

the royal prerogative to issue his two declarations of indulgence in favour of Catholics and Protestant dissenters (4 and 27 April), brought on an increasingly determined Anglican resistance which was to result in the trial and acquittal of the Seven Bishops, the point from which the King, who seemed at first to have outflanked his opponents, began to lose control of the situation. On 10 June, however, occurred an event which to some Catholics seemed miraculous, to others a telling stroke of providence at the least. After a series of miscarriages and of children lost in infancy Queen Mary was safely delivered of a son, thus providing a Roman Catholic heir to the throne. To a political nation the majority of whom now took legal hereditary kingship as their foundation this event was profoundly disturbing, for it seemed to ensure a Catholic monarchy for the future. The King's revolutionary measures could not now be ridden out by patience and a wise procrastination, as many had hoped. The lines of opposition hardened; within a few weeks a small number of carefully self-chosen aristocrats and churchmen secretly invited the ready Prince of Orange to invade. This development Dryden had already foreseen with remarkable accuracy; and yet God was surely showing his hand? As Milton had said of Cromwell that God was at his side, so Dryden in his verse panegyric *Britannia Rediviva* could now write:

> God is abroad, and wondrous in his ways,
> The Rise of Empires, and their Fall surveys;
> More (might I say) than with an usual Eye,
> He sees his bleeding Church in Ruine lye,
> And hears the Souls of Saints beneath his Altar cry.
> Already has he lifted high, the Sign
> Which Crown'd the Conquering Arms of *Constantine*.
>
> (ll. 75–81)[33]

'By this sign ye shall conquer': this was the vision of the cross of Rome's first Christian emperor, an adroit invocation by Dryden since Constantine, the Christian head of state, had in earlier times been part of the Protestant argument against the temporal claims of the Papacy. In this poem lavish praise of the baby prince mingles with considered advice to the King. The prayer against further civil war, a recital of English ills modelled on a passage in the Second Ode of Horace's First Book, serves as a serious and as it

[33] *Works*, iii. 212.

turned out prophetic warning though uttered without overt criticism of James:

> Enough of Ills our dire Rebellion wrought,
> When, to the Dregs, we drank the bitter draught;
> Then airy Atoms did in Plagues conspire,
> Nor did th'Avenging Angel yet retire,
> But purg'd our still encreasing Crimes with Fire.
> Then perjur'd Plots, the still impending Test,
> And worse; but Charity conceals the Rest:
> Here stop the Current of the sanguine flood,
> Require not, Gracious God, thy Martyrs Blood;
> But let their dying pangs, theyr living toyl,
> Spread a Rich Harvest through their Native Soil:
> A Harvest ripening for another Reign.
>
> (ll. 152–63)[34]

Joy is thus balanced with an awareness of danger in the vision of this panegyric; and it is the balance of justice to control these which the poet, *laudando praecipere*, here attributes to the king whose responsibility it is to hold all together.

> Life and State
> Are One to Fortune subject, One to Fate:
> Equal to all, you justly frown or smile,
> Nor Hopes, nor Fears your steady Hand beguile;
> Your self our Ballance hold, the Worlds, our Isle.
>
> (ll. 357–61)[35]

Dryden's last work before the Revolution was his translation of Dominique Bohours's *Life of St Francis Xavier* with its Dedication to Queen Mary (published July 1688). The poet's motives for bringing out this work at this time are complex,[36] but chief, surely, was the example of the great missionary at a time when it was hoped that the crown would win fresh converts to Catholicism in England. The life of the saint also offered a more acceptable example of a Jesuit than some then at court and on the Privy Council.[37] Further, in a tactful speculative question, Dryden alludes to the part allegedly

---

[34] *Works*, iii. 215.
[35] See J. D. Garrison, *Dryden and the Tradition of Panegyric* (1975), esp. 182–92.
[36] See *Works*, xix. 449–56.
[37] eg. Father Petre, the figure chiefly glanced at in the Martin, in the Panther's tale of the swallows.

played by prayer to this saint in ending the twenty years' barrenness of Anne of Austria, to give birth to the prince who became Louis XIV. Could the birth of the Prince of Wales possibly be due to prayers for the intercession of Saint Francis? The tone of this Dedication is humble and devout. When Dryden wrote it he had, perhaps, more real hope that James and his policies would survive than Milton, in *A Readie and Easie Way*, had that Parliament would establish a free commonwealth. Again, a political tract contributing to a wide public debate is a very different form from a dedication to a pious queen. Yet, when all these differences have been allowed for, one is still struck by the absence in Dryden in 1688 of that fierce confidence of judgement mixed with tragic despair at the trend of events with which Milton, twenty-eight years earlier, had responded to the prospect of another revolution. It is as though the longer history of the seventeenth century had schooled the later poet to patience.

The ways of Divine Providence are incomprehensible, and we know not in what times, or by what methods, God will restore his Church in *England*, or what farther tryals and afflictions we are yet to undergo. Onely this we know, that if a Religion be of God, it can never fail, but the acceptable time we must patiently expect, and endeavour by our lives not to underserve. I am sure if we take the example of our Soveraigns, we shall place our confidence in God alone: we shall be assiduous in our devotions, moderate in our expectations, humble in our carriage, and forgiving of our Enemies. All other Panegyricks I purposely omit. . . .[38]

Only three months later there began to be heard in the streets of London the mocking strains of a very different kind of work, Thomas Wharton's *Lilli Burlero*, whose ventriloquized Irish voices and sprightly air gave Catholicism the face of the hated Irish, their hour come round at last, and struck a telling popular blow against the religious policies of James and Mary.[39]

What now took place in James II's three kingdoms, the revolution which one strand in the English-speaking tradition has called 'glorious', was not the popular revolution of 1660. The invitation to the Prince of Orange represented no widespread desire to depose King James, while William, unlike Charles II, arrived at the head of an army of invasion. There was no manifest previous collapse of

[38] *Works*, xix. 3.
[39] *Poems on Affairs of State* (New Haven, 1963–75), iv, ed. G. M. Crump (1968), 309–15.

government, as in 1659–60, but James had, nevertheless, lost control of events and thus given William the opportunity he desired. The strongest force for change came from Holland where William needed to secure England in his struggle against Louis XIV. The tragic dilemma of the Anglicans, the whole basis of whose creed was the alliance of altar and throne, has obscured the international origins of 1688. Doubtless William felt a Protestant's concern at James's pro-Catholic innovations, but his single-minded aim was not to rescue the Church of England but to secure the crown. He connived at James's flight, rejected the proposal of a regency, and obliged the Convention Parliament to fall back on the fiction that the King had abdicated, leaving a vacant throne. The more plausible conclusions that James had been deposed or overcome by force of arms were quite unacceptable to all but minorities of the political nation. The appearance of legality had to be kept up, if only to make William and Mary look more secure.[40]

Three pieces of personal evidence throw light on Dryden's new situation. In a passage cancelled from the Dedication to *King Arthur* (1691) he wrote of the new regime as 'A Government which has hitherto protected me (and by a particular favour wou'd have continued me what I was, if I could have comply'd with the terms which were offered me.') As Winn points out, Dryden's 'old friend and patron Dorset' was Lord Chamberlain by 13 February 1689, and the condition was almost certainly the poet's rejection of the Catholic faith. A passage from the 'Discourse Concerning Satire' (pub. October 1692 but dated 1693) acknowledges Dorset's financial generosity to the poverty-stricken Dryden at that earlier moment, and says that on this account 'I must not presume to defend the Cause for which I now suffer' since Dorset is committed against it. Finally, a letter to Elizabeth Steward in 1699 speculates about some possible support from William's administration, saying that his 'acquiescence under the present Government, & forbearing satire on it' could be promised, but 'I can never go an Inch beyond my Conscience & my Honour'.[41] The 1692 statement means, probably, only that Dryden would not attempt to defend his 'Cause' in

---

[40] J. P. Kenyon, *Revolution Principles: The Politics of Party, 1689–1720* (Cambridge, 1977). See too John Miller, 'Proto-Jacobitism? The Tories and the Revolution of 1688–89', in Jeremy Black and Eveline Cruickshanks (eds.), *The Jacobite Challenge* (Edinburgh, 1988), 7–23.

[41] Winn, *John Dryden*, 434; *Works*, iv. 23; *Letters*, ed. Ward, 123.

the 'Discourse': in any case the context of his gratitude to Dorset renders his remark less than a full, formal, undertaking of the sort he seems to have had in mind seven years later. What emerges from these remarks is that, though willing at times to make some practical concessions, and certainly reluctant to embarrass Dorset, Dryden never in fact agreed not to write against the post-revolutionary government. He was of course subject to all the usual cautions, and was especially vulnerable as a papist. A Jacobite publisher was hanged for treason in 1693.[42]

III

In *Paradise Lost* Milton turned to sacred history and the Virgilian epic. He went to the Bible as the fountain-source of history: to the Old Testament narrative of the creation and fall of man as the point from which all later history and historical interpretation flowed. A rigorous classical humanist, he set aside the multiple narrative structure of Ariosto and his admired Spenser, with their rich freight of chivalric romance, and followed the example of Tasso back to the single action of classical epic. He was undoubtedly aware of the links of the *Aeneid*, and indeed of Virgil's other poems, with the princeps Augustus.[43] He may also have been aware, though unpersuaded, of a Constantinian interpretation of Virgil, sometimes associated with Eusebius and printed in his works, according to which the epic is read as the pilgrimage of the Christian soul from the city of destruction, Troy, to the heavenly city, the promised establishment of the Roman empire.[44] Too modern a humanist to think that Virgil really wrote prophetic Christian allegory, Milton could have found the Eusebian reading suggestive when he came to abandon his drama of 'Adam Unparadised' and cast his Christian narrative into Virgilian form.

It is at least striking that the first words uttered within *Paradise Lost*:

[42] This was William Anderton. See Howard Erskine-Hill, 'Literature and the Jacobite Cause', in Eveline Cruickshanks (ed.), *Ideology and Conspiracy: Aspects of Jacobitism, 1689–1759* (Edinburgh, 1982), 51.

[43] From Virgil's own texts in the first place, eg. *Aeneid*, i. 288–94, vi. 791–7; viii. 678–81. Also from Aelius Donatus's Life of Virgil.

[44] Eusebius, *The Ancient Ecclesiasticall History* . . ., trans. Meredith Hanmer, fifth edn. (1650), Constantine's Oration to the Clergy, p. 89. ('by *Troy* he allegorically signifieth the whole world').

If thou beest he; but O how fallen! how changed.

(i. 84)

echo not only Isaiah's 'How art thou fallen from Heaven, O Lucifer' (14: 12) but, more closely, the words addressed by Aeneas to the disfigured shade of Hector, amidst the burning ruins of Troy (ii. 274). The verbal link points to something important in the design of each poem, the opening books of which are dominated by a vision of destruction and fire. The single action of course allows a strongly oriented narrative, and the movement of the poem from Satan's fall towards man's redemption may be compared with the movement of the *Aeneid* from the fall of Troy to settlement in Italy with the Rome of Augustus in the prophesied future. The same Virgilian dynamic is to be observed. This does not mean that Milton is imitating Virgil in any narrow sense. Indeed the independence of his Virgilian architecture can be seen from the fact that, while the Augustan poet devoted the central Book VI of his poem to the descent to the underworld, Book VI of Milton's twelve-book epic is set in Heaven. Celestial warfare, not underworld prophecy, fills the dominating vision of the central books of *Paradise Lost*.

To remember the *Aeneid* (and one of its Homeric predecessors, the *Odyssey*) is of course to recall their heroes as voyagers. As the first words uttered in Milton's poem recall words of Aeneas, so, it has long been obvious, their utterer, Satan, has, in his career through *Paradise Lost*, some relation with the voyaging hero of the classical epic. In this area of the poem, where Holy Scripture holds so little basis for Milton's fiction, the initial invitation held out by the text, to a reader who has not yet read the chronologically prior narrative of Satan's revolt in Heaven, is to consider Satan as one who acts out the paradigm of the voyaging epic hero, not now traversing seas unknown but the unknown spaces of the Christian cosmos.[45] And as has again long been obvious, the voice of the epic narrator, by clear implication or overt warning, repeatedly urges that Satan is an epic hero with a difference; not *pius Aeneas* or Odysseus claiming his own, he aims at an utterly different goal though it can be seen in epic terms from the viewpoint of Hell. But as Satan the epic hero, commanding our admiration and even

[45] Christopher Kendrick, *Milton: A Study in Ideology and Form* (New York and London, 1986), notes that 'Satan seems to inhabit an almost exclusively classical epic, that he is somehow more classical than the other characters' (p. 151).

sympathy, is through Milton's narrative brought morally down, Adam and Eve, mankind, are, through their fall, raised up into a heroism of a very different kind. Eve falls through Satan's deceit, not knowing what she does; unlike Aeneas who deserts Dido to obey the god, Adam has full knowledge and yet falls, eating the fruit for love of Eve and fear of being again alone. Unlike Satan's fall this fall is, in its motivation, redeemable, and Milton is able to devote the later books of his poem to the setting forth of another kind of heroism than that subverted and exhausted in the figure of Satan. Adam and Eve are now Christian heroes in the terms explained in the opening of Book IX (ll. 1–47), repenting, obedient, and of no small moral stature as they face life in the fallen world they have themselves brought forth. The symmetry of Milton's Christian epic, itself a response to the epic symmetries of the *Aeneid*, thus holds in formal balance the classical hero and the Christian hero: in the new mono-theistic Christian cosmos Satan's rebellion can only betray and destroy, while Adam's responsibility and humility can still create. *Paradise Lost* bridges classical and Christian as the *Aeneid* bridged Greek and Roman, *Iliad* and *Odyssey*. As Dryden was to put it in 1688 in perceptive compliment:

> Three *Poets*, in three distant *Ages* born,
> *Greece*, *Italy*, and *England* did adorn.
> The *First* in loftiness of thought Surpass'd;
> The *Next* in Majesty; in both the *Last*.
> The force of *Nature* cou'd no farther goe:
> To make a *Third* she joynd the former two.[46]

That *Paradise Lost* should so conspicuously have occupied the high biblical and poetic ground, above the cut-and-thrust of imme-diate political justification, as exemplified in *The Tenure of Kings and Magistrates*, *Pro Populo Anglicano Defensio*, *Defensio Secun-da*, and *A Readie and Easie Way*, no doubt helped to deter the watchful censor, the least of Milton's considerations, perhaps, but still a significant one.[47] From here we may take our lead from a classic essay by Mary Ann Radzinowicz who, rejecting both the argument that in *Paradise Lost* Milton put politics behind him, and that the text of the poem encodes a political position and political

---

[46] *Works*, iii. 208.
[47] Annabel Patterson, *Censorship and Interpretation: The Conditions of Writing and Reading in Early Modern England* (Madison, 1984).

allusions, contends that teacher and public servant are now sub-
sumed in the calling of the heroic poet, and that the poem 'con-
stitutes a course in political education' from first principles and
experience.[48] Radzinowicz thus seems to rescue *Paradise Lost* for
political ideology, or vice versa, while still seeing the text as disen-
gaged from Milton's current or recent historical situation. She has
no difficulty in dealing with 'political ideas as an overt subject in the
poem', leaving 'remoter levels of signification' to discussion of a
different kind.[49]

An important conclusion can be learned from this argument.
From the very fact that the epic, unlike the tracts, has no apparent
persuasive design on the reader its 'political moments' (if for the
moment for the sake of argument they may be so called) have a
different and perhaps more telling impact. They have the character
of spin-offs, reliable discoveries, the more trustworthy simply be-
cause the energies of the writer are so obviously invested in the
achievement of a different goal. Radzinowicz mentions the ant,
*'which having no prince, ruler, or lord, provides her meat in the
summer, and gathers her good in the harvest'*: this ant from Proverbs
6: 6–8 is cited by Milton in *A Readie and Easie Way*[50] and *Paradise
Lost* (vii. 484–9),

> Pattern of just equality perhaps

How lightly yet tellingly this point is touched on in the later text,
during an angelic discourse to Adam *de rerum natura*! A further
instance cited by Radzinowicz,[51] recalls *A Readie and Easie Way*
equally significantly. In Book XII Michael describes to Adam the
migration of the Israelites from Egypt:

> the race elect
> Safe towards Canaan from the shore advance
> Through the wild desert, not the readiest way,
> Lest entering on the Canaanite alarmed
> War terrify them, inexpert, and fear
> Return them back to Egypt, choosing rather
> Inglorious life with servitude.
>
> (xii. 214–20)

---

[48] Mary Ann Radzinowicz, 'The Politics of *Paradise Lost*', in Kevin Sharpe and
Stephen N. Zwicker (eds.), *The Politics of Discourse: The Literature and History of
Seventeenth-Century England* (1987), 204–6.
[49] *Works*, iii. 206.   [50] *Prose Works*, vii. 427.
[51] Radzinowicz, 'Politics of *Paradise Lost*', 219.

The collocation of 'not the readiest way' with the echo of *A Readie and Easie Way*'s 'returne them backe to *Egypt*. . . . a captain back for *Egypt*' clinches the allusion, and stresses the glory of hardship when it constitutes the surest if not the readiest way; it raises the issues of freedom and servitude in a manner which supplies specific content to these abstractions while at the same time taking an almost self-reproving glance back at the tragic urgency of the 1660 tract. Finally, we might look at the passage early in Book 1 which John Toland later reported to have been found possibly subversive by Charles II's Licenser for the Press:

> his form had not yet lost
> All her original brightness, nor appeared
> Less than archangel ruined, and the excess
> Of glory obscured: as when the sun new risen
> Looks through the horizontal misty air
> Shorn of his beams, or from behind the moon
> In dim eclipse disastrous twilight sheds
> On half the nations, and with fear of change
> Perplexes monarchs.
>
> (i. 591–9)

Less politically explicit than the two previous instances, this does indeed have more that a censor would be alert for: it is menacing in its hint of a present fear of change among kings. But it is done with consummate art, for the origin of the menace is Satan, described in the past tense, and only linked by simile to contemporary eclipse. Yet in the poetic realm here shown Satan it is who has the power to make thrones unsafe. The implication of this for Satan himself will be pursued shortly; here it is relevant to note the almost provocative placing of the passage early in Book 1. It is a mocking challenge yet, as soon as it is noticed, it dissolves back into the infernal atmosphere: it is only a simile, it alludes to all kings, and what is being said against kings if it is said they are menaced by Satan? The passage is a perfect example of what the apparently politically unpartisan epic can do in a political way. The glancing stroke as the narrator hastens on draws blood and leaves a small but revealing scar.

In an important respect the politically educative process to which Radzinowicz refers involves argument from significant absence. The alleged origin of monarchy in patriarchy, the derivation of kingship from Adam, was one of the strongest arguments for kingship in the seventeenth century, grounding the institution in Eden at the head of sacred history. Though Sir Robert Filmer's full statement of this theory in his *Patriarcha* was not published until the Exclusion Crisis, in 1680, his views, briefly published during the civil war period, were an articulation of a widespread view.[52] For a patriarchalist the subject of *Paradise Lost* was a superb opportunity to display the early and God-given origin of kingship. Milton's disregard of this opportunity, hardly objectionable perhaps to a Restoration censor, makes the political trend of the poem very clear, more so than his avoidance in Book XII of the difficult episode in 1 Samuel 8 where the Hebrews demand a king.[53] It may be that argument from absence is a dubious strategy, but in this case Milton finally underlines its significance. In Books XI and XII, where so many lessons are made clear to Adam and the reader, Adam perceives that:

> He [God] gave us only over beast, fish, fowl
> Dominion absolute; but man over men
> He made not lord; such title to himself
> Reserving, human left from human free
>
> (xii. 67–71)

which Michael endorses:

> Justly thou abhorr'st
> That son, who on the quiet state of men
> Such trouble brought, affecting to subdue
> Rational liberty.
>
> (xii. 77–82)

This exchange about Nimrod, whose 'proud ambitious heart' breaks the original 'paternal rule' to arrogate dominion (xii. 24–32), raises a further argument about kingship, a further hypothesized

---

[52] Sir Robert Filmer's *Patriarcha* was composed between 1635 and 1642, and first published in 1680. Several significant shorter works were printed during the Interregnum: *Observations on Aristotle's Politiques . . .* and *Observations Concerning the Originall of Government*, both in 1652. See too *The Anarchy of a Limited or Mixed Monarchy* (1648). See Peter Laslett (ed.), *Patriarcha and Other Political Writings* (Oxford, 1949) for these works, and for a discussion of the influence of patriarchal thought 20–43.

[53] Noted in his Commonplace Book (*Prose Works*, i. 440) and used in *Tenure of Kings and Magistrates* (*Prose Works*, iii. 207–9).

source for which was in conquest. This, it might be thought, would hardly be welcome to royalists but was in fact more acceptable, not to say credible, to them than the theory of original contract which Milton himself had espoused in *The Tenure of Kings and Magistrates*. In the later sixteenth century Jean Bodin and King James VI were unembarrassed to find a mediate basis of kingship in conquest.[54] Nimrod was not invariably execrated, or in all respects, and Bodin, as we have seen in Chapter 1, allowed for the evolution of the legal, hereditary 'royal' monarch from conquerors. Milton's presentation here is emphatically hostile. Yet at the same time it should be noticed that at no point in the poem does Milton include a contractual account of the origin of government. *Paradise Lost* appears to underwrite an original, non-kingly, paternalism. It repudiates, though with little sound and fury, a patriarchal origin of kingship, remains silent on contractualism and assails conquerors, 'sword-law' (xi. 672), and the rule of force, in which, if anywhere, the human origin of kingship is to be found.

But emphasis must be laid on the word 'human'. In a fine short study of *Paradise Lost*, Stevie Davies shows how the image, concept, and associations of kingship are distributed throughout the poem: 'every major character in *Paradise Lost* is alluded to by Milton as a king, and the more minor ones are all in the service of a monarchy.'[55] As if to signify this wide dispersal of kingship within the realm of the poem, a repeated line sounds the motif:

> Thrones and imperial powers, offspring of Heaven
> Ethereal virtues;
>
> > (Beelzebub, ii. 310)

(Cf. Satan's line at ii. 11, where 'Thrones' are not mentioned.)

> Thrones, princedoms, powers, dominions I reduce.
> > (God to Christ, iii. 320)

> Thrones, dominations, princedoms, virtues, powers
> > (God to the angels, v. 601)

---

[54] *Political Works of James I*, ed. C. H. McIlwain (Cambridge, Mass., 1918; repr. 1965); Jean Bodin, *Les Six Livres de la république* (1576).
[55] Stevie Davies, *Images of Kingship in Paradise Lost: Milton's Politics and Christian Liberty* (New York, 1983), 6.

Thrones, dominations, princedoms, virtues, powers
(Satan to his supporters, v. 772)

Thrones, dominations, princedoms, virtues, powers
(Abdiel to Satan's supporters, v. 840)

him thrones and powers,
Princedoms, and dominations ministrant
Accompanied to heaven gate.
(the poet, of Christ, x. 86–7)

Thrones, dominations, princedoms, virtues, powers
(Satan to the devils, x. 460)

Deriving from a passage in Colossians 1: 16, which sees Christ as the agent in the creation of heavenly and earthly powers and supreme over them, the line is significant in its variations. Seen chronologically within the poem, God's first use of it gives its true meaning; in his second, but first public, use of the line the word 'virtues' (not in the New Testament source) is added, suggesting good will and judgement to be on a par with power and title. This is then seized on by Satan who interprets it as a list of 'magnific titles' (v. 773) merely, and is quoted back at him by Abdiel in defiant explanation. It is next echoed by Beelzebub (ii. 310–11) with a similar misunderstanding to that of Satan who, in his final use of the line, takes 'virtues' as synonymous with 'thrones' and as such capable of *de facto* vindication by power as a royal title is *de jure*.[56]

The idea and image of kingship is thus to be seen poetically deployed throughout the narrative, from 'Moloc, sceptered king I. . . the strongest and the fiercest spirit I That fought in heaven' (ii. 43–6) to the 'naked majesty' of unfallen Adam (iv. 290), to

the true
Anointed king Messiah . . . [who] shall ascend
The throne hereditary, and bound his reign
With earth's wide bounds, his glory with the heavens.

(xii. 358–71)

The pervasive use of royalism in the poem may strike us as nothing less than extraordinary from an embattled republican. It has partly contributed to well-known hypotheses of unconscious bias towards Satan (Blake), covert criticism of God (Empson), and of underlying

---

[56] See Radzinowicz, 'Politics of *Paradise Lost*', 221, 226.

cultural royalism (Mackenzie Ross).[57] But two things should be remembered, one concerning effective modes of communication, one concerning religious belief. Like the angelic narrator Raphael in Books V and VI, Milton may 'what surmounts the reach | Of human sense . . . delineate so, | By likening spiritual to corporeal forms, | As may express them best' (v. 571–4): he may seek in the image of kingship the most appropriate and effective metaphor consistently to convey the nature of God and the image may have a Neoplatonic function (v. 574–6). Further, Milton's own poetic procedure affords the reader a priority of images, for in the opening of Book III 'God is light' and 'fountain' (iii. 1–8) before he is referred to as 'High throned above all highth' (iii. 58): it is when he deals with divine action and relationship that Milton needs the metaphor of royalty—images of babaric or corrupt kingship applied to the devils are, of course, no problem. But, secondly, metaphor is only part of what we encounter here, for Milton certainly acknowledged the kingship of the Messiah:

It is no 'recommendation of royal government' to say that Christ was sprung of royal stock [he argued back against Salmasius], any more than to call Christ their descendant is a recommendation of the worst of kings. 'The Messiah is king.' This we recognise, it brings us joy and we pray for his speedy advent: for he is worthy and there is none like him or resembling him. (iv. 367)[58]

Milton was a political republican in opposing men who seemed to arrogate to themselves what was proper to God alone. That this is a misunderstanding of the divine right of kings is neither here nor there. The republican poet had in common with royalist readers that he was a metaphysical royalist: the two sides of his thought are complementary, indeed symbiotic. This I think is a coherent view of Milton's consistent attitude before and after the revolution of 1660, whose restoration of the legitimate monarchy reanimated the metaphor of kingship. The poet's mind was of wide resource, capable of discretion without betrayal of conviction. His belief in the kingship

---

[57] William Blake, *The Marriage of Heaven and Hell, Complete Poems*, ed. David Erdman and W. H. Stevens (1971); William Empson, *Milton's God* (London, 1961; Greenwood Press repr. 1978), ch. 2 and 3 esp.; Malcolm Mackenzie Ross, *Milton's Royalism: A Study of the Conflict of Symbol and Idea in the Poems* (Ithaca, NY, 1943), ch. 3. I am in debt to their discussion.
[58] 'This does not mean that all kings are tyrants', he adds (*Prose Works*, iv. 367) (see also 370, 427), and in *Defensio Secunda*, as is well known, he praises Queen Christina of Sweden in high terms (*Prose Works*, iv. 606).

of the Messiah enabled him to reach out in his poem to a readership beyond that of falling or defeated republicans. Further, his desire to offer a political education through Christian epic is admirably fulfilled in its wide application of the image and terms of kingship, genuine and spurious, throughout the narrative.

Stevie Davies has a further argument, of great interest. Noticing that only certain forms of kingship are applied to God and His Son, she points out that one of these is monarchy in a conspicuously feudal form. In a brilliant passage she then shows that certain sixteenth-century French writers on the obligations and limitations of kings—François Hotman in his *Franco-Gallia*, the author of *Vindiciae Contra Tyrannos*, and, one might add, the early Bodin— writers cited by Milton in his Commonplace Book, base their argu- ment on the late-lingering feudal phase of the French monarchy.[59] It now becomes clear why contract as an overtly alleged origin of kingship did not need to appear in *Paradise Lost*. Davies does not address herself specifically to this problem, but it is evident that Milton used some of the forms of feudal kingship to convey the reciprocal character of God's royal relation with all his subordi- nates, a point which Abdiel well understood in his great defiance of Satan at the rebellious gathering in the North (v. 826–48).

Conspicuous among these 'Thrones, dominations, princedoms, virtues, powers' is Satan, the most educative instance of all, and in no merely pedagogical sense. Just as not all forms of kingship are applied to God, or to Adam, not all are applied to Satan. Christ's throne is finally pronounced 'hereditary' (xii. 370): with Satan this is not the case. The introduction of Satan enthroned at the opening of Book II seems of lasting significance:

> High on a throne of royal state, which far
> Outshone the wealth of Ormus and of Ind,
> Or where the gorgeous East with richest hand
> Showers on her kings barbaric pearl and gold,
> Satan exalted sat, by merit raised
> To that bad eminence.
>
>   (ii. 1–6)[60]

---

[59] Davies, *Images of Kingship*, 130–3. See *Prose Works*, i. 409, for a reference to Bodin's *Six Livres* in the Commonplace Book.

[60] Claes Schaar, *The Full Voic'd Choir: Ventrical Context Systems in Paradise Lost* (Lund, 1982), exhaustively discusses this passage, save from the viewpoint of Bodinian thought about monarchy, 217–24.

If Book I displayed Satan the heroic military leader (albeit in defeat, and in what cause will become clear in Books V and VI), Book II shows that leader enthroned in 'royal state'. This tells us what kind of monarch Satan is: he is, explicitly, 'by merit raised | To that bad eminence'. Bodin would have recognized the paradigm of the 'lordly monarch' or conqueror (he could also be the tyrant, but this is not yet clear): he is certainly not the 'royal monarch', legal, hereditary, but one who has come to his throne by leadership and force. Like Marlowe's Tamburlaine or Shakespeare's Bolingbroke he is the type of monarch who does not come to a throne through a dynasty, but seeks to found a dynasty. As Fowler puts it in a note to Book I, line 98, 'Satan conceives merit in terms of might'. But, later in the passage, consent and right are claimed (ii. 24, 37).

So far it has been possible to discuss affairs of state in *Paradise Lost* at the level of political ideas: kinds of government, types of kings, the basis and origin of rule. But it would be quite naïve to suppose that either Milton or his readers would wish to separate these arguments in their mind from recent history. Milton's projected drama 'Adam Unparadised' would hardly have afforded scope to narrate, even retrospectively, the war in heaven, Satan's overthrow and rally, 'the great consult', and Satan's epic journey to discover earth. *Paradise Lost* picks up 'Adam Unparadised' with Satan's soliloquy in Book IV and goes much beyond it in later stretches of the narrative. The turn from drama to epic allowed Milton to draw on what his generation of English poets uniquely had lived through: an unparalleled and prolonged crisis in the state, civil war, war parliaments in London and Oxford, the emergence of a military leader of extraordinary powers, the illegal and hasty execution of a king, that military leader's equally arbitrary dismissal of the parliament he had served, his later dismissal of what were by comparison with those of Elizabeth, James, and Charles, puppet parliaments, his assumption of a monarchical role in all but name, his long, ambiguous contemplation of the offer of the crown before his prudent refusal, and final, ceremonious, oath-taking as Lord Protector. As the Member of Parliament Lister said in Cromwell's last parliament, 'You are making his Highness a great prince, a King indeed, . . . Ceremonies signify much of the substance in such cases. . . . I would have him provided with a robe of honour.' (At this point some hearers thought he had said 'rope'.) Cromwell therefore was provided for this oath-taking as Protector with a purple robe lined with ermine, as well as a Bible, a sceptre, and a sword.[61] What did the poet who in early 1660 was to write of the reinstated Rump as 'our old Patriots, the first Assertours of our religious and civil rights' (vii. 356) think about the man who had expelled the Rump by the sword now becoming 'a King indeed', virtually a king in ceremony, backing off only from the name? What did he think of Cromwell's protracted contemplation of the offer of the crown at this time, and the long, evasive, and amorphous speeches to 'parliament' (so different from his once stirring oratory) in which he said neither yes nor no to the offer?[62] Was God still at his side? Or had the one-time 'Chief of Men' grown into a military despot, a Sulla, and betrayed the revolution of the 1640s? The Independent John Hutchinson thought so. Did Milton come to think the same?

The question may most usefully be put in critical form. It is hardly controversial to suggest that Milton's experience during the civil wars, commonwealth, and protectorate contributed to the salient developments in *Paradise Lost*. But how far did Milton wish or expect his readers to be reminded of recent history, and in what ways? The allusion to *A Readie and Easie Way* in Book XII (and all that that implies) is one sign that Milton did see his Christian epic reflecting back upon recent history, and it is surely natural that the abstract politics of the poem should recall specific events at such a time. Much literature of the 1640s and 1650s, from epic to prose romance, did allude to specific historical figures and events under other names, though in no precise and simple fashion; Spenser himself, as we have seen, would have afforded Milton a model for complex, multiple, allusion to historical figures and events.[63] In *Milton and the English Revolution* Christopher Hill has proposed some unusually specific references. He likens Satan's rebellion from the north to Charles I raising his standard in the north (i.e. Nottingham), the indecisive first day's battle in heaven to Edgehill, the angelic mountain-hurling to the *levée en masse* of Parliament's new

---

[61] Oliver Cromwell, *Writings and Speeches*, ed. W.C. Abbott (Cambridge, Mass., 1947), iv. 559.

[62] Ibid. 453–5. See also John Milton, *Sonnets*, ed. J. S. Smart (Glasgow, 1921), 92.

[63] Paul Salzman, *English Prose Fiction, 1558–1700* (Oxford, 1985); Patterson, *Censorship and Interpretation*; since A. H. Nethercott, *The Muse's Hannibal* (1931), Cowley's *Davideis* has been thought to convey contemporary political allusion. See too David Trotter, *The Poetry of Abraham Cowley* (1979), and Howard Erskine-Hill, 'On Historical Commentary: The Case of Milton and Dryden', in id. and Richard A. McCabe, *Presenting Poetry* (Cambridge, 1995), 53–6.

recruits from London, the intervention of the Son to the New Model Army, Satan's resolve to fight back after defeat to the continuing resistance of the Stuarts after Naseby, and his temptation of Eve to the idiom of a royal masque.[64] Such an approach is at present desperately unfashionable, and even those eager to read *Paradise Lost* in a political way flinch from such particular suggestions.[65]

Yet it is quite probable that Milton's first readers approached the poem in this way; that, at any rate, they tried the text for identifications and allusions. It is clear from Hill's suggestions that he wishes to nudge Satan in the direction of the royalists in the civil war; on the other hand he rejects the *roman-à-clef* as a critical model and professes liberality of interpretation. More specifically he identifies some features of Ranter thought in Satan (ideas that he says helped betray the revolution of the 1640s) and acknowledges the general possibility that 'the character of Satan alludes to some of the ways in which the Good Old Cause had gone wrong'.[66] That Satan the degenerating hero has lessons for both, indeed all, sides in the civil wars is the readiest religious truth, but it is of more interest if he can be shown to display a coherent pattern of political allusion.

Not all Hill's proposals seem plausible. The rebellion from the north is certainly more than a theological reference (cf. Fowler's note to v. 689), and one could add to Hill's political examples the Pilgrimage of Grace, and the rising of the earls against the Protestant Tudors, and the 'rebellion' in *1 Henry IV*. But can Charles I be said to have possessed 'the quarters of the north' and raised his standard there? The comparison of the *levée en masse* seems to lack a sense of proportion, even allowing for the magnifications of the epic, and something similar is troubling in the likening of Christ's power on the third day to the New Model Army, however idealized according to an Independent, Cromwellian, and epic view. (Some would think the devils' use of gunpowder a better analogy to the New Model Army.) Finally, balancing these suggestions, and in the same critical mode, it may be proposed that Satan's first speech of seduction to his supporters (v. 771–802), with its abrupt shifts from loyal senti-

[64] Christopher Hill, *Milton and the English Revolution* (1977), 371–2, 396–7, 366, 380, 398.
[65] See Andrew Milner, *John Milton and the English Revolution* (Totawa, NJ, 1981), 204–5.
[66] Hill, *Milton*, 366, 396, 398 (for his rejection of the *roman-à-clef* model, and support for liberality of interpretation).

ment to resentful defiance, recalls the extraordinary speech with which Cromwell dismissed the Rump in 1653, first doffing his hat and praising the assembly, then donning it and denouncing the parliament in the most violent terms before expelling it by armed guard.[67] It seems plausible that there are specific moments in the text of *Paradise Lost* in which differing parties to the conflicts of 1642–60 were meant to see something quite particular of themselves in Satan. Dual political application, seeing King Charles and Cromwell, the two mighty opposites, in both Satan and God, at different moments, will appeal to most readers. Yet that balanced conclusion seems not quite fully true to the poem. Satan is still undeniably the powerful leader 'by merit raised | To that bad eminence' of a throne: only on that basis does he claim the 'consent' of his supporters to a royal title, imperial dignity, and the succession of sin and death. Specific moments apart, such a career can never in general allude to King Charles, while if there were one character thrown up by the conflicts of the mid-seventeenth century who resembled Satan in his courage, leadership, cunning, opportunism, persuasiveness, and destructive egoism, above all in his rise to a throne, it is Cromwell.[68] In my own un-unique view, Milton's Satan not only draws on Cromwell but is a transparent though not formal allusion to him. This is not of course to argue for identity. J. B. Broadbent has called Satan 'the devils' Cromwell' and that puts it very well.[69]

[67] Cromwell, *Writings and Speeches*, ed. Abbott, ii. 641–2. Other accounts, naturally perhaps, remembered the denunciation only (ii. 642–4).
[68] This view of Cromwell's career I base on Abbott's edition of *Cromwell's Letters and Speeches*, 4 vols. which takes us closer to the chief evidence of his life than conventional biography.
[69] J. B. Broadbent, *Some Greater Subject* (1960), 115. See his whole discussion, 110–20. Broadbent considers the possibility that Milton 'might even be satirising Cromwell' (115). Northrop Frye, *Five Essays on Milton's Epics* (1966; first published in Toronto, 1965, as *The Return of Eden*), 115, says Milton 'is willing to consider Oliver Cromwell as an emergency leader'. Jackie DiSalvo, in *War of the Titans: Blake's Critique of Milton and the Politics of Religion* (Pittsburgh, 1983), writes of 'Satan as Republican Hero' (247–55) but from a Blakeian viewpoint. Christopher Kendrick, in *Milton: A Study in Ideology and Form* has shrewd remarks about political analogies in *Paradise Lost* (92–3), but has perhaps too simple a notion of 'Milton's known political sympathies' (93) at the conscious level, and thus reaches too readily for what seems symptomatic of a dislocated ideology. Herman Rapaport, in *Milton and the Postmodern* (Lincoln, Neb., and London, 1983), discusses Satan in connection with Hitler and Lenin; and stresses Milton's 'complicity' with 'totalitarian action' (172–3). Historically speaking I think there can be little doubt about this last point. The three last commentators notice problems which the links here posited between Satan and Cromwell might be thought to solve. For further consider-

From this it may be proposed that the apparent unconscious bias towards Satan, the alleged 'contradictions' and ambiguities in his presentation, have a relatively simple explanation in the doubleness of Milton's historical experience. Satan has the qualities which originally induced the poet to see Cromwell with God at his side; he also has the qualities which history subsequently revealed in the sword-law of a military dictatorship. Through his early commitment to Cromwell, Milton became locked into a position of support for the sword. To cast this doubleness into the narrative of the degenerating classical hero was a brilliant response on Milton's part, and constitutes the most powerful example we have of the Renaissance rhetoric of temptation (as expounded by Stanley Fish among others[70]) made possible in poetry by the very depth of Milton's experience and involvement in affairs of state. The mighty opposites had collapsed into one; kingship claimed them both; and it is thus the more important to qualify Stevie Davies's thesis by noticing that Adam and Eve, 'naked majesty' and lordship over the beasts conceded, are, as human and Christian heroes, the least be-kinged of all the major figures of Milton's poem.

IV

A salient difference between the publishing histories of Milton and Dryden is that while Milton said the bare minimum about his three great poems, Dryden loved to surround his poems and plays with a setting of critical discourse and intriguing allusion. In his 'Dedication of the *Aeneis*' (1697) Dryden fully states, perhaps deliberately overstates, the role of the *Aeneid* as a complimentary court poem, making a series of allusions to Romans of that era of the Augustan principate. He shows a clear understanding of the role of Augustus in relation to recent Roman history and of Aeneas in relation to the kingdom of Priam. Aeneas was not the heir to Priam's crown; Augustus, though in a more than nominal sense restoring the Roman Republic, was changing the basis of its government according to its previous laws. While Milton enhanced the monolithic

---

ations supporting a link between Cromwell and Milton's Satan, see Erskine-Hill, 'On Historical Commentary', 65–8, 73–4.

[70] S. E. Fish, *Surprised by Sin* (London and New York, 1969).

appearance of his three post-revolutionary poems by his relative silence, Dryden openly situates Virgil's epic and his own English version, displaying in his discourse to Lord Sheffield the circumstances, choices, and procedures of the two poems. A consequence of Drydens's Dedication is that the reader of Dryden's *Aeneis* is immediately put on the alert, even for the detail or word which might point the Virgilian text.

At the end of his Dedication Dryden acknowledges his debt to Richard Maitland, Earl of Lauderdale, whose slightly earlier translation of Virgil was made available to him in manuscript. Lauderdale was a Protestant Jacobite in exile in France, and what seems not to have been known to the two modern editors of Dryden's Virgil is Lauderdale's MS Dedication to Queen Mary of Modena of the earliest parts of his translation (*Aeneid*, iv, vi, and viii), dated 1 January 1691 at Saint-Germain-en-Laye. Since Dryden is on record as having wished to dedicate his own translation to a restored James II, it is clear that each translator had the exiled dynasty in mind. Lauderdale's openly Jacobite dedication reveals much that could only lurk in the subtext of Dryden's, especially the relation they saw between the text of Virgil and their contemporary realm of politics. Lauderdale tells his Queen that 'I begun yᵉ 6ᵗʰ [book of the *Aeneid*] in England above a year agoe, when I durst not appear for yᵉ Usurpers' (fᵒ. 5ᵛ) and desires that his translation may 'be useful one day' to 'yᵉ Prince our rising hope' (fᵒ. 6ʳ and ᵛ). In a most interesting passage he declares that he has *found* the *Aeneid* relevant to 'yᵉ affairs of England' in the 1680s and 1690s, while disclaiming that he has forced Virgil's sense to yield a Jacobite reading:

I have endeavour'd to express yᵉ Author's meaning as near as possible, & I have kept as close to his words as yᵉ different ideoms of yᵉ two languages would bear; there are some things in yᵉ affairs of England, such as Staffords murder; Doctour Oates his testimony, the unnatural Usurper & some of his chiefe Agents, wᶜʰ any body may think I have made of designe for them, yet I have kept as close to Virgil's words in these few lines, as in yᵉ others . . . (fᵒ. 6ᵛ)

Significant here is the fact that Lauderdale began his translation with that book of the *Aeneid* which seemed to him most relevant to his times, and that Dryden closely follows him in many phrases of the passage of *Aeneid*, Book VI, which deals with the punishment of the wicked (vi. 548–624), and which modern commentators on

Dryden have recognized as expressing a Jacobite view. Lauderdale's explanation, I think, means that he has not as translator invented new *matter* to vindicate his own stand in favour of his *de jure* king, under the seeming authority of Virgil. However, I do not believe that his Dedication disclaims his phrasing his translation so as to point a contemporary moral. Further, it is worth noting that Lauderdale suggests no continuous parallel between the *Aeneid* and contemporary history: he does not, for example, attempt to turn his translation into a Jacobite allegory in which Aeneas stands for James II, however much he may, at some points, remind us of him. Lauderdale's practice is compatible with the careful political distinctions Dryden makes in his own Dedication concerning the status of Aeneas and Augustus (neither an hereditary king), and Latinus and Turnus. Each translator sees the *Aeneid* as a poetic text for the understanding of history, much perhaps as people read the Bible to interpret their own times. Neither seeks to appropriate Virgil's poem, so as to turn it into a Jacobite *Absalom and Achitophel*.[71]

Unlike the first-time reader of *Paradise Lost* when he encounters the eclipse which perplexes monarchs, Dryden's reader carries Virgil's and Dryden's worlds with him, watching for political allusion from the start. And from the start he finds it, though not quite in the simple parallel he might have expected:

> Arms, and the Man I sing, who, forc'd by Fate,
> And haughty *Juno*'s unrelenting Hate,
> Expell'd and exil'd, left the *Trojan* Shoar:
> Long Labours, both by Sea and Land he bore,
> And in the doubtful War, before he won
> The *Latian* Realm, and built the destin'd Town:
> His banish'd Gods restor'd to Rites Divine,
> And setl'd sure Succession in his Line:

[71] 'Dedication to the Aeneis', in Dryden, *Works*, vi. 872 (*The Works of Virgil in English*, ed. William Frost (Berkeley and Los Angeles 1987)). For Dryden's intentions to dedicate his Virgil to James II, see his *Letters*, ed. Ward, 85–6. For Lauderdale's dedication and translation of the *Aeneid*, IV, VI, and VIII, see the National Library of Scotland, Department of MSS, 221/62. I am grateful to Edward T. Corp (ed.), *La Cour des Stuarts a Saint-Germain-en-Laye au temps de Louis XIV* (Paris, 1992), item 265, p. 201, for drawing my attention to this MS. David Bywaters, *Dryden in Revolutionary England* (Oxford, 1991), 147–62, offers an acute account of Dryden's Dedication with due attention to Jacobite principle and experience.

From whence the Race of *Alban* Fathers come,
And the long Glories of Majestick *Rome*.

(i. 1–10)[72]

The implications of this opening are now well understood.[73] Virgil's 'profugus' does not in context primarily mean 'exile' or even precisely 'forc'd' though that is nearer. It is expanded by Dryden into 'forc'd', 'Expell'd and exil'd', the later two words suggesting human agency. All these words were precise terms for the departure of James VII and II from England in 1688 according to the Jacobite view: 'forc'd away' was a specific term applied.[74] 'Banish'd Gods', an expression suggesting human agency more strongly still and with no warrant in Virgil, leads to a richly entwined political pun in 'Rites Divine':[75] the restoration of James as Defender of the Faith would restore the rights and rites of the persecuted papists by the hereditary prerogative of the rightful king, who would also secure the royal succession, as the ousted laureate now does in his line and narrative. There is a high degree of poetic self-consciousness here.

There is no doubt that the repeated hopes and disappointments of the Jacobites since 1688, the flights, voyages, refuges, storms, landings, victories, defeats, embassies, and strategies brought, to men of Dryden's political sympathy, a special understanding of the 'Long Labours' of Aeneas which formed the body of Virgil's poem. More than in 1649–60, even, these labours seemed to figure the exile of the Stuarts, and it was indeed after the end of the great Irish civil war and the departure of Sarsfield and his forces for France that the Jacobite diaspora throughout Europe really began. The *Aeneid* could seem thus intensely contemporary, and it is of course notable that at this time the Jacobite Lauderdale was writing, in exile, that translation of the *Aeneid* from which Dryden drew so much.[76] And

---

[72] *Works*, v. 343.

[73] Ibid., v and vi *The Works of Virgil in English*, ed. William Frost; Berkeley and Los Angeles, 1987, vi. 965; Winn, *John Dryden*, 487–8.

[74] Howard Erskine-Hill, 'Literature and the Jacobite Cause', in Eveline Cruickshanks, *Ideology and Conspiracy: Aspects of Jacobitism, 1689–1759* (Edinburgh, 1982), 62, citing Sir James Montgomery, *Great Britain's . . . Just Complaint* (1692), 22.

[75] Not noted in Frost's volumes in *Works*, cf. vi. 965.

[76] *Works*, vi. 866–70. Among the first to notice specific allusions to contemporary history in Dryden's *Aeneis* were his editor G. R. Noyes, and L. Proudfoot, *Dryden's Aeneid and its Seventeenth-Century Predecessors* (Manchester, 1960), 197–207. See also Howard Erskine-Hill 'Dryden the Poet and Critic', in Roger Lonsdale (ed.), *Dryden to Johnson* (1971; rev. edn. 1986), 29–30.

yet Dryden is not offering a parallel between Aeneas and James, certainly not between Aeneas and William.[77] As Virgil's Aeneas was hardly exiled, banished, or expelled from the kingdom of Troy, for Troy was in ruin and he *profugus*, so, again unlike James, he was not king in succession of his line. He was, of course, in the political position of Milton's Satan, the false Aeneas, a leader of princely rank who seeks by courage and conquest to establish a royal line of his own: '*Aeneas*, Author of the *Roman* line' seeks to be the positive example of what Bodin had categorized as the Lordly Monarch. While Satan sank from Lordly Monarch to tyrant, however, *pius Aeneas*, an epithet Dryden seizes on and magnifies, is further fortified, not by having God at his side for surely never have so many gods opposed a hero, but by his constant reverence for the gods and the particular prophecies he seeks to fulfil. Dryden's near-contemporary translator of the *Aeneid*, J. R. de Segrais, considered Aeneas to have been modelled on Augustus, and directed his version towards his own 'glorieux Monarque'. By contrast Dryden sees Aeneas as 'a monitory ideal' to William, and a hero who served to highlight the sufferings, piety, and destiny of the exiled Stuarts.[78]

Of course Dryden does not sustain the density of contemporary allusion in Book I, lines 1–10, throughout the narrative. While it certainly heightens the reader's awareness of the word exile, frequently found without warrant of the original,[79] and hence diffuses itself into the general story of the Trojan wanderings, Dryden is, more clearly than Milton, using that logic of political allusion found in epic poetry whereby an apparently 'universal', lofty, or exotic narrative, with its own autonomous goals and wisdom, suddenly signals its awareness of recent affairs of state. As before, the judgement is the more convincing because it is hardly the overt design of the whole epic to drive it home. The reader is not repeatedly reminded of the Jacobite cause as he follows Aeneas on his various wanderings from Troy to Carthage and Carthage to 'the *Cumaean* Coast' (vi. 21)[80] but, here in the central book of the *Aeneis*, whose final vision of Roman destiny so clearly orients the mazy narrative, as Abdiel's denunciation of Satan in *Paradise Lost*, Book VI lines 111–88, had vainly pointed *his* right course, Dryden's text suddenly and unmistakably looks at post-revolutionary England again.

[77] *Letters*, ed. Ward, 93.
[78] I would thus modify the otherwise excellent formulation of Frost (vi. 873–4).
[79] e.g. v. 818 (*Works*, vi. 1024).   [80] *Works*, v. 527.

Among the damned of the realm of 'awful *Rhadamanthus*' (vi. 764;)[81] after a considerable Virgilian list of sinners recounted by the Sybil, we find those

> who Brothers better Claim disown,
> Expel their Parents, and usurp the Throne;
> Defraud their Clients . . .
>
> (vi. 824–5)[82]

This is a stunningly direct reference to Mary II, William III, and the 'Glorious Revolution'. Not so many lines later that the point has been forgotten, we read (for Virgil's 'nec veriti dominorum fallere dextras'–613) of

> Hosts of Deserters, who their Honour sold,
> And basely broke their Faith for Bribes of Gold:
>
> (vi. 832–3)[83]

where 'Hosts of Deserters' seems to recall the melting away of James's large army opposing William on Salisbury Plain (especially, perhaps, the notorious desertion of Churchill). Thus, when the Virgilian 'dominumque potentem | Imposuit' (vi. 621–2) arises, Dryden can translate it straight and know that his readers will think of England:

> To Tyrants others have their Country sold,
> Imposing Foreign Lords, for Foreign Gold.
>
> (vi. 845–6)[84]

To put your political opponents in hell may not be subtle, but Dryden was hardly the first great poet to resort to it. Thus the 1688 Revolution was brought under the judgement of the *Aeneid*.

At the transition from Book VI to Book VII—to simplify greatly— the *Aeneid* turns from a narrative of voyaging to one of warfare on land, though the special uncertainties of the sea are frequently recalled. The last six books are political in the sense that conflicts of

---

[81] *Works*, 554.
[82] Proudfoot, *Dryden's Aeneid*, 201; Erskine-Hill, 'Dryden, Poet and Critic', in *Dryden to Johnson*, ed. Roger Lonsdale (1971, rev. 1986), 30.
[83] *Works*, v. 556.
[84] Ibid. These instances are notably close to Lauderdale's rendering (*Works of Virgil*, 1709, 221–2: vi. 741–3, 748–50, 759–62).

(*a*) The crown offered to William III, 1689, by Anton Meybusch. The word 'vici' on the reverse concedes the claim, denied by Parliament, that James II was expelled by force of arms.

(*b*) James II and James, Prince of Wales, 1699.

(*c*) The succession of Prince James, 1699.

FIG. 5. Woodcut representation of 1690s medals drawn from Edward Hawkins, *Medallic Illustrations* (1885), i. 657–8, ii. 202 and 204.

states and peoples, alliance, rupture, battle, treaty, and duel, domi-
nate the tale.[85] The migration of a new people into a land long
settled and ruled is a subject commanding that compassionate un-
derstanding which is the very hallmark of Virgil's vision. The
anxiety of Latinus, the intelligible hostility of Turnus, the tragic
emotion of the tyrant Mezentius at the death of a son who had
but just protected his life—these emotions are now weighed against
the readers' sympathy with the sufferings of the Trojans. In accord-
ance with this epic turn of attention the viewpoint of Dryden's
allusions to current affairs of state shifts also, and the exiled
prince becomes the allegedly providential invader: what the Prince
of Orange seemed in 1688–9. This is first signalled early in Book
VII:

> An ancient Augor prophesy'd from hence:
> Behold on *Latian* Shores a Foreign Prince!
> From the same parts of Heav'n his Navy stands,
> To the same parts on Earth: his Army lands;
> The Town he conquers, and the Tow'r commands.
>
> (vii. 102–6)[86]

and proceeds, pointedly enough as Steven Zwicker observes, in a
valuable chapter of his *Politics and Language in Dryden's Poetry*,[87]
to the presentation of Lavinia, promised as a bride to Turnus but
destined for Aeneas, as:

> The Nymph who scatters flaming Fires around,
> Shall shine with Honour, shall herself be crown'd:
> But, caus'd by her irrevocable Fate,
> War shall the Country waste, and change the State.
>
> (vii. 117–20)[88]

These terms go beyond Virgil, who speaks only of fame, fortune,
and war. The words 'herself be crown'd' point again to Mary II, not
merely consort of William but queen in her own right if the decision

---

[85] See the excellent discussion by William Myers, *Dryden* (1973), 163–9.

[86] *Works*, vi. 574.

[87] S. N. Zwicker, *Politics and Language in Dryden's Poetry: The Arts of Disguise*
(Princeton, 1984), 198–9; for Frost on Aeneas, as model for an elected prince, see
Works, ed. Hooker, Swedenberg, *et al.*, vi. 873. The term 'foreign prince' is also used
by Lauderdale, and Vicars in 1632 (ibid., vi. 1046 n. 103). Loeb Virgil gives
'externum cernimus' (vii. 68). So does the Ruaeus *Virgil* (1722 edn.), 581.

[88] *Works*, vi. 574.

of the Convention Parliament were held legal. Later Juno, in an angry and ironical speech to Jupiter on the wrongs of the Italians, is made to declare:

> You think it hard, the *Latians* shou'd destroy
> With Swords your *Trojans*, and with Fires your *Troy*:
> Hard and unjust indeed, for Men to draw
> Their Native Air, nor take a Foreign law:
>
> (x. 112–15)[89]

The last two lines have no basis in Virgil, and bespeak a native resentment against the Dutch newcomers. Thus it will be seen that the Jacobite vision of these pointings and additions to Virgil's text has not changed from Books I–VI: it is the role of Aeneas in relation to that vision which has now altered. The example of Aeneas has been turned within the revolution of the state to display a different aspect.

   Dryden goes further. The tyrant Mezentius, Virgil tells us, ruled his city by savage force until his subjects expelled the monster by arms, and he fled to Turnus (viii. 478–93). In Dryden's version Mezentius 'Assum'd the Crown, with Arbitrary Pow'r' and, when the people 'fire his Palace' and 'execute his Friends', he, 'favoured by the Night, | To *Turnus* friendly Court directs his Flight' (viii. 631–47).[90] Virgil here gave Dryden the opportunity to give a reminder of James II from a Whig point of view, and he took it. Though his rendering of his Latin text is straightforward, 'Arbitrary Pow'r' obviously spoke to Dryden's times, while the small detail of escape by night (not in Virgil) further points to James, who left Rochester at one in the morning on 23 December 1688 for refuge at the friendly court of Louis XIV.[91] It need hardly be said that the pious and constant James was neither the 'Atheist' Dryden later thinks of Mezentius as being, nor the monster introduced by Virgil. Dryden's tactic in exploiting Virgil here is subtle and effective. The committed extreme Whig is, as it were, invited in and catered for by the politically hospitable story. But a little consideration should then bring that reader up short. How understandable that the people should expel the sadist tyrant Mezentius! How unjustified, by comparison, to expel the pious James! Further, Dryden knows that the later development of the narrative will in a measure work for him.

---

[89] *Works*, vi. 682.   [90] *Works*, vi. 628.
[91] Evelyn, *Diary*, ed. De Beer, iv. 612 n. 4. Cf. Frost, *Works*, vi. 875.

In the Argument to Book X he invites the reader to compare the deaths of the young Lausus, and the atheist Mezentius, his father. The point here is that the death of Lausus is an outstanding example of filial heroism on behalf of a tyrant father, an extreme case of loyalty to the patriarchal monarch despite his crimes. How differently Mary II had treated her own so different royal parent Dryden underlined in Book VI (see p. 206 above). Mezentius is now fighting in the cause of Turnus and Latinus, both hereditary kings. And as Virgil responds to the human grief of Mezentius at his son's death, Dryden is well able to follow him, as ll. 1251–1313 show, of which I shall only quote the end.

> For this, this only Favour let me sue,
> (If Pity can to conquer'd Foes be due)
> Refuse it not: But let my Body have,
> The last Retreat of Human Kind, a Grave.
> Too well I know th'insulting People's Hate;
> Protect me from their Vengeance after Fate:
> This Refuge for my poor Remains provide,
> And lay my much lov'd *Lausus* by my side:
> He said, and to the Sword his Throat apply'd.
> The Crimson Stream distain'd his Arms around,
> And the disdainful Soul came rushing thro' the Wound.
>
> (x. 1303–13)[92]

What completes the pattern of allusion to affairs of state in the second half of Dryden's *Aeneis* is the wise and relevant example offered by Aeneas himself, in the provisions he makes in case of defeat or victory in the proposed duel with Turnus (xii. 272–91): if he won and espoused Lavinia he would not take the crown from Latinus, the hereditary king, but ask only 'Altars for my weary Gods'.[93] In the altered viewpoint of political allusion from the first to the second half of Dryden's *Aeneis* we may see a creative response to Virgilian symmetry. Aeneas as a defending example for James is succeeded by Aeneas as a monitory example for William: the two are brought together here, so that what, in a larger view, is a minor feature of Dryden's handling of Virgil is nevertheless imbued with something of Virgil's strategic skill and breadth of vision.

[92] *Works*, vi. 717–18.
[93] Zwicker, *Politics and Language in Dryden's Poetry*, 186–7.

By comparison with *Paradise Lost* the political allusions we have been tracing in Dryden's *Aeneis* are, perhaps, more persistent. In common with Milton's poem such allusion appears local—at least at first sight—and all the more telling for seeming so. In *Paradise Lost*, however, there lay something larger and less definable, also political, partly beneath the surface of the poem: the complicity between the figure of Satan and the historical career of Cromwell, and the probable allusion to Cromwell arising from it; and this took us into the larger dynamic of Milton's epic. The figure of Aeneas, as he moves through the narrative of Dryden's *Aeneis*, is constantly shaped and modified by the poet's choice of word, management of contrast,[94] and reference to recent history. But as in *Paradise Lost* it is essential to observe the subtler pervasion of historical concern within a poem which is, after all, neither a political tract, nor an apolitical epic with discrete political allusions thrown in. In Book V of the *Aeneis* there is a remarkable passage describing the equestrian display and mock-battle of the Trojan boys, their contribution to the heroic games of that book. The movement of the sport perhaps gives Dryden a special opportunity for his style of verse:

> Th'unfledged Commanders, and their Martial Train,
> First make the Circuit of the sandy Plain,
> Around their Sires: And at th'appointed Sign,
> Drawn up in beauteous Order form a Line:
> The second Signal Sounds; the Troop divides,
> In three distinguished'd parts, with three distinguish'd Guides.
> Again they close, and once again dis-join,
> In Troop to Troop oppos'd, and Line to Line.
> They meet, they wheel, they throw their Darts afar
> With harmless Rage, and well-dissembled War.
> Then in a round the mingl'd Bodies run;
> Flying they follow, and pursuing shun.
> Broken they break, and rallying, they renew
> In other Forms the Military shew.
> At last, in order, undiscern'd they join;
> And march together, in a friendly Line.

(v. 753–68)[95]

---

[94] G. R. Noyes, James Kinsley, and William Frost in *Works*, vi. 1086–7. The point is also well made in T. W. Harrison, 'Dryden's *Aeneid*', in Bruce King (ed.), *Dryden's Mind and Art* (Edinburgh, 1969), 143–7.

[95] *Works*, v. 513.

The precision and symmetry of the military exercise can be mimed by the balanced and paradoxical heroic couplet ('Flying they follow . . .'), with all the division and turning between the 'beauteous Order' of the 'friendly Line' (ll. 756, 768) at the beginning and end. The particular movements of the boys are more fully mimed and traced by Dryden than in the description by Virgil, and I think it begins to grow clear as we read the passage that its moving quality arises from the way it is a harmonious response to the tragic turns, divisions, and repetitions of the migrating Trojans' experience. This war game played with magical discipline is both reminiscent and proleptic, expressing in its perfect skill and control what skill could not control without error and death in the repeated disappointment and effort of the Trojans to re-establish their line. Some of this is made clear in the similes which follow:

> And, as the *Cretan* Labyrinth of old,
> With wand'ring Ways, and many a winding fold
> Involv'd the weary Feet, without redress,
> In a round Error, which deny'd recess;
> So fought the *Trojan* Boys in warlike Play,
> Turn'd, and return'd, and still a diff'rent way.
>
> (v. 769–74)[96]

The Trojans are in the world, to the threshold of which Adam and Eve come with their 'wandering steps', and, with appropriate paradox, the military show is both inspiring and ominous: inspiring because the poet shortly tells us that the Trojans brought it to Italy, where it became in due course the *ludus Troiae*, part of the Roman Games; ominous because, just after this glimpse of the future, the goddess Iris in disguise utters to the Trojan women the complaint of the Trojans,

> toss'd from Shores to Shores, from Lands to Lands,
> Inhospitable Rocks and barren Sands;
> Wand'ring in Exile, through the stormy Sea . . .
>
> (v. 816–18)[97]

—a complaint meant to persuade them to burn their fleet and put an end to their struggle. The repeated pattern of the *ludus Troiae*, here an image of history, conveyed tragic tenacity and loss as well as ultimate victory, and this, it may be thought, is the wider political experience of both *Aeneid* and Dryden's *Aeneis*.

And loss means death. Surely the *Aeneid* could hardly be more full of the deaths of characterized individuals? Here Dryden's *Aeneis* must contrast markedly with *Paradise Lost* for, strangely perhaps in a poem about how man's fall 'Brought death into the world' (i. 3), there is little individual death in Milton's Christian epic. None can die in the wars in Heaven, and while Death is allegorically presented and much discussed in general, neither the sorrow nor the release of individual death greatly occupy Milton's vision. The salient exception is the death of Abel (xi. 429–47) and here, as it happens, Milton resorts to a characteristically Virgilian description:

> he fell, and deadly pale
> Groaned out his soul with gushing blood effused.

> (xi. 446–7)

The extraordinarily tense conflict of *Paradise Lost* owes something to the rarity of moments such as this. It is 'a round Error' which denied the 'recess' of death. Death's release of physical and spiritual is seldom allowed. In the *Aeneis* the death of Dido permits such catharsis:

> The strugling Soul was loos'd; and Life dissolv'd in Air.

> (iv. 1009)[98]

The gods give this release. A different end meets Rhoetus, a probably drunken victim of Nisus's and Euryalus's night attack:

> The Wound pours out a Stream of Wine and Blood,
> The Purple Soul comes floating in the flood.

> (ix. 470–1)[99]

There are many variations on this mordant line in the later books of the poem (cf. x. 484–6, 849),[100] indeed it may be said to perform the same role in the *Aeneis* as 'Thrones, dominations, princedoms, virtues, powers' in *Paradise Lost*. The death of Pallas is a notable case, where, since a spear has pierced his heart, it is useless to tug it out:

> The Soul comes issuing with the vital Blood:

> (x. 680)[101]

---

[98] *Works*, v. 484.   [99] *Works*, vi. 656.   [100] *Works*, vi. 693, 704.
[101] *Works*, vi. 698.

The youthful and heroic Lausus is another example, a life which, after the gallant defence of Mezentius, Aeneas would like to spare. He calls to Lausus with 'friendly threat'ning' (brilliant rendering by Dryden of Virgil's x. 810!) but the young man defies him and meets death at his hand:

> The purple Streams thro' the thin Armour strove,
> And drench'd th'embroider'd Coat his Mother wove:
> And Life at length forsook his heaving Heart,
> Loath from so sweet a Mansion to depart.
>
> (x. 1160–3)[102]

This staining of clothing and armour with blood from the death wound is shortly to be seen again in the death of Mezentius (x. 1312–13). At that moment Dryden, mindful perhaps of the character of Mezentius, chooses to speak explicitly of this stain, with wordplay ('distain'd his Arms', 'disdainful Soul') which must be designed to convey the dishonour and fury of this ruler:

> And the disdainful Soul came rushing thro' the Wound.
>
> (x. 1313)[103]

The unbroken alexandrine (cf. iv. 1009)[104] needfully expresses an extraordinary release of angry vigour and will.

As has often been noticed, Dryden closely echoes the closing couplet of Book X (the death of Mezentius) with the concluding couplet of the *Aeneis* itself (the death of Turnus). Virgil does not do quite the same though the mordant line is there in each case. The later poet certainly wished to underscore the iterative effect and use the very end of his poem to remember what, describing the fall of Troy far back in Book II, he translated as the 'frequent Funerals' (l. 491): the cost in deaths of the cause of empire. It seems too that he wanted a closer link between Mezentius and Turnus than Virgil allowed; though the suicide-like death of the former is contrasted with the shining, heroic, sword of Aeneas at the end of Book XII, yet the energy and resentful anger of Aeneas' two great foes are now drawn into formal resemblance by the use of the same line:

> at the Word,
> Deep in his Bosom drove the shining Sword,
> The streaming Blood distain'd his Arms around:

---

102 *Works*, vi. 714.   103 *Works*, vi. 719.   104 *Works*, v. 484.

And the disdainful Soul came rushing thro' the Wound.

(xii. 1374–7)[105]

Virgil, having used no word to afford a basis for 'disdainful' at the end of Book X, speaks at the end of Book XII of the indignant life ('vitaque . . . indignata') of Turnus. The sense of 'disdainful' which almost approximates to 'indignant' barely warrants (in terms of translation) the masterful baroque gesture with which Dryden thus concludes his poem. Like Milton he saw that gore becomes spirit in some of these deaths of Virgil: the soul has the colour and streaming energy of the heart's blood. As an image of historical process Milton's repeated line is explicitly political, moral, and commanding, Dryden's heroic, physical, perhaps sacrificial. Defeat for Milton springs from a series of crucial decisions, by Satan, Eve, Adam; the sacrificial cost of the redeeming victory is rather abstractly prefigured. Defeat for Virgil and Dryden is a datum of the poem; the cost of ultimate victory is far more copiously conveyed. If the hypothesis connecting Satan with Cromwell has validity, defeat sprang from the moral fall of one man, compounded, admittedly, by a backsliding and unelect populace. After his Dedication of the *Life of Saint Francis Xavier* to Queen Mary, even after the cruel visions of *Hind and the Panther*, Part III, Dryden needed the pagan pantheon to convey, imaginatively, the experience of the defeat through which he lived in 1688–9, and the seemingly endless pattern of hope and disappointment and further hope thereafter. Much of the *Aeneid* came perfectly to his purpose, and his *Aeneis* was the result.

[105] *Works*, vi. 806.

7

Post-Revolutionary Tragedy

SAMSON AGONISTES and *Don Sebastian* are tragedies of alien setting, of the Hebrew faith in Philistia, of the Christian faith in Africa. When they were made public their authors were something like internal exiles. The London Milton had praised in *Areopagitica*, the London Dryden had praised in *Annus Mirabilis* had been overthrown by the revolutions of 1660 and 1688 respectively. For each poet the good city did not abide: alienation sharpened the metaphor of the wilderness. I shall explore briefly what the wilderness meant to each poet, as introduction to their post-revolutionary tragedy.

The wilderness is a threatening place, very different from an important or acknowledged position within the structures of the state. That there was drudgery for Milton in translating the State Letters is obvious; that Dryden's 'little Sallary' was 'ill paid' he tells us;[1] but each was at least needed or recognized by the existing political order, before the revolutions with which we are here concerned. But political supremacies could be seen more clearly, perhaps, from the distanced and deprived vantage point of the wilderness. When Dryden became a Catholic he joined the religion of the king, but once he sought to share the privileges of the established church with papists and dissenters the king was no longer part of the establishment. Having joined the disestablished Catholic community, Dryden shows us how his papist Hind, 'Panting and pensive' (a phrase nicely chosen to portray her animal form and religious character)

> rang'd alone
> And wander'd in the kingdoms, once Her own.
> The common Hunt, though from their rage restrain'd
> By sov'reign pow'r, her company disdain'd:
> Grinn'd as They pass'd, and with a glaring eye

---

[1] John Dryden, *Works*, ed. E. N. Hooker, H. T. Swedenberg, *et al.*, 20 vols. (Berkeley and Los Angeles, 1961–), iv. 23.

Gave gloomy signs of secret enmity.
(*The Hind and the Panther*, i. 25–30)[2]

In *Paradise Regained* (1671) Christ, in 'pathless desert, dusk with horrid shades' (i. 296) is likewise in danger though unmolested by savage beasts: 'the Lion and fierce tiger glared aloof' (i. 313).

From this position both Christ and the Hind have their vision of secular monarchy: Henry VIII and Tiberius, an interesting pair, as Johnson must have thought when he came to compose his portrait of Cardinal Wolsey in *The Vanity of Human Wishes*.[3] In the view of the Catholic Hind the Protestant monarchy begot a secular church:

> A *Lyon* old, obscene, and furious made
> By lust, compress'd her mother in a shade;
> Then, by a left-hand marr'age weds the Dame,
> Cov'ring adult'ry with a specious name:
> So schism begot; and sacrilege and she,
> A well-match'd pair, got graceless heresie.
> God's and kings rebels have the same good cause,
> To trample down divine and humane laws:
> Both wou'd be call'd Reformers, and their hate,
> Alike destructive both to church and state:
>
> (i. 351–60)[4]

Dryden's diagnosis of a political and religious fall, stemming from lust and masquerading as reformation is now driven home in an extraordinary sequence of five triplets, the expected closure repeatedly opening up into yet further degradation:

> The fruit proclaims the plant; a lawless Prince
> By luxury reform'd incontinence,
> By ruins, charity; by riots, abstinence.
> Confessions, fasts and penance set aside;
> Oh with what ease we follow such a guide!
> Where souls are starv'd, and senses gratify'd.
> Where marr'age pleasures, midnight pray'r supply,
> And mattin bells (a melancholy cry)
> Are tun'd to merrier notes, *encrease* and *multiply*.

---

[2] *Works*, iii. 123–4.
[3] In his *Vanity of Human Wishes* (1749) Johnson parallels Juvenal's Sejanus with Cardinal Wolsey, and thus the Emperor Tiberius with Henry VIII.
[4] *Works*, iii. 133.

> Religion shows a Rosie colour'd face;
> Not hatter'd out with drudging works of grace;
> A down-hill Reformation rolls apace.
> What flesh and bloud wou'd croud the narrow gate,
> Or, till they waste their pamper'd paunches, wait?
> All wou'd be happy at the cheapest rate.

(i. 361–75)[5]

One might note in passing that if puritanism means religious and moral strictness, a distrust of liberal tendency, Dryden's tone is not un-Puritan here. In displaying a vaster and more ancient degeneration Milton exploits the coming of Christ on earth in the reign of Tiberius, his earlier reading of Machiavellian argument against the superstate being briefly evidenced in Satan's observation that:

> Judaea now and all the promised land
> Reduced a province under Roman yoke,
> Obeys Tiberius; nor is always ruled
> With temperate sway; oft have they violated
> The Temple, oft the Law with foul affronts,
> Abominations rather, as did once
> Antiochus: and think'st thou to regain
> Thy right by sitting still or thus retiring?

(iii. 157–64)

Satan brilliantly appeals to the predicament of the small nation, intensely conscious of its own identity and religion, overwhelmed by a larger; his tone modulates rapidly from restraint to outrage ('nor is always . . .' to 'Abominations'). He offers Christ the heroic example of Judas Maccabeus, who prevailed against Antiochus Epiphanes, founded a new Jewish dynasty, and was sometimes considered a type of Christ.[6] (One might add that Maccabeus has something in common with Samson.) Tiberius is reintroduced in Book IV as the climax of an extraordinary vision of Rome, its buildings, roads, dignitaries, administration, geographical range,

> Civility of manners, arts, and arms,

(iv. 83)

---

[5] *Works*, iii. 133–4.
[6] *John Milton, Poems*, ed. John Carey and Alastair Fowler (1968), 1122 (ll. 165–70 n.).

the corrupt centre of the great and apparently virile empire:

> This emperor hath no son, and now is old,
> Old, and lascivious, and from Rome retired
> To Capreae an island small but strong
> On the Campanian shore, with purpose there
> His horrid lusts in private to enjoy,
> Committing to a wicked favourite
> All public cares, and yet of him suspicious,
> Hated of all, and hating;
>
> (iv. 90–7)

Satan concisely states the Machiavellian paradox of ancient Rome, now a 'victor people' under 'servile yoke!' (iv. 102), wishing to underline the extraordinary opportunity for a new political Messiah, or new Prince. Christ in his reply accepts but goes beyond this political diagnosis, tracing an almost Polybian or Tacitian pattern in the rise and degeneracy of the Romans as an imperial people, to the point where they are 'by themselves enslaved'. The self-enslaved, he declares, cannot be freed, not, at least, by any political liberator (iv. 143–5). Meanwhile 'the means' whereby a very different renewal of 'David's throne' may be accomplished cannot be divulged to Satan (iv. 146–53). The relevance of this picture of Rome, outwardly impressive but corrupt at heart, to the royalist milieu of the Restoration need hardly be insisted on:[7] Milton's desert vision is designed to pierce what he would have regarded as the Roman masquerade of the restored Stuarts. Yet despite Dryden's prominent use of Roman parallel in his panegyrics and other public poems there is quite a lot in common between these two visions of decline. In each case corruption seems to start at the top and might be, but is not, resisted from below. It is worth remarking that Christ's eventual means of redeeming the self-enslaved, his self-sacrificial death and founding of the church militant, is betrayed, among other times and places, by the degeneration of the priesthood in Dryden's Counter-Reformation history of England.

The parallel between *Paradise Regained* and *The Hind and the Panther* might be taken further, particularly in their treatment of the places of respite in the wilderness, where one notices the links and

---

[7] See John Ogilby's *Entertainment of His Most Excellent Majestie* . . . (1662), introd. Ronald Knowles (Binghamton, NY, 1988), and Howard Erskine-Hill, *The Augustan Idea*, (1983) 213–22.

contrasts between Christ's *dream* of holy sustenance, the accepted offer of the Hind's humble hospitality—and the lowly house of Evander which has received a god in *Aeneis*, Book VIII, and which Dryden's poem both recalls and anticipates.[8] These are places of succour and instruction, not abiding cities. In the case of Christ the sustenance is purely spiritual; in the case of the well-provided Panther she only accepts the lowly fare out of prudence. Dryden hopes still for a mediate success, suggested by James's 'late nocturnal victory' over Monmouth; Milton puts all quasi-secular hope of that kind behind him, in Christ's rejection of the kingdoms. Ultimately the goal of each wanderer, oriented or bewildered, is a messianic but not political triumph.

I

Judas Maccabeus and Samson were both considered types of the Messiah. So, in Christian allegorizing, was Hercules, the god received by the humble house of Evander in the *Aeneid* (such allegorizing is recalled in Milton's sonnet: 'Methought I saw my late espoused saint'). As it happens the subject of Dryden's first major post-revolutionary work, *Don Sebastian, King of Portugal* (first performed late in 1689) was the object of a Renaissance messianic cult. Sebastian disappeared in the midst of disastrous military defeat in the Battle of Alcazar, in North Africa, thus opening the way for Spain, Portugal's mighty neighbour, with a fair dynastic claim not recognized by Dryden, to take over the small, intensely self-conscious nation and its vast seaborne empire. The belief of the oppressed Portuguese that Sebastian was *rex quondam et futurus*, that he would appear again to rule Portugal until the Second Coming of Christ, seems to be referred to by Dryden in the Preface to his *Don Sebastian, King of Portugal* (first performed late in 1689):

'Tis most certain, that the *Portugueses* expected his return for almost an Age together after that Battel; which is at least proof of their extream love to his Memory; and the usage which they had from their new Conquerors, might possibly make them so extravagant in their hopes and wishes for their old Master.[9]

---

[8] *Works*, iii. 407.   [9] *Works*, xv. 67–8.

That Dryden does not refer to any merely short-term hope that Sebastian would prove to have survived the battle is clear from the words 'almost an Age' and 'so extravagant'. That he also invites the reader to compare the new situation in Britain with that of Portugal after the disappearance of Sebastian, with 'new Conquerors' and an 'old Master' in each case, is also as clear as it could possibly have been in a published Preface of 1690.[10] There is no mistaking the conspicuously equivocal position Dryden adopted with the publication of *Don Sebastian* in 1690. The Prologue openly reminded the audience that the author was the deposed laureate and a Catholic; the Preface spoke of new conquerors, a usurpation, and an old Master; but also of how 'History' afforded him the 'groundwork' of his play, some of it well known through the mediation of prose romance.[11]

These signals are, as we have seen, characteristic of Dryden but uncharacteristic of Milton. In the case of Milton's post-revolutionary drama, *Samson Agonistes*, we are faced with the poet's most enigmatic work, quite different from the explicit *Paradise Regained* which resists the attempts of even recent criticism to subtilize it.[12] Further, the drama's very period of composition is in dispute from lack of clear circumstantial evidence. Internal evidence there is, as we shall see, but this can never be so fully satisfactory.[13] What must be the basis of any attempt to read *Samson Agonistes* politically, as many critics of Milton do, is its date of publication. Licenced 2 July

[10] See Howard Erskine-Hill, 'The Providential Context', *TLS* (12 Aug. 1977), 988; C.R. Boxer, *The Portuguese Seaborne Empire, 1415–1825* (1969), ch. 16.
[11] Dryden's chief source was almost certainly *Don Sebastian King of Portugal. An Historical Novel. In Four Parts. Done out of French by Mr Ferrand Spence* (1683). See *Works*, xv. 383–91, for a full discussion.
[12] See the proposals of J. A. Wittreich in *Milton and the Lines of Vision* (Madison, 1976), and the responses of A. H. A. Rushdy, 'The Empty Garden', Ph.D. Diss. (University of Cambridge, 1989).
[13] The case for an early date of composition, ?1647–53, proposed by W. R. Parker, is summarized and accepted by Carey and Fowler in their edition of Milton's *Poems*, 330–2. The most powerful case for the traditional late date, after the Restoration, is put by M. A. Radzinowicz in *Towards Samson Agonistes: The Growth of Milton's Mind* (Princeton, 1978), 387–407. The whole weight of her book backs the hypothesis of a late date, but her evidence is critical and internal, resting on her judgement of the evolution of Milton's thought. In 'Scholarship as Humanism', *Essays in Criticism*, 39:1 (Jan. 1979), 46–7, I attempted to show what differences in interpretation the proposed different dates of composition might involve. The hypothesis that *Samson* was begun early, but completed and shaped as a poem for the Restoration is not less plausible than the others. My interpretation here rests on the date of publication, and some internal features of the work, no more.

1670, registered 10 September of the same year, it was published early in 1671 with *Paradise Regained*, 'To which is added *Samson Agonistes.The Author, John Milton*', as the title-page said. Whether or not first composed in 1647–53 (and it may have been begun then but modified and finished later), *Samson Agonistes* was bound to be read, as Milton must have recognized, as a work of his own, in the light of his personal and public history. While his self-presentation in *Paradise Lost* is certainly not simply autobiographical, and blindness, obscurity, and hardship (iii. 22–6; vii. 21–31) are endowed with fit symbolic importance within the poem, still such self-presentation was noticeable. When, therefore, the same notorious or celebrated poet, the blind defender of regicide, providentially punished and disgraced as many thought, chose to publish a tragedy on a champion overthrown, blinded, and disgraced, it would have been too much to expect that its first readers would approach it as a biblical drama merely, with no allusion to its author and recent times. This must have been the case whatever subsequent qualification, demural, or adjustment between personal, secular, and sacred history the text might compel. That well-qualified readers did react in this way is surely borne out by lines in Marvell's commendatory poem to *Paradise Lost* which appeared three years later in 1674:

> the argument
> Held me a while misdoubting his intent,
> That he would ruin (for I saw him strong)
> The sacred truths to fable and old song
> (So Sampson groped the Temple's post in spite)
> The world o'erwhelming to revenge his sight.[14]

The anti-autobiographical bias of New Criticism would make nothing of this point,[15] but a broader historical approach must include questions of authorial and biographical awareness. If Milton recognized that his readers would look for 'The Author John Milton' in *Samson Agonistes*—as it was satirically said they had sought and found him in *Paradise Lost* but not in *Paradise Regained*[16]—it follows that he considered his readers would expect in the text some bearing on the present and recent past: the historical events of Milton's lifetime. The critical question then resolves into

---

[14] *Poems*, 455.   [15] It is dismissed in *Poems*, 331.
[16] J. Milton French (ed.), *The Life Records of John Milton* (New Brunswick, NJ, 1949–58), v. 32.

this: how far does the text of the tragedy satisfy or deny such expectation?

Sacred history was read for its contemporary relevance. Nothing is more obvious than that religion and politics were inseparable in the mid-seventeenth century. If *Samson Agonistes* as we now have it were completed in the period 1647–53 Samson himself might have figured the people of England aroused, as he did in *Areopagitica*,[17] 'a noble and puissant Nation rousing herself like a strong man after sleep, and shaking her invincible locks', and his final act might then have expressed the destruction of England's 'kingdom old' and its ancient laws.[18] That Samson breaks out of bondage, rather than awakes from sleep (an image of 1644), would perhaps be no great difficulty. But what the text of *Samson* unmistakably puts before us is opportunity lost. As Samson rhetorically asks, in seeking to justify himself to the Chorus of the people of Israel,

> But what more oft in nations grown corrupt,
> And by their vices brought to servitude,
> Than to love bondage more than liberty,
> Bondage with ease than strenuous liberty;
> And to despise, or envy, or suspect
> Whom God hath of his special favour raised
> As their deliverer . . .

> (ll. 268–74)

This sounds in the middle lines like Christ on the corruption of the Romans under Tiberius; it also reminds us of the Digression on the Long Parliament in Milton's *History of Britain*, now at last recently redated by Austin Woolrych.[19] This is not to say that Samson speaks wholly for Milton: the question of who lords over whom is decisively rejected by the Christ of *Paradise Regained*, while *A Readie and Easie Way* leads one to doubt the later Milton's trust in individual deliverers. But the passage puts the pain of recent historical disappointment plainly before us while, in the general formulation of the central lines ('What more oft . . .') certainly carrying wider implications. Take a further case, the utterance not this time of Samson himself but of the Chorus after the Episode with Manoa:

[17] John Milton, *Complete Prose Works*, ed. Douglas Bush *et al.* (New Haven, 1953–82), ii. 557–8.
[18] Erskine-Hill, 'Scholarship as Humanism', 46.
[19] Austin Woolrych, 'The Date of the Digression in Milton's *History of Britain*', in R. Ollard and P. Tudor Craig, (eds.), *For Veronica Wedgwood, these* (1986), 217–46.

God of our fathers, what is man!
That thou towards him with hand so various,
Or might I say contrarious,
Temper'st thy providence through his short course,
Not evenly, as thou rul'st
Th'angelic orders and inferior creatures mute,
Irrational and brute.
Nor do I name of men the common rout,
That wandering loose about
Grow up and perish, as the summer fly,
Heads without name no more remembered,
But such as thou hast solemnly elected,
With gifts and graces eminently adorned
To some great work, thy glory,
And people's safety, which in part they effect:
Yet towards these thus dignified, thou oft
Amidst their height of noon,
Changest thy countenance, and thy hand with no regard
Of highest favours past,
From thee on them, or them to thee of service.
   Nor only dost degrade them, or remit
To life obscured, which were a fair dismission,
But throw'st them lower than thou didst exalt them high,
Unseemly falls in human eye,
Too grievous for the trespass or omission,
Oft leav'st them to the hostile sword
Of heathen and profane, their carcases
To dogs and fowls a prey, or else captived:
Or to the unjust tribunals, under change of times,
And condemnation of the ingrateful multitude.

(ll. 667–96)

Nothing could be more bland or unremarkable than a general reflection on the mysteriousness of divine providence. How unsurprising that those of special power and merit should be cast down! What makes this meditation on change in affairs of state remarkable, quite the reverse of bland, is the pained simplicity with which the Chorus sets out the whole matter of its bewilderment and grief at the divine ordering of history. Further, it is not merely a meditation on historical mutability, because the concept of the elect, of those who surely have God at their side, is at the centre of the Chorus's consciousness. Expectation that Milton would in some way reflect on the events of his lifetime is hardly denied or deflected by this choric ode; as usual the formal scope of the sentiments is broad, applicable in principle to Britain after the withdrawal of Rome or on the coming of the Normans, for example, not to say the story of Samson himself; but who surviving from high Common-wealth or Cromwellian office into the Restoration could have helped thinking, when he came to the list of punishments and fates at the end, 'under change of times', of the revolution of 1660 and all it meant? *Samson Agonistes* is no *roman-à-clef*, but, W. R. Parker to the contrary, it is not foolish to think of Cromwell, Ireton, Brad-shaw, Harrison, Hugh Peters, and others here, not to mention Milton himself.[20] What puts the last revolution at the centre of these general reflections is the way they gather point in relation to the known history of the poet himself. And notable in this choric passage is the almost customary distinction for Milton between 'the common rout' (l. 674) and 'the people' (l. 681): this characteristic dislocation, similar to speeches of Cromwell invoking the support of 'the people of England, the good people',[21] was the fatal weakness in Milton's defence of the regicide state, as Salmasius recognized.[22]

The general political remarks of the drama (passing over the political extenuations of Dalila which are rejected not as inherently wrong but as hypocritical) focus finally on conquest and command (ll. 1205–7). Here, though the sentiments are recognizably Miltonic (violence against conquest is justifiable), they do not easily fit the contemporary situation, in so far as the Stuart restoration, unlike the Commonwealth and Protectorate, was not established by con-quest. Here then the text, which to a substantial degree has been hospitable to contemporary application, marks a salient difference. While the debate about violence is relevant, the play stops short of being a full description of the times.

A final passage which commands attention here is that famous sequence of images comparing Samson to flame under ashes (l. 1691), 'an evening dragon' (l. 1692), an eagle (l. 1695), and, back to ashes and flame, to 'that self-begotten bird' the Phoenix, which, 'from out her ashy womb now teemed, | Revives, reflourishes, then

[20] See Christopher Hill, *Milton and the English Revolution* (1977), 435–6; W. R. Parker, *Milton: A Biography* (Oxford, 1968), i. 316–17.

[21] Oliver Cromwell, *Writings and Speeches*, ed. W. C. Abbott, iii. 453: 'all men, the best of men', (Cambridge, Mass., 1947).

[22] See Milton, *Prose Works*, ed. Wolfe, iv, part I, 113–14.

vigorous most | When most unactive deemed' (ll. 1699, 1793–5).
These may all be images capable of messianic interpretation, with
most prominent the Phoenix reminding of Samson as a type of
Christ, risen from his own death. Yet the emphasis of the images is
rather on terror and power than love, or even than the aloofness
above power of the Christ of *Paradise Regained*. The basis of the
image, the capacity of fire to lurk hidden only to rise as a terrible
destroyer, would remind Londoners of the Great Fire of 1667, and
perhaps what Dryden had made of the experience politically in his
Annus Mirabilis, where it is figured as 'some dire Usurper' surpris-
ing and (at first) overwhelming 'His Prince' (stanzas 213–20). In
these lines Milton's text appears to respond to recent experience and
perhaps to a prominent poem that dramatized it. His image affords
us an opportunity of transition to *Don Sebastian*, where it is also
used to suggest unexpected revolution after apparently final defeat:

BENDUCAR. A Secret party still remains
  Like Embers rak'd in ashes—wanting but
  A breath to blow aside th'involving dust,
  And then they blaze abroad.

                    (II. i. 75–9)[23]

What is common to the two poets here is the political substratum:
the knowledge of how defeat, secrecy, opportunity, can flare up into
a change of state. Milton builds on this foundation to give (at a
learned and hermeneutic level) a proleptic figure of Christ which
retains all the political terror latent in a fundamentally historical
image. Dryden too voices a political threat, but without, at this
point, reaching for Christian ratification. The new establishment in
the England of 1689 is, by analogy with the events of his drama, as
vulnerable as earlier supremacies to subversion by residual loyalty.

  By comparison with *Samson Agonistes, Don Sebastian* teems with
provocative political opinion, much of it topical, yet topical with a
difference from both Milton's practice and that of the pre-revol-
utionary Dryden. New readers of *Samson Agonistes*, remembering
Paradise Lost, would have been likely to look for symbolic autobio-
graphy; those first seeing or reading *Don Sebastian*, remembering
Absalom and Achitophel, The Hind and the Panther, and *The Duke
of Guise*, would have probably expected a 'parallel' with the times.

        [23] *Works*, xv. 104.

A consideration of political utterance in *Don Sebastian*, and then of its characters and structure, reveals how far the text allows and transforms this expectation. A salient example, noted by several commentators,[24] occurs in the mobile or crowd scene, in IV. iii, where Captain Mustapha addresses his ready rabble:

MUSTAPHA. Do you remember the glorious Rapines and Robberies you have committed? Your breaking open and gutting of Houses, your rummaging of Cellars, your demolishing of Christian Temples, and bearing off in triumph the superstitious Plate and Pictures, the Ornaments of their wicked Altars, when all rich Movables were sentenc'd for idolatrous, and all that was idolatrous was seiz'd?

(IV. iii. 124–30)[25]

This unmistakably recalls the mob violence against Roman Catholic chapels and houses in London, immediately after the flight of James II. But this is a Mohametan mob (Mohametans like Puritans hated idolatry and 'superstitious pictures') and the moment of self-recognition for Londoners confirms a running parallel in which Mohametans are Protestants, and Christians Catholics, and spurs on a continuous attack on rebellious dissenters and trimming, equivocating, Anglicans epitomized by the Mufti. Thus Antonio, the man of pleasure threatened with a whip in a slave-market, remarks: 'I see the Doctrine of Non-Resistance is never practis'd thoroughly but when a Man can't help himself' (I. i. 521–2). The Anglican doctrine of non-resistance to kings had been compromised, under James II, not by the peaceful protest of the Church of England at the king's pro-Catholic measures, but by the acquiescence of all but the Non-Jurors in the subsequent invasion by the Prince of Orange.[26] The point is expounded more widely and dramatically in the comic melodrama of an exchange between the new Emperor Muley-Moluch and his holy man, the Mufti. 'Cancel me that Marriage' demands the Emperor, on hearing that the princess he lusts after has married Don Sebastian, but the Mufti demurs, finding no warrant in the Alcoran. Taking him by the throat the Emperor asserts:

[24] J. R. Moore, 'Political Allusions in Dryden's Later Plays', *PMLA* 73 (Mar.–June 1958), 41–2; David Bywaters, 'Dryden and the Revolution of 1688: Political Parallel in *Don Sebastian*', *JEGP* 85 (July 1986), 363; J. A. Winn, *John Dryden and His World* (1987), 440.

[25] *Works*, xv. 173.

[26] J. P. Kenyon, *Revolution Principles: The Politics of Party, 1689–1720* (Cambridge, 1977), 2–3.

'Know I am Law' and threatens him with deprivation and death.
The Mufti then responds:

> 'Tis true, our Law forbids to wed a Christian;
> But it forbids you not to ravish her.
> You have a Conqueror's right upon your Slave.

> (III. i. 95–7)[27]

The Moorish Princess, Almeyda, was a convert to Christianity
before her marriage to Sebastian. The scene pointedly recalls
Dryden's treatment of Henry VIII in *The Hind and the Panther*
('Cancel me that Marriage' was after all the origin of the Anglican
Church) but also broadly mimes the most recent history of Church
and State in England as the Catholic Dryden saw it. With Dryden's
usual acute vision of the future it anticipates those arguments that
the success of William III must mean the approval of God (a very
Miltonic position) which were shortly to become notorious in the
contention of William Sherlock that William's conquest must by
definition be of God.[28] In this connection nearly all the religious
references of the drama take on strong contemporary significance,
under a comic masking that repeatedly says that Protestants are no
better than Turks: 'That your Emperor is a Tyrant is most manifest',
says the Mufti to the crowd, 'for you were born to be *Turks*, but he
has play'd the *Turk* with you; and is taking your *Religion* away' (IV.
iii. 81–3).[29]

   This announcement is one of several which prompt the realization
that while a consistent parallel may run through the play in regard
to Moslems and Christians and Protestants and Catholics, thus
giving a certain primacy in interpretation to matters of religion, no
such parallel is to be found in regard to the question of legitimate
kingship. The comment of the Mufti quoted above reminds one
irresistibly of the Catholic measures of King James II, but the ruler
here referred to in the play is the tyrant Emperor Muley-Moluch. If
any figure of the play is continuously a reminder of James II it is Don
Sebastian himself, a Christian, legitimate, hereditary king, suffering
the consequences of defeat overseas and away from his native

---

[27] *Works*, xv. 129.
[28] Howard Erskine-Hill, 'Literature and the Jacobite Cause: Was There a Rhetoric
of Jacobitism?', in Eveline Cruickshanks (ed.), *Ideology and Conspiracy: Aspects of
Jacobitism, 1689–1759* (Edinburgh, 1982), 50–2; George Every, SSM, *The High
Church Party, 1688–1718* (1956).
[29] *Works*, xv. 172.

kingdom. This is a point to which we will return. What is here to be learned is that the expectation of political parallel takes the interpreter of *Don Sebastian* some distance but not the whole way.

Other political remarks point to other political matters, though always linked to those of religion. Many of these focus on change of state in kingship and on the field of battle, as we might expect. Sebastian, defeated in the cause of Almeyda, legitimate Queen of the Africans in her own right, and a Christian convert, puts the providential question to her:

> And is't not strange, that Heav'n shou'd bless my Arms
> In common Causes, and desert the best?
> Now in your greatest, last extremity,
> When I wou'd ayd you most, and most desire it,
> I bring but Sighs, the succors of a Slave.
>
> (II. i. 511–15)[30]

Notable here is that the experience of having been, apparently, deserted by providence, is focused by the defeated champion not on his own desolation, but the need of another. This is a real contrast with Milton's opening presentation of Samson, though it should be recalled that the antecedents of Dryden's drama in seventeenth-century prose romance afford some precedent for regarding Almeyda as symbolic of the legal and Christian honour of England.[31] Dryden approaches the mood of *Samson* more closely in a speech of Almeyda herself in Act III:

> Farewell, my last *Sebastian*!
> I do not beg, I challenge Justice now.
> O Pow'rs, if Kings be your peculiar care,
> Why plays this Wretch with your Prerogative?
> Now flash him dead, now crumble him to ashes.
>
> (III. i. 312–16)[32]

---

[30] *Works*, xv. 118.
[31] Cf. the role of the Princess Cloria in Sir Percy Herbert's romance of that title (1661): see Paul Salzman, *English Prose Fiction, 1588–1700* (Oxford, 1985), 157–8. Annabel Patterson, *Censorship and Interpretation: The Conditions of Writing and Reading in Early Modern England* (Madison, 1984), in her chapter 'The Royal Romance', is one of the few recent commentators on political allusion in 17th-cent. literature to discuss the relatively neglected genre of prose romance.
[32] *Works*, xv. 136.

'This Wretch' is the Emperor Muley-Moluch, *de facto* monarch, by conquest. Again, there can be little doubt that the flight of King James and the triumph of the Prince of Orange are in the mind's eye here, focused by that crucial contemporary word 'Prerogative', by virtue of which alone King James had issued the Declarations of Indulgence which precipitated his fall. As in Milton, so here, the questioning of providence is far from occluding more contingent explanations of the turns of state. This is to be seen in the centrally important figure of Dorax, supporter of his king, Sebastian, through 'Fifteen hard Campaigns' (i. i. 91),[33] yet now a renegade in religion, and a fighter against Sebastian in the recent battle. The grievances of Dorax, which involve a measure of pride and a measure of misunderstanding, are disclosed later in the play: it is what he says about the tyrant on whose behalf he has just successfully fought that, as several commentators have noted,[34] bears so clearly on the affairs of 1688-9. Tempted by the treacherous courtier Benducar to betray his new monarch, Dorax, in a most revealing disclosure of conflicting views, cannot bring himself to do it:

He trusts us both; mark that, shall we betray him?
A Master who reposes Life and Empire
On our fidelity: I grant he is a Tyrant,
That hated name my nature most abhors;

. . . .

But, while he trusts me, 'twere so base a part
To fawn and yet betray, I shou'd be hiss'd
And whoop'd in Hell for that Ingratitude.
BENDUCAR. Consider well what I have done for you.
DORAX. Consider thou what thou woud'st have me do.
BENDUCAR. You've too much honour for a Renegade.
DORAX. And thou too little faith to be a Fav'rite.
    Is not the bread thou eat'st, the Robe thou wear'st,

33 *Works*, xv. 83.
34 Moore, 'Political Allusions in Dryden's Later Plays', 40; Bywaters, 'Dryden, the Revolution of 1688, and *Don Sebastian*', 359-60; Winn, *John Dryden*, 440-1. See also John Wallace, 'John Dryden's Last Plays and the Conception of a Heroic Society', in Perez Zagorin (ed.), *Culture and Politics from Puritanism to the Enlightenment* (Berkeley and Los Angeles, 1980), 115-23. Wallace's emphasis on generosity and obligation in late 17th cent. English society is especially apt when we notice how, from before the Restoration, the Duke of York seems to have attempted to build up a clientele of people, of all kinds, who were obliged to him. It did him some good in his years of crisis as king, but not enough to enable him to keep his throne. See also Winn, *John Dryden*, 441.

Thy Wealth, and Honours, all the pure indulgence
Of him thou wou'dst destroy?
And wou'd his Creature, nay his Friend betray him?
Why then no bond is left on human kind.

(II. i. 288–91, 296–307)[35]

Gratitude to a tyrant may seem no very strong ground for fidelity (certainly not to Milton and the contractualists), especially not when the tyrant in question (Muley-Moluch) is not the legitimate monarch in any case. Dorax is impressive at this moment because the 'Master' primarily in mind is James, deserted by so many he had trusted and honoured, and represented in this text chiefly by Sebastian, whom Dorax had betrayed. Dryden could then hardly have found a better way of commending the doctrine of political gratitude, uttered by a politician against himself, and in favour of a ruler so manifestly more atrocious than the pious and hardly tyrannical James II. Dorax's response to the temptation of Benducar is, of course, only a crucial stage in the tragic exposition which, through the play, is to bring him back to fidelity and Sebastian. So that any who saw in the quoted exchange a lesson of loyalty to William would, though not wrong in the short term, be wrong in the long term.

The issue between James and William is perhaps most sharply portrayed not in relation to Sebastian, but Muley-Moluch and Benducar. When the latter seizes his moment for supreme power, and to this end attempts to coerce Almeyda into marriage, she, in the same remarkable mobile scene, throws herself on the mercy of the mob, speaking to them as their lawful Queen:

Now *Affricans*,
He shows himself to you; to me he stood
Confest before, and own'd his Insolence
T'espouse my person, and assume the Crown,
Claym'd in my Right: for this he slew your Tyrant;
Oh no, he only chang'd him for a worse,
Imbas'd your Slavery by his own vileness,
And loaded you with more ignoble bonds:

(IV. iii. 250–7)[36]

This could hardly be more sharply topical, and yet is no simple mirror of the times. William claimed the English throne mainly

[35] *Works*, xv. 111.   [36] *Works*, xv. 178.

through his marriage to Mary, elder daughter of James, who thus betrayed a father's crown in favour of a husband's, together with the orthodox principle of male primogeniture which set a son before an elder daughter. That James had been a tyrant through use of force (the resort to the royal prerogative) was a Whig argument; that William secured the crown by force (his armed invasion) was a Jacobite view shared by Dryden. In each case the image of rape—an image of political and social violence almost invariably sharpened by its sexual meaning—was prominent in the opposing rhetoric. Whatever the sources of this rhetoric, *Don Sebastian* appears to be the first, major, post-revolutionary text to seize upon it and to deploy the sexual and political trope in a consistent and evidently influential way (see pp. 227–8 above for other examples). It was to remain a dominant concept and image in the public debate for over twenty years. Here the revelation of Almeyda's speech is that the people have overthrown one tyrant (Muley-Moluch) only to receive a worse (Benducar). Once again the sharp political application emerges without there having been any consistent political parallel: Whigs are enticed into seeing Muley-Moluch as James, momentarily, which leads them to see Benducar as William, and be told that he is the worse tyrant, having the same goals but more cunning. The view that, in 1689, England was out of the frying pan into the fire, was not uncommon.[37] Jacobites could see in this episode a dreadful example of what happened when a crown changed hands by coercion rather than succession: slavery. Williamites were pointed to this judgement too. Finally, each party was offered something in the figure of Almeyda. Williamites could reflect that Mary II had been regularly married to William of Orange before the English crown entered its crisis: no case of coercion there. Jacobites could reflect that this speech against the coercion of usurpers was delivered by a queen in her own right, not one who, acquiescing in conquest, pretended to be a queen. Almeyda would remind each party of Mary II, not because she is a historical portrait of the Stuart princess, but because she raised all the issues of Mary's historical role.

A final political comment marks the orientation of the play. It is by Sebastian to Dorax, who has just revealed to him his true identity:

[37] See e.g. Charlwood Lawton, *A French Conquest Neither Desirable Nor Practicable* (1693).

I have not yet forgot I am a King;
Whose Royall Office is redress of Wrongs:
If I have wrong'd thee, charge me face to face;
I have not yet forgot I am a Soldier.

(IV. iii. 397–400)[38]

Not yet forgot I am a King: this speaks of legitimate kings in exile or deposed. When followed up, in the plain pattern of the speech, and after the military metaphor, with: not yet forgot I am a soldier, this must in 1689 be a clear reminder of James, a 'warlike prince' with much military experience; and the speech is of course also a clear statement of the duties of kings. A little later in the same scene Sebastian commands the renegade Dorax: '. . . know me for thy King' and Dorax replies: 'Too well I know thee; but for King no more: | This is not *Lisbonne* . . .'. I shall argue that Sebastian more or less regularly reminds us of James; but, taking these two moments as a local allusion alone, there can be no doubt that they point to the contemporary political situation.

II

The chief figures of the two dramas fortify the political concerns of their authors more prominently displayed in uttered political sentiment. How close, or distant, were the minds that conceived, for example, Manoa—and Alvarez and Dorax; Dalila—and Johayma and Almeyda? The Chorus of Hebrews and the mobile provide a different basis of comparison, while, dominating the action of each play, their two great protagonists, Samson and Sebastian, command our attention. Even such selective listing brings out the austerity of structure in *Samson Agonistes*, the copiousness of *personae dramatis* in *Don Sebastian*. It also reveals the comic aspects of Dryden's vision. Female deception is allowed a due and often cynically amusing role in Johayma, in a play which also displays innocent sexual attraction in Morayma and Antonio and a high royal heroine in Almeyda. By contrast with Milton's grave Chorus, Dryden's political crowd, crucial in a single scene, is full of comic intelligence in its unscrupulous volatility. It is *so* receptive that it seems to parody the assumptions of all those who seek to exploit it. Dorax refers

[38] *Works*, xv. 183.

contemptuously to the crowd at the end of this scene (IV. iii. 353–8);[39] this is Dryden's characterization of Dorax. His own presentation of the crowd has a different tone.

Despite these differences it seems fair to say that each poet creates character as symbolic type. This does not preclude considerable psychological exposition, especially in Samson and Sebastian, and in figures such as Manoa and Dorax. Manoa is perhaps the active inner exile. He represents the attitude of accommodation to alien rule while never endorsing it, and his skill is to ameliorate the present situation by personal diplomacy, a role he plays right up to the death of his son, and despite Samson's rejection of his proposal (ll. 487–540). One might think Manoa the most near to naturalistic of all the figures of Milton's drama, and it need hardly be stressed that Milton must have been indebted to those who acted as Manoas on his behalf early in the Restoration. This key role of Manoa is not in the biblical narrative. It is possible that Milton knew of a Manoa in Admiral Sir William Penn, who used his connections with the Duke of York to attempt to release from prison and jeopardy his son, William Penn, the then warrior-like young puritan who would become the great Quaker. (Both Penns had, by 1670, ample experience of imprisonment, and release through good offices.)[40] Manoa is the honest courtier surviving in an alien supremacy. Dryden's Alvarez is a similar type, but his diplomatic solution is to save his master from a sin his master does not yet know is committed. In each case the poet recognizes the goodwill of such men but sees a limit to what they can achieve.

Dalila, like Harapha and the Officer, is a less continuous figure in the drama than Manoa or (of course) the Chorus of Hebrews. Confined by the simple classical structure Milton develops from the *Prometheus* and *Oedipus Coloneus*, she has small opportunity to engage our interest in her response to an unfolding series of crises, as Almeyda does in *Don Sebastian*. She epitomizes fatal temptation, and, as Milton handles the episode, one might wonder whether her gender is more than the alluring form of that temptation, woman as the temptress, though the usually austere idiom of *Samson Agonis-*

---

[39] *Works*, xv. 181.

[40] See *DNB* in each case. The earliest biography of William Penn the younger would appear to be that prefaced to *A Collection of the Works of William Penn*, 2 vols. (1726), i. 1–238. The life of Penn senior is found in Granville Penn, *Memorials of the Professional Life and Times of Sir William Penn, Knt . . .*, 2 vols. (1833). See Appendix III.

tes reaches for remarkable lavishness and delicacy in her presentation. Her function in the tight spiritual and psychological structure of the drama is so evident (Samson must be put to the test again and withstand, if he is ever again to receive special grace from Heaven) that it is easy to ignore the slight and uncertain motivation she has for visiting him at all (once again the biblical story affords no precedent). Almeyda, courageous queen and lover, belongs, like much else in *Don Sebastian*, to the more spacious world of prose romance. She has relative autonomy by comparison with Dalila, and, in Dryden's fable, there is parity of sin between herself and her lover Sebastian: each enters, impetuously, unknowingly, into an incestuous marriage. It is not, as in Milton, a case of one less deceived than the other. As queen and Christian convert, doomed in the act of returning the love of a Christian king and warrior, all that is most worthy of her love, Almeyda holds the bewilderment, despair, and idealism of the play within her theatrical arc. She is a perfect example in Dryden, not of the political figure of the *Absalom and Achitophel* kind, but of the political figure deeply imbued with wider experience.

With Harapha, an addition to the biblical story of Samson, we enter the world of Almansor, Morat, or Muley-Moluch—as is often pointed out.[41] The *miles gloriosus* as theatrical type strongly informs this character, a fastidious (ll. 1106–7), lordly giant, sensitive to insult, but the core of his significance is as a representative of arrogant conquest. In this play it is his claim that Samson's god has deserted him that cuts deepest, yet Samson can respond to this taunt of the cavalier giant, no longer with direct physical threat, but with an acknowledgement of his own error, and his wish to be worthy to fight for God again. Again, Milton's single-minded focus on Samson provides in Harapha just what is needed to bring him towards his final act. *Don Sebastian*'s Muley-Moluch, for his part, represents, in the end almost pathetically, the vulnerability of bloodthirsty, unashamed, conquest. If Samson sends Harapha away crestfallen, Muley-Moluch is too pliable in the hands of his cunning courtier Benducar. As the latter puts it: 'I can sin but once to seize the Throne. | All after Acts are sanctify'd by pow'r' (IV. ii. 187–8).[42]

[41] Eugene M. Waith, *The Herculean Hero* (1962).
[42] *Works*, xv. 161.

The type of the corrupt courtier informs Benducar, as the *miles gloriosus* Harapha. Cunning as he is, empire is snatched away from him at the very moment of triumph because he has not foreseen the effect on the crowd of a speech by their true queen. It is, however, in his sinuous approaches to this moment that Benducar displays his remarkable theatrical life. Within the first fifty lines of the play Benducar, courtier to the new conqueror, has laid his plot to bring in a more pliable prince:

MULEY-ZEDAN. My Father!
BENDUCAR. My future King! (auspicious *Muley-Zeydan:*)
    Shall I adore you? No, the place is publick;
    I worship you within.

. . . .

                    [*after Muley-Zeydan's exit*]
    Him I can manage, till I make him odious
    By some unpopular act, and then dethrone him.
                                (I. i. 39–42, 63–4)[43]

Here he is the Achitophel to Absalom, Shaftesbury to Monmouth. We follow then how Benducar, as chief minister and favourite of Muley-Moluch, advises him in such a way as to appear the pattern of loyalty while steadily betraying him. He is eloquent (and sometimes barely beyond the frontier of comedy) in his treachery:

BENDUCAR. The thoughts of Kings are like religious Groves,
    The Walks of muffled Gods:
                                (II. i. 2–3)

BENDUCAR. [*in disorder*]
    . . . The Name of Treason shakes my honest Soul
                                (II. i. 68–9)

BENDUCAR. If I must personate this seeming Villain,
    Remember 'tis to serve you.
                                (II. i. 108–9)[44]

Benducar becomes the perfect double agent—but in his own ultimate interest. And here he does not fully resemble Shaftesbury, always more open in his strategies, but, as J. R. Moore seems to have been the first to point out, Robert Spencer, Earl of Sunderland, 'premier minister' of James II,[45] a politic Catholic convert, and

---

[43] *Works*, xv. 81.   [44] *Works*, xv. 101–5.
[45] John Evelyn, *Diary*, ed. E. S. De Beer (Oxford, 1955), iv. 501.

encourager of the King's politically fatal religious policies.[46] On James's fall Sunderland fled to Holland, whence he issued his apologia, *The Earl of Sunderland's Letter to a Friend*, copies of which Evelyn was distributing to his parliamentary friends in March 1689. It was a denunciation of '*the Romish party and Others for the Subverting of the Protestant Religion and the Laws of the Kingdom*', as its full title ran, correctly implying that Sunderland now denied his conversion to Rome.[47] He was, as anyone might see (and Dryden had had some acquaintance with him in the past),[48] managing his transition into the favour of William, apparently achieved by 24 April 1691.[49] There is thus recent historical experience behind this character; the generalized type of the treacherous courtier is sharpened by specific memory. It is not, however, clear that Benducar is a *portrait* of Sunderland.[50] The text of Dryden's play responds to the Sunderland phenomenon more broadly, for one of the most salient features of his recent career, his facility in religious conversion, is taken up in the Mufti's readiness to trim religious opinion to political demand, and in the conversion from Christianity of Dorax.

If Benducar walks the tightrope between the sinister and dextrously comic, the Mufti is a figure of contemptuous comedy altogether. To the recent suggestion that he portrays Burnet,[51] perhaps the most pro-Williamite Anglican, one may respond by saying that he better represents the Anglican Church itself; the Mufti is a comically staged development of those features Dryden had found in 'The Lady of the spotted-muff': the Panther herself in *The Hind and the Panther* (i. 572). Her special alliance with power, her love of a comfortable, uncelibate, establishment, are Dryden's focus here, and nearly all the satiric thrusts that suggest Burnet, suggest him as a representative of his Church as seen by the Catholic Dryden. (Only

[46] Moore, 'Political Allusions in Dryden's Later Plays', 40–1; Bywaters, 'Dryden, the Revolution of 1688, and *Don Sebastian*', 362–3.

[47] Published in *Somers Tracts*, 16 vols. (1748–51), ed. Sir Walter Scott, 13 vols. (1808–15), x. 321–4. See J. P. Kenyon, *Robert Spencer, Earl of Sunderland* (1958), chs. 4–7, for Sunderland's role in the reign of James II.

[48] Evelyn, *Diary*, ed. De Beer, iv. 317–18 (Evelyn and Dryden dined at the Earl of Sunderland's in distinguished company, on 17 June 1683).

[49] Evelyn, v. 49 n.

[50] Winn, *John Dryden*, 617 n. 39, rightly argues against an 'identification' of Benducar with Sunderland.

[51] See Bywaters, 'Dryden, the Revolution of 1688, and *Don Sebastian*', 360–2. The strength of Bywaters's discussion, however, lies in his recognition that 'the Portuguese and the Moors represent the Catholic and Protestant subjects of England' (354).

later, in his tale of the Poor Parson, would Dryden recognize the
integrity of the Anglican Non-Juror position.)

With Dorax Dryden moves decisively out of the comic ranges of
his drama. Conversion in his case sprang from hatred—or what he
took to be hatred—of Sebastian. In Dryden's broad, baroque depic-
tion of the relations of loyalty and religious faith, Dorax is a figure,
not only of the sharpest contemporary relevance, but one who is
treated so as to have considerable mythic implication. A less com-
mon type than the braggart, conqueror, or cunning courtier, Dorax
is, eventually, the repentant deserter. Played by Betterton himself,
the leading tragic actor of the day, Dorax moves through the play in
quest of honourable revenge and, with Almeyda and Sebastian,
provides its tragic focus. Dryden's art with Dorax is to use him as
an effective witness for the loyalty he has abandoned. 'My Master',
he asks, 'By what title?'

> Because I happened to be born where he
> Happen'd to be a King?
>
> (I. i. 86–8)[52]

But he goes on from this reductive scepticism to speak with pain of
his years of service to his king, and of Sebastian's qualities:

> Yet I must do him right; he was a Man,
> Above man's height, ev'n towring to *Divinity*.
> Brave, pious, generous, great and liberal.
>
> (I. i. 101–3)[53]

Hard as it may be to credit in retrospect, this was how James seemed
from his later years of exile in the Low Countries and Scotland until
his accession, especially to those of his party and interest. Dorax's
admiration of his king becomes clear almost in the same breath as
he says he hates him. The fount of this conflict is uncovered in IV.
iii, the scene so admired by Sir Walter Scott, in which Dorax charges
Sebastian with 'Inhumane Tyranny' (l. 386) and Sebastian gives his
own account of his breach with his old supporter and servant.
Ingratitude is Dorax's accusation. Disappointed of reward after his
long service, he was jealous of Enriquez, his successful competitor in
love, and apparently the King's favourite. The unwarrior-like Enri-
quez nevertheless died in battle protecting the body of his king

---

[52] *Works*, xv. 83.   [53] *Works*, xv. 83.

(there may here be a reminiscence of the death of Falmouth, on the ship of James, Duke of York, off Lowestoft). At this revelation all Dorax's accusations fall. Enriquez was as worthy and loyal as he had been himself; indeed Dorax covets his death. At this point he repents; his imminent fight with his sovereign is halted; Sebastian forgives him.

It is not my purpose here to display the remarkable dramaturgy and powerful poetry of this scene, but to note some of the features of the situation disclosed. It is redolent of court politics, and here it is relevant to recall that Sunderland's conversion to Rome was his last desperate throw to retain power and his master's favour. James's court was riven between the counsel of the loyal Protestants, and those of the moderate, and of the hard-line, Catholics, these last led by the handsome, courtier-like, but injudicious Earl of Melfort, who had, however, gone into exile with James. Something of Sunderland's experience is picked up in Dorax, and if the story of Dorax, Sebastian, and Enriquez reads like prose romance there is much court reality behind it. No doubt this is why prose romance continued to be read. The court of James II in particular resembles a late honour society, so many of his supporters having been steadily elevated from comparative obscurity in recognition of their ability and personal devotion to their patron, from far back during Charles II's reign. In such an honour society, service and gratitude are essential to the political bond, and Dorax's resentment was caused by another's being preferred before him, despite his own service.[54] Thus described, resentment at the promotion of another begins to recall something greater. The association has been prepared by Benducar's reference, in I. i. 130–1,[55] to Lucifer's drawing a 'third part' of the 'Heav'ns'. That was said of Sebastian's side, but then it was Benducar who drew the analogy. In IV. iii, Sebastian asks Dorax to judge who best deserves his favour:

> I knew you both; (and durst I say) as Heaven
> Foreknew among the shining Angell host
> Who would stand firm, who fall.
>
> (IV. iii. 581–3)[56]

In a moment Dorax embraces the simile, 'Alonzo', he says, alluding to his name when he was still a Christian,

[54] See Wallace, 'John Dryden's Last Plays and the Conception of a Heroic Society'.
[55] *Works*, xv. 84.   [56] *Works*, xv. 189.

> *Alonzo* was too kind a name for me.
> Then, when I fought and conquer'd with your Armes,
> In that blest Age I was the man you nam'd:
> Till rage and pride debas'd me into *Dorax*;
> And lost like *Lucifer*, my name above.
>
> (IV. iii. 617–21)[57]

Aware of the Miltonic example at least since he attempted *The State of Innocence* (composed by 1674), Dryden has here responded more creatively to it. In Dorax the traitor and renegade he has taken the qualities of Milton's Satan, the prowess, pride, hatred, and residual recognition of goodness, and, in this world of royalist romance, has believably turned the example. Here a potentially Satanic figure is reconciled to what is godly in his king:

> DORAX. O stop this headlong Torrent of your goodness:
>   It comes too fast upon a feeble Soul,
>   Half drown'd in tears, before;
>
> (IV. iii. 628–30)[58]

Christian epic is thus invoked—though in a cause which would have provoked Milton's angry sarcasm—to commend an example of repentant loyalty. J. R. Moore and David Bywaters are surely right to see in the career of Dorax an appeal to the many Protestant leaders and noblemen who had deserted James II in 1688—particularly perhaps men like John Churchill, and the Earl of Dartmouth, whom he had raised from nothing—to return to their allegiance.[59] That this is no simple political appeal, however, may be seen from what befalls Sebastian himself in the last act of Dryden's tragedy. But first we must turn back to Milton's Samson.

III

Physical champion though he is, Samson's role in Milton's drama is that of a vessel of grace. No predestinarian Calvinist,[60] Milton has

---

[57] *Works*, xv. 190.   [58] *Works*, xv. 190–2.

[59] Moore, 'Political Allusions in Dryden's Later Plays', 40; Bywaters, 'Dryden, the Revolution of 1688, and *Don Sebestian*', 359–60. See *DNB* on John Churchill and the Earl of Dartmouth.

[60] Radzinowicz, *Towards Samson Agonistes*, 339, on the 'contingent predestination' of Milton's drama.

no vision of the religiously unregenerate nevertheless being arbitrarily elect. Samson must make good the causes of his fall, before, however unworthy he might still be, God can make him his champion again. The five classical episodes of this drama bring Samson to the point of this readiness, as the first four acts of *Don Sebastian* bring Dorax to reconciliation with his king. This process of psychological and spiritual growth (an orthodoxy of Milton criticism not quite unchallenged)[61] brings him from blame of others to self-blame, in the episodes of the Hebrews and of Manoa; from near despair to a renewing moral self-confidence, in the episode of Dalila; to a spirit of resistance newly attentive to God's will, in the episode of Harapha; while the important episode of the Officer, that most functional of all figures in the drama, begins to alert him to Hamlet's recognition that 'The readiness is all' (v. ii. 168). Such a summary ignores much significant fluctuation of mind, but it is not seriously misleading: the drama thus acts out the self-admonishment found early in the opening soliloquy, living out the precepts, rather as Prince Hal acts out, not without heat and dust, the programme of behaviour he proposes for himself at the end of Act I, scene ii, of *1 Henry IV*.

The champion Samson as the self-betrayed and enthralled people of England, not now as in *Areopagitica* a champion awakening to his strength for the first time, but one who recovers it in a new form after dire defeat, is a resonant mythic figure. He embraces the royalist myth of the historical John Milton, physical blindness now serving as a metaphor for the misguidedness of the people of England, only to turn it as the drama develops against the Restoration supremacy. The bond between Milton's vision of himself and his vision of the people of England serves to point the contemporary relevance of the way the drama seizes on royalists' vision and uses it as a weapon against them. He certainly also appeals to those who knew the Old Testament story of Samson through the Bible, and also through popular sixteenth-century and seventeenth-century ballad narrative.[62] The desolation of the utterly self-betrayed and

---

[61] Most recently, perhaps, by S. E. Fish in a series of lectures on *Samson Agonistes*, delivered at the National Humanities Center, North Carolina, 1988–9. Fish argued that we cannot know anything about the mind of Samson.

[62] William Empson, *Milton's God* (1961), 217; Hill, *Milton and the English Revolution*, ch. 31; Andrew Milner, *John Milton and the English Revolution*, (Totowa, NJ, 1981), 181–2. (Milner's argument is turned, overconfidently, to a solution to the problem of the date of *Samson Agonistes*. But he is surely correct to

defeated can, with the bestowal of God's light and grace, take on terrible power. It is this simple and appalling power which, in the daylight vision of the Hebrew *nuntius*, is revealed at the culmination of the drama. After the physical constraint and spiritual remorse of the great body of the play, the agonized questioning of providence, self-questioning, accusation of others, self-accusation, even the dubious sounds of catastrophe beyond the presented scene, the beginning of the Messenger's formal narrative constitutes an extraordinary release:

> Occasions drew me early to this city,
> And as the gates I entered with sun-rise
> The morning trumpets festival proclaimed
> Through each high street: little I had dispatched
> When all abroad was rumoured that this day
> Samson should be brought forth to show the people
> Proof of his mighty strength in feats and games;
> I sorrowed at his captive state, but minded
> Not to be absent at that spectacle.
> The building was a spacious theatre,
> Half round on two main pillars vaulted high,
> With seats where all the lords and each degree
> Of sort, might sit in order to behold,
> The other side was open, where the throng
> On banks and scaffolds under sky might stand;
> I among these aloof obscurely stood.

(ll. 1596–1611)

But the spring is steadily tightened again as the narrative focuses once more on Samson, not now in the mental theatre of Milton's Hebrew classical drama only, but also in the great state theatre of the Philistines, recalling theatres for gladiatorial display in ancient Rome, and, with its strong pillars, the emblem of their ordered, hierarchical society, as architecture was often taken to be.[63] Here he performed for his conquerors, as the Messenger from his high and distanced position saw. Here—it was afterwards reported—Samson asked to rest. Here the Messenger saw him in the posture of prayer,

---

see the publication of the drama as a political challenge.) On the ballad Samson, see *The Roxburghe Ballads*, ed. William Chappell, FSA (1824), ii. 459–64.

[63] See Howard Erskine-Hill, 'Heirs of Vitruvius', in id. and Anne Smith (eds.), *The Art of Alexander Pope* (1979), 144–56.

> with head awhile inclined,
> And eyes fast fixed he stood, as one who prayed,
> Or some great matter in his mind revolved.

(ll. 1636–8)

Such is the scrupulous observation of a stranger. The reader or onlooker at the drama, privy not only to Samson's exchanges with others, which the Chorus of Hebrews know, but also to the opening soliloquy, which they do not know, can have small doubt that Samson both prayed and 'some great matter in his mind revolved'. This is the moment of bestowal of divine grace. Only now is he regenerate, for grace can never be won but only prepared for and bestowed. The word 'revenge', given to Samson himself at this point in the biblical narrative (Judges 16:28) is taken from him by Milton and given to the Chorus; likewise occluded here is the question of suicide ('Let me die with the Philistines': Judges 16:30), it having been explored and exhausted earlier, when we saw Samson develop beyond the desire of death.

And now the Semichorus utter their savage ode of triumph:

> While their hearts were jocund and sublime
> Drunk with idolatry, drunk with wine.

(ll. 1669–70)

The first Semichorus halt at their vision of the Philistines 'with blindness internal struck' (l. 1686). The theme of blindness is then taken up by the second Semichorus:

> But he though blind of sight,
> Despised and thought extinguished quite,
> With inward eyes illuminated
> His fiery virtue roused
> From ashes into sudden flame.

(ll. 1687–91)

We now reach (in the process of the play) those images of 'evening dragon', 'eagle', phoenix, and fire considered earlier in this discussion.[64] When the Chorus are, as here, characters in the drama—

---

[64] It is sometimes considered that Milton uses the word 'holocaust' (l. 1702) in the modern sense; indeed Murray's *Oxford English Dictionary* says so (sense 2c). This seems not to be the case, the crucial word being 'erewhile': Samson's life *has been* like a holocaust, or burnt offering, until his final moment of grace and power. The idea of the burnt offering was probably picked up from the story of Samson's birth in Judges 13:23.

Milton's classical chorus is not like those in Shakespeare's *Romeo and Juliet* or *Henry V*—no quasi-authorial voice pronounces the end. This is quite traditional. The Chorus cannot be demonstrated to utter Milton's whole truth; that they are meant to utter some truth, however, it would be merely perverse to deny. Their hymn of triumph is a hymn of hate and warning. The triumph of God and his elect nation spells destruction to the prevailing order, and if we attempt to soften this by postulating an unspoken compassion for the dead, a resistance in the career of Samson to interpretation of any kind, or even an intertextual contrast with *Paradise Regained* in which the savagery of *Samson Agonistes* is 'placed', we shall emasculate the last poetic work Milton published. It is not in the end very Christian, but in the depths and intensity of its sheer primitive triumph it is unique in English literature, and perhaps nearer to early Old Testament religion ('I will sing to the Lord, for He hath triumphed gloriously; The horse and his rider he hath thrown into the sea': Exodus 15:1) and to Athenian tragedy, than anything else the English seventeenth century can afford.

IV

While both *Samson* and *Don Sebastian* open with battle in the background and the protagonist a prisoner, only *Samson* culminates in physical violence. *Don Sebastian* culminates not in destruction but withdrawal from the world. This is generated by something very different from the process of Milton's drama; if *Samson* constitutes a drawing away from error and sin as it approaches divine violence, *Don Sebastian* impetuously consummates, as the centre of its action, the unknowingly incestuous love felt by Sebastian and Almeyda before the battle in which they suffer military overthrow. Dryden's art of revelation is, however, strategic. Our first impression of Sebastian is of his Christian stoical courage as, a prisoner and in mean habit, he draws the black lot which means death. As he accepts this lot he announces his kingship:

> Then there's no more to manage! if I fall
> It shall be like my self; a setting Sun
> Shou'd leave a track of Glory in the Skies.

Behold *Sebastian* King of *Portugal*.

(I. i. 338–41)[65]

He is a proud spirit, 'Souls know no Conquerors' (l. 369), but still moved to compassion for those who fell fighting for him in battle:

> Wou'd·I had a Soul
> For each of these: How gladly wou'd I pay
> The Ransom down: But since I have but one,
> 'Tis a King's life, and freely 'tis bestowed.
> Not your false Prophet, but eternal Justice
> Has destin'd me the Lot, to dye for these:
> 'Tis fit a Sovereign so shou'd pay such Subjects;
> For Subjects such as they are seldom seen,
> Who not forsook me at my greatest need;
> Nor the base Lucre sold their Loyalty,
> But shar'd my dangers to the last event,
> And fenc'd 'em with their own.

(I. i. 387–400)[66]

As a by-product of its expression of compassion, this speech glances at what was notorious in James's situation in Jacobite eyes: his desertion by so many who had been indebted to him. Less obvious, save in the light of the play's whole action, is the almost too heroic style with which Sebastian speaks of death and sees his royal role as virtually redemptive.

In Act II, in response to Muley-Moluch's threat if not to marry then to rape Almeyda, she and Sebastian reaffirm their love, and consider, and in Christian spirit reject, the notion of heroic suicide. As Sebastian says, charging a dramatic irony which is to be felt in Act V,

> *Brutus* and *Cato* might discharge their Souls,
> And give 'em Furlo's for another World:
> But we, like Centry's, are oblig'd to stand
> In starless Nights, and wait the 'pointed hour.

(II. i. 526–9)[67]

To Almeyda's wonderful response to this instruction (does Milton give so fine a speech to a woman?):

> If shunning ill be good, then Death is good
> To those who cannot shun it but by Death:

[65] *Works*, xv. 92.   [66] *Works*, xv. 93–4.   [67] *Works*, xv. 119.

> Divines but peep on undiscover'd Worlds,
> And draw the distant Landshape as they please:
> But who has e'er returned from those bright Regions,
> To tell their Manners, and relate their Laws?
> I'll venture landing on that happy shoar
> With an unsully'd Body, and white Mind;
> If I have err'd, some kind Inhabitant
> Will pity a stray'd Soul, and take me home.
>
> (II. i. 530–9)[68]

Sebastian now, with a sophistry the full implications of which emerge only at the play's end, slides his Christian instruction against suicide into persuasion to human love, albeit love to be consummated in marriage:

> Beware of Death, thou canst not dye unperjur'd,
> And leave an unaccomplish'd Love behind:
> Thy Vows are mine; nor will I quit my claim:
> The tyes of Minds are but imperfect Bonds,
> Unless the Bodies joyn to seal the Contract.
>
> (II. i. 540–4)[69]

Before his urging prevails, the two debate the warnings, mysterious, or apparently contradictory, which they have heard against their marriage. The play is here close to *Oedipus Tyrannus* and the Dryden/Lee *Oedipus*, though, unfortunately, the warnings are crudely handled, as is some of the poetry in this specific area of the play. Not so the dramatic irony when Almeyda speaks of her love for Sebastian:

> Mine is a flame so holy, and so clear,
> That the white taper leaves no soot behind;
> No smoak of Lust; but chaste as Sisters love,
> When coldly they return a Brothers kiss,
> Without the zeal that meets at lovers mouths.
>
> (II. i. 576–80)[70]

Through the plotting of Benducar, and the cupidity of the Mufti, the courage of Sebastian and Almeyda attains, by the second half of IV. iii, mastery of the situation. Then occurs the *éclaircissement* between Dorax and Sebastian, in which light is cast not on his love,

---

[68] *Works*, xv. 119.   [69] *Works*, xv. 119.   [70] *Works*, xv. 119–20.

as in the previous two acts, but his justice and forgiveness as a
master. All is now set for that moment of precarious joy which
opens Act v:

DORAX. Joy is on every face, without a Cloud:
  As, in the scene of opening Paradice,
  The whole Creation danc'd at their new being:
  Pleas'd to be what they were; pleas'd with each other.

(v. i. 1–4)[71]

It is with the re-entry of the released Alvarez that all the warnings
and omens, some natural, some contrived, some verging on the
blatant, begin to be fulfilled and Sebastian finds himself an Oedipus,
Almeyda his sister. It certainly cannot be said that the revelation of
incest is arbitrarily added; warnings and omens apart, the headlong
courage of both brother and sister now becomes explicable, and is
now less admiringly displayed in a more than Oedipus and Jocasta-
like contempt for the selfless representations of Alvarez. To his
explanation of the sin of Sebastian's father, Sebastian bursts out:

  Base groveling Soul, who know'st not honours worth;
  But weigh'st it out in mercenary Scales;
  The Secret pleasure of a generous Act,
  Is the great minds great bribe.
ALVAREZ. Show me that King, and I'le believe the Phoenix.
  But knock at your own breast, and ask your Soul
  If those fair fatall eyes, edg'd not your Sword,
  More than your Fathers charge, and all your vows?
  If so, and so your silence grants it is,
  Know King, your Father had, like you, a Soul;
  And Love is your Inheritance from him.

(v. i. 298–308)[72]

Alvarez has recognized the nature, not so much of Sebastian's
motives, but of the emotions that fired them. Love rather than
disinterested chivalry spurred him in the fight. Once the proof of
incest has gone home, Sebastian's physical impetuosity turns on
himself. His horror at his own sin now drives him towards that very
suicide (cf. II. i. 530–1)[73] which the lovers had rejected before.
  The final turn of the tragedy occurs when the reconciled Dorax
urges that Sebastian be not prevented from suicide but allowed to

[71] *Works*, xv. 192.   [72] *Works*, xv. 202.   [73] *Works*, xv. 119.

kill himself. Sebastian hails him as 'My last, my only Friend' (l. 480). Once again he may be thought to speak lightly of death, the implication of which is brought out in some highly effective, terse, dialogue between the two. Death, says Sebastian, is 'but a petty reparation too; | But all I have to give.'

DORAX. Your pardon, Sir;
   You may do more, and ought.
SEBASTIAN. What, more than death?
DORAX. Death? Why that's Children's sport: a Stage-Play, Death.
   We Act it every Night we go to bed. . . .

   .   .   .   .

SEBASTIAN. To expiate this, can I do more than dye?
DORAX. O yes: you must do more; you must be damned. . . .

   .   .   .   .

SEBASTIAN. How, damn'd?
DORAX. Why, is that News?

(v. i. 501–17)[74]

Dorax's tactics have been to bring home to Sebastian the spiritual consequence of 'self-Murder' (l. 517), a deliberate sin which unknowing incest, if not knowingly prolonged thereafter, is not. Sebastian is thus driven to propose his only other course: 'To live alone to Heav'n: and dye to her': 'to turn an Anchoret' (ll. 545–6). Praised now by Dorax as 'A Soul fix'd high, and capable of Heav'n' (l. 558), Sebastian thus becomes the hidden king of Sebastianism: the old master whose return his people will long for almost an age after.

The problem which now confronts the commentator on the play is to discover how the copious reference to contemporary affairs of state can cohere with the more evidently tragic character of the incest plot which comes to the fore in Act V. One recourse is to deny or attempt to minimize the political reference, making of it a minor distraction, chiefly in the *mobile* scene, from an enduring tragic concern of Dryden which transcends the political. This is the policy of the Clark editors.[75] The trouble with this is that Sebastian, Dorax, and Almeyda move through the play as political figures, though not, to be sure, political figures only. Further, political concern and the well-being of Sebastian's kingdom are consistently represented in

---

[74] *Works*, xv. 210.
[75] Specifically Earl Miner, *ibid.* 404. One must sympathize with a desire to resist the premature limitation of the play's meaning, but there is no reason why contemporary political allusion should not open out into further meanings of the text.

Act v by the now important figure of Alvarez. In justice to the possibility that Dryden's play might be coherent, some more comprehensive critical formula must be sought. Such a formula is, in all probability, suggested by the contemporary response of a hostile critic, who wrote of the play,

> Which abdicated laureate brings
> In praise of abdicated kings.[76]

It is now well known that in 1689 the majority of those who did not wish to see King James return, or who, in tragic conflict, set Church above Crown, settled for 'de facto theory' and the fiction that the King had abdicated, leaving the throne vacant.[77] The opportunity for a contemptuous thrust against Dryden was afforded by recognition of an allusion to James in the figure of Sebastian, not primarily the Sebastian of the earlier acts but the spiritual as well as martial hero who renounces his throne in Act V. Indeed a general, idealizing, allusion in Sebastian to James seems to run through the text: in a drama so filled with references to the Williamite revolution, and of appropriate reflections upon it, Sebastian is its one legitimate king, a warrior monarch who has lost his throne. (That sentiments relevant to the rebellion against James have been uttered in the rising against Muley-Moluch is not denied, but *Don Sebastian* is not 'a parallel'.)

This returns us to the questioning of defeat so central to *Paradise Lost* and *Samson Agonistes*, and raised explicitly by both Sebastian and Almeyda in Dryden's play. At the simplest level people ask the question: what secret sin causes the apparently virtuous and pious to be overthrown under providence? At a level more appropriate to the complex awareness of *Don Sebastian* it may be suggested that the theme of unknowing incest works as a metaphor for the inexplicable defeat of truth and right within a providential vision of history. For a papist particularly, reflecting on the overthrow of a papist prince and the consequence for those loyal to him, the idea of unknowing incest might express that terrible proximity of love for what seemed most to warrant love with a breathtakingly swift defeat.

Such an hypothesis, if apparently far-fetched, has some support from the firm ground of the character of Sebastian. Despite the overt

---

[76] John Dryden, *Four Tragedies*, ed. L. Beaurline and Fredson Bowers (1967), 281.
[77] Kenyon, *Revolution Principles*, 21–34.

praise for this prince which runs through the play, its progressive dramatic revelation displays, not indeed base or sinful motives in the protagonist, but motives a good deal more self-interested and per-haps self-admiring than have been professed. We have seen Alvarez bring these to light. The heroic Sebastian and his chivalric enter-prise—an enterprise to support a convert to the true faith—have been in some measure flawed. And despite his justice and generosity Sebastian has been, almost to the end, a primarily physical hero. He really does not fear death, and his readiness to take his own life is, as Dorax perceives, almost an easy gesture. He has not yet thought beyond death, as Almeyda had begun to do in the love scene in II. i. What the incest theme brings into intense drama is what might otherwise have been the unremarkable general reflection that the best of rights, the most heroic of enterprises, and the holiest of aims, can be brought to nothing by human frailty. Samson and Sebastian both have great pride, which history humbles, and Samson's self-admonishment: 'O impotence of mind, in body strong!' (l. 52) has some bearing on the later hero. Each dramatist uses all his resources to enlarge a true but trite moral into the tragic life of history, and one way in which this was done was by remembering the times and aiming at affairs of state as they currently were.

Some differences between the two tragedies need not, perhaps, concern us here. Dryden's drama, deriving from prose romance, has features which are contrived and sensational in a stage play (the double poison which saves Dorax for example, the rehearsal of early warnings against the marriage, all of which might have passed off well enough in a discursive prose style and a spacious narrative). Even *Samson*, if it does not put a foot wrong, halts at times, especially in some of the experimental choric odes in the middle of the play. What is relevant to recognize is the way in which Milton's political charge is laid deep in the classically shaped fable. Contem-porary originals who prompted or contributed to the play (one might suggest Admiral Penn behind Manoa, William Penn behind Samson) there may conceivably have been, but the text is not full, like that of Dryden, of commentary on recent events. The choric ode 'Many are the sayings of the wise', with its complaint at the down-fall of the elect is the exception. The salient difference between these two post-revolutionary tragedies, however, is their choice of fable from the viewpoint of what should constitute their respective en-dings. Samson pulls down the temple but Sebastian becomes a hermit. There can be little doubt which is the more Christian end to a political story. Curiously, however, each poet seems to thrust against the trend of events as they must have appeared, at least by the time of publication or performance. Thus Dryden's royal patron seemed to have seized back his kingdom of Ireland, where he was poised to fight William, or to invade Scotland or England. By 1670 the various small risings and rumours of risings against the restored monarchy seemed to have subsided.[78] Yet Milton's elect nation rises in his play to fight back and bring down divine destruction, while Dryden, who wanted and seems to have expected the return of James,[79] has his royal hero withdraw from the political arena of the world 'To live alone to Heav'n' in holy retreat. Neither poet is depicting things as they are. Each uses poetic power to produce a challenging image, with many implications for the future. Milton's publication of *Samson* at the time he published seems an unmistakable threat. With Dryden the question of possible prescription is more subtle. It is not out of the question that Dryden remained loyal to James at this time while wishing to recommend recourse to pious retreat. His play certainly offers an image of genuine abdication, in contrast with the fictional abdication of 1689 '*de facto* theory'. Generally, the tragedy explores the issues of legitimate kingship, loyalty, and love for the individual caught amidst the revolutions in affairs of state, and the political and religious picture thus drawn may be thought to be that more specific 'Moral' which in his Preface Dryden says is 'couch'd under every one of the principal Parts and Characters' (ll. 18–19).

[78] See Hutton, *The Restoration*, 150–2, 178–9. Milner, *John Milton and the English Revolution*, 181–2, seeks to link *Samson Agonistes* forward to the Succession Crisis.

[79] See Dryden to the Earl of Chesterfield, 17 Feb. 1697 (*Letters*, ed. Charles E. Ward (Durham, NC, 1942), 85–6). Dryden's hope and expectation of James's return must, presumably, have been stronger still during 1689.

Conclusion

How can we characterize that political consciousness which exploration of Elizabethan and seventeenth-century poetry reveals? Perhaps by saying that the poetic texts that have been discussed here constitute a prolonged, pragmatic, and religious meditation on the nature and conditions of kingship. True we have seen a *politique* fascination with republican polities; true Milton and some like him committed themselves to a kingless commonwealth in reaction against the Stuart monarchy and the prospect of its restoration. But just as Marvell's 'republican' 'Horatian Ode' is dominated by two monarchical figures, so the concept of kingship was ever present even in the absence of a king. Whether seen as an opportunity, an ideal, or a warning, kingship is the one dominant landmark in the political terrain between the late sixteenth and the later seventeenth centuries.

Kingship was generally the target of political aims and the goal of conflicting ideologies. The way to gain your own end was not, usually, to overthrow the crown, but to influence it, control it, even coerce it. This rather than any picture of growing parliamentary liberty is what study of the poetic evidence seems to reveal. The crude struggles to gain possession of the person of Mary, Queen of Scots, only underline later and subtler attempts to capture the will of the monarch, for example the efforts of militant Protestants such as were supported by Spenser to win over Elizabeth I, or the determination of re-established Anglicanism after 1660 to uphold the crown as a pillar of the Church. The impolitic refusal of James II to play this role in the expected way led to his downfall. Much that occurred during the seventeenth century was prefigured in Shakespeare's Histories. With English Tudor and Scottish Stuart history to reflect on, Shakespeare had no difficulty in recognizing a diversity of struggles to control the crown, and how such struggles could, in extremity, pass through coercion into deposition. It is no accident that both

Elizabeth I and James II pondered the example of Richard II as a political portent.[1]

Is it strange that Shakespeare's apparently Bodinian attitude to the establishment of new dynasties in the 1590s should have been so little assimilated by 1688 that the deposition of James II should have caused civil war in two kingdoms, and more than half a century of future rebellions in his interest and that of his heirs? Was the late seventeenth century *more* committed to indefeasible hereditary right than the late sixteenth century? Probably not, though the events of the mid-seventeenth century may have sharpened royalist ideology for the later decades. There are two important points to be made. First, it was conflict of interest as well as constitutional disagreement which kept the dynastic issue alive after 1688. Secondly, it was manifest in the 1590s that the Tudor dynasty was reaching its period with the life of Elizabeth. To challenge hereditary right on the ending of one royal line was a very different thing from the execution or deposition of a reigning hereditary ruler, hereditary right being enshrined in existing law.

In his 'Horatian Ode' Marvell writes of the king and the 'kingdom old', and of Cromwell, the Lord General, already beginning to assume the features of a new Augustan prince. He writes also of the 'republick' which happens to have been the form of government established at the time of writing. Yet the new republic makes nothing like so vivid an impression on the reader as the fallen king or the rising general. This, perhaps, underlines the mental alliance between poetry and the realm of politics in the period we have explored, with all their subtle interrelation and natural allusiveness. To consider what was undeniably important politically, the record of dynasties and the character of kings, was also, as it happened, to reflect on all the contingency of human experience and personal character. Even Milton, even Harrington, could hardly create in literary terms the ideal of a republic, let alone any underlying social or economic laws which affected the logic of history. Poetry and the realm of politics were, we may fancy, twin pillars of the great theatre of the world.

---

[1] See Ch. 1 above and S.W. Singer (ed.), *The Correspondence of Henry Hyde, Earl of Clarendon*, 2 vols. (1828), ii. 211. I am indebted for this reference to Professor John Miller.

APPENDIX I

A CONNECTION between Lord Darnley's murder and *Hamlet* was first proposed by Lilian Winstanley in *Hamlet and the Scottish Succession* in 1920. Her argument is not on the whole well conducted. While denying that Shakespeare meant to portray the Darnley tragedy in any complete and realistic sense, she does seem to strive to demonstrate a parallel, including an allusion in the murder of Polonius to the murder of Rizzio. She sometimes uses modern histories to establish what a situation looked like to Shakespeare, and she is not always convincing on the compatibility of her hypotheses. Yet when all these criticisms have been voiced she did, in my judgement at least, see the resemblance between the opening situation of *Hamlet* and the Darnley murder, and she did understand that it was necessary to see how the Scottish events had been portrayed in sixteenth-century propaganda. Above all, she saw the importance of Buchanan's *Detectio* as a source. (In a later article Winstanley extends her argument to suggest, among other things, that something of the family history of the Earls of Essex and Leicester contributed to *Hamlet*. This is possible; but if so it is more likely to have been a partial source than a deliberate allusion. See Lilian Winstanley, 'Hamlet and the Essex Conspiracy', *Aberystwyth Studies*, 6 (1924), 47–66; 6 (1925), 37–50.)

Scottish poems on the Darnley murder and its aftermath, one of which is quoted by Winstanley (50) are collected in James Cranstoun (ed.), *Satirical Poems of the Time of the Reformation*, 2 vols. (1891), i. 30–81. *Ane ballat declaring the Nobill and Gude Inclination of our King* (?May 1567), a poem full of classical allusion, states: ' "With Clytemnestra I do not fane to fletche, | quhilk slew hir spous the greit Agamemnon' (ll. 145–6). This and *The Testament and Tragedie of Umquhile King Henrie Stewart of Gude Memorie* were broadside ballads in black letter, perhaps by the famous Sempill.

In 1587, John Gordon, a Scot at the court of Henry III of France, wrote the following Latin poem about the murder of Lord Darnley:

> HENRICI Scotorum REGIS MANES AD IACOBVM VIium filivm
> Discite Rectores Populorum, Discite Reges,
> Obsignata Dei Decreta Iura tueri,
> Et quod Naturæ, quod Gentibus omnibus æquum,
> Seruare, ac nullo rescindere fœdera facto.
> Ni facitis, Vindicta manet certissima Culpam.
> In reliquos homines quam magna Potentia Regum,

Tàm Deus Imperio Reges supereminet ipsos.
Vna Exemplorum, si quæritis, Insula turmas
Suggeret, æquoreo surgit, quæ maxima Ponto,
Tot Regum, et toties fuso maculata Cruore,
Quos me salua licet Fortuna, recenseat inter,
At non Culpa Reum tamen arguit. Integer ad vos
Descendi, ô Maiorum Animæ. Nec credite Crimen,
Vxorem nimium nisi Crimen amare Marito est.
Tene mihi, ô Vita Coniux iucundior ipsâ,
Averso tantum mutatam Pectore, ob Iræ
Iustæ tot Procerum, Populique indigna ferentis
Condonatum vnum Nebulonem! Impurane tanti
Cerdonis tibi Vita fuit Cytharædica tanti,
Regii uti Decoris Famæque oblîta, Veneno
Tentatum primùm, excusso mox mente timore,
Me ferro incautum, flammisque agressa necares!
Nec stetit hic scelus indignum, Bothuelius ille,
Dis Caput inuisum, tanti tibi criminis Auctor,
Qui post sacra Thori violata impunè, Mariti
Vxorem docuit respergere sanguine Palmas,
Nostros infamis thalamos calcauit Adulter,
Non tulit adiunctum Sceleri Rhamnusia Fastum,
Securos est passa diù nec ludere Amantes.
Nam subitò Procerum exorta Indignatio Pacem
Sustulit, atque nouos turbauit Marte Hymenôeos.
Ipse fremit Populus, quacumque vagantur et illi
Cincti Armis, Cædisque meæ, Infantisque tenellæ,
Nequicquam in Cunis tollentis bracchia Cœlo,
Cœlâtam Effigiem passim per Compita Miles
Circumgestat Ouans, et Probris Crimen acerbat.
Vnde Ignominia Confusus, ad Orcadas ille
Fugit, et hinc Cimbros delatus, turpitem actam
Turpiter obscuro clausit sub Carcere Vitam.
Illa sed extemplò dulci viduata Columbo
Deserit augustos conscensa naue Penates,
Et dubiis (famam Huperno commiserat olim)
Fortunam commisit Aquis Regina ferendam,
Et tandem inuisis Anglorum allabitur Oris.
Hic quoque misceret cœco quum cuncta tumultu
(Ausa, immane nephas, Germanam tollere ferro)
Penè decem et totidem vigili Custode per Annos,
Postquam habita est, tandem infœlix percussa securi est.
Anglis in Scotos tantum licuisse dolendum,

Et dolui. Sed me summi Moderator Olympi
Longius errare hic Umbram non passus inultam.
Has Cineri Inferias, hæc misit Februa nostro.
Tàm seræ haud alias Caussas iam quærite Pœnæ.
At tu, de tanto superas qui parua Tabella
Naufragio, Mater cui vix irata pepercit,
Nate, Caledoni, nunc ô Spes Vnica Sceptri,
Si meus es, si Rectum audis, Me Disce Magistro
Iustitiam colere, et magnos non temnere Diuos.
Tu fuge Adulentum Occursus, Fuge Subdola, cautus,
(Quantum, Nate, potes) liuentis Spicula Linguæ.
Quid Regno expediat, quid rerum postulet Vsus,
Quid Populi commissa Salus, hoc, sedulus, Vrge;
Cætera Rumorum Securus neglige Vulgi.
Frustrà etenim si quid secus audes, Nate, laboras,
Nec tantùm debes Maternâ Morte moveri,
Vindictâ quantum Cædis gaudere Patêrnæ.

                                        I. G. st.
                                        Me. Martio
                                        1587

   Geoffrey Bullough, in *Narrative and Dramatic Sources of Shakespeare*
(1957–75), vii, is aware of the possible reference of the plot of the old play
of *Hamlet* to the general story of Mary, Queen of Scots, and King James VI,
though what he has chiefly in mind is the expectation that James might find
some way of avenging his mother's execution. He is also well aware of the
topicality of Denmark and things Danish (18–20, 40–5). He does not
mention Winstanley's book, though he includes in his volume an item
tending to support her argument (125–7).
   Another modern commentator aware of the possible connection between
Hamlet and the Darnley murder is Roland Mushat Frye, *The Renaissance
Hamlet: Issues and Responses in 1600* (Princeton, 1984), 31–7.

THE following points are worth putting on record:

(i) Orsino's words to Antonio (v. i. 65) 'Notable pirate, thou salt-water thief' remind us of 'One Raguzine, a most notorious pirate' (*Measure for Measure*, IV. iii. 68), and we may wish to consider whether the name Raguzine itself did not link in Shakespeare's mind with Ragusa. Did he loosely associate Ragusa with piracy (see (iv) below)? This is a possibility, though the name Ragazonius could have been found in the pages of Knolles's *General Historie of the Turkes* (1603), as G. R. Hibbard '*Othello* and the Pattern of Shakespeare Tragedy', *Shakespeare Survey*, 21 (Cambridge), 46, points out.

(ii) Viola's suggestion to the Captain (I. ii. 52) 'Thou shalt present me as an eunuch to him [Orsino]' certainly suggests, as Lothian and Craik observe (New Arden edition, 10) an 'Eastern Mediterranean' court: in this case something Turkish that Viola expects but does not find.

(iii) The inconsistency of the style of Orsino ('Duke' in the stage-directions and three times in the text (I. ii and i. iv), but elsewhere 'Count' or 'County') has been cited as evidence for the view that the text of *Twelfth Night* was set up from foul papers, rather than a satisfactorily revised version. But this diagnosis has not found general support, and it may be worth suggesting that the 'inconsistent' usage would accord with the practice of Ragusa which elected its 'Duke' monthly: when it is a question of referring to the ruler as such, 'Duke' is used; when the individual only, the hereditary title.

(iv) There are two major sources of *Twelfth Night*: *Gl'Ingannati*, and *Riche His Farewell to Militarie Profession*, the latter direct while the former may be indirect. In the former the setting is Modena, in the latter Constantinople. If Shakespeare sought to combine his two sources he would have needed for his setting a place midway between the two. Ragusa was such a place, perhaps the best possible example of a situation between the Italianate and the Oriental. The most recent discussion of the setting and sources of *Twelfth Night*, Leo Salingar's *Shakespeare and the Traditions of Comedy* (Cambridge, 1974), observes that: 'Whatever else Illyria meant to Shakespeare (such as a haven for the "notable pirates" and "salt-water thieves" with whom the duke identifies Antonio), it was the region of Epidamnus and hence the setting for [Plautus's] *Menaechmi*, the prime example for the Renaissance of festive masquerade. It was the typical land of comedy' (241). The region of Epidamnus returns us once again to the southern part of the eastern coast of the Adriatic in which Ragusa was the chief city and only sovereign state.

(v) The First Officer's words to Orsino ('...this is that Antonio | That took the Phoenix and her fraught from Candy...', v. i. 56–7) may, as Professor Veselin Kostić has pointed out to me, be most interestingly glossed by his discovery that a Ragusan merchantship, 'the Phoenix', made the voyage to London in 1602, and may also have done so before the probable date of completion of *Twelfth Night* towards the end of 1601 (Historical Archives of Dubrovnik, Noli e sicurtà, vol. 43, fos. 238, 244–5^v, and vol. 44, fos. 43^v–44^v). These points do not, in my opinion, show that by 'Illyria' Shakespeare meant Ragusa. Rather, they are a set of clues which, taken together, suggest that his 'Illyria' was not simply a classical setting but a blend of classical and modern, and that Ragusa may have been in his mind when the comedy was written. It is, however, very plain that he did not wish to identify 'Illyria' with any modern state, as he plainly did in his exploitation of Venice in *The Merchant* and *Othello*. For *Twelfth Night* a more delicate sense of place was required; a designated local habitation would only have destroyed the rich and strange allusiveness of the text.

APPENDIX III

A USEFUL popular account of Penn the younger is Catherine Owens Peare, *William Penn: A Biography* (Philadelphia and New York, 1957). See also Samuel M. Janney, *The Life of William Penn* (1851; repr. New York, 1970). Penn was briefly imprisoned with other Quakers in Cork in Sept. 1667. He was next imprisoned, for his tract *The Sandy Foundations Shaken* (1668) in December of that year, and not delivered into the custody of his father until July 1669. He was arrested and imprisoned again, under the Conventicle Act on 14 August 1670, and was not released until July 1671. Milton could have known about Penn through Thomas Ellwood, the Quaker. Both Penn and Ellwood were under the influence of the Quaker Thomas Loe, early in the Restoration (*The History of the Life of Thomas Ellwood*, ed. C. Y. Crump (1910), 62–6). As a youth Penn was notable for his stalwart and martial appearance (see the armour-portrait illustrated in Granville Penn, *Memorials*, ii, facing p. 431, and in Peare's *William Penn*, *frontispiece*). An educated and accomplished young man in the 1660s, he devoted his life more and more to his religious vocation, the earliest experience of which, vaguely referred to by later biographers, was recorded by Aubrey: 'The first sense he had of God was when he was 11 yeares old at Chigwell, being retired in a chamber alone. He was so suddenly surprized with an inward comfort and (as he thought) an externall glory in the roome that he has many times sayd that from thence he had the seale of divinity and immortality, that there was a God and that the soule of man was capable of enjoying his divine communications.—His schoolmaster was not of his perswasion' (John Aubrey, '*Brief Lives*', *Chiefly of Contemporaries ... Between 1669 & 1696*, ed. Andrew Clark (Oxford, 1898), ii. 132). It may finally be noted that, while today we associate the Quakers with pacifism, in the last years of the Interregnum and the first of the Restoration they appeared a widespread and well-organized revolutionary sect: on this see Ronald Hutton, *The Restoration: A Political and Religious History of England and Wales*, 1658–1667 (Oxford, 1985), 53, 121, 178, 344 n. 144. This would have struck Milton. They were then among the most arrested and imprisoned people of the early Restoration period, their later passive resistance stemming from this experience.

In 'Milton, *Samson Agonistes*, and the Restoration', Gerald Maclean, ed. *Culture and Society in the Stuart Restoration* (Cambridge, 1995), pp. 111–35, Blair Worden argues for the bearing on Milton's text of further revolutionary figures of the early Restoration.

Select Bibliography

Place of publication is London unless stated otherwise

PRIMARY

ANDERTON, WILLIAM, *Remarks on the Present Confederacy* (1693).

AUBREY, JOHN, *'Brief Lives', Chiefly of Contemporaries . . . between 1669 & 1696*, ed. Andrew Clark (Oxford, 1898).

BALE, JOHN, *King Johan* (rev. 1561); ed. J. H. P. Pafford (1931).

BELLEFOREST, FRANÇOIS DE, *Histoire des neufs roys Charles de France* (Paris, 1568).

—— *Histoire tragiques* (Paris, 1570).

—— *L'Innocence de la tresillustre, treschast, et debonnaure Princess, Madame Marie Royne D'Escosse . . .* (1572).

BLOUNT, CHARLES, *King William and Queen Mary Conquerors* (1693).

BODIN, JEAN, *Les Six Livres de la République* (1576), trans. Richard Knolles (1606), ed. K. D. McRae (Cambridge, Mass., 1962).

—— *Methodus ad Facilem Historiarum Cognitionem* (1566).

BUCHANAN, GEORGE, *Ane Detection of the doings of Marie Quene of Scottes, touchand the Murder of hir husband, and hir conspiracie . . . with the Erle of Bothwell* (1571).

BULLOUGH, GEOFFREY (ed.), *Narrative and Dramatic Sources of Shakespeare*, 7 vols. (1957–75).

BURNET, GILBERT, *A Pastoral Letter . . . to the Clergy of his Diocess* (1689).

CAMDEN, WILLIAM, *Annals (Annales rerum Anglicarum et Hibernicarum regnante Elizabetha)* (1615, 1627); trans. R. Norton (3rd edn., 1635).

Certayne Sermons appoynted by the Queenes Maiestie . . . [The Book of Homilies] (1569) (1587).

CONTARINI, GASPARO, *De Magistratibus et Republica Venetorum* (Venice, 1543), trans. Lewis Lewkenor (1599).

CRANSTOUN, JAMES (ed.), *Satirical Poems of the Time of the Reformation*, 2 vols. (1891).

CROMWELL, OLIVER, *Writings and Speeches*, ed. W. C. Abbott (Cambridge, Mass., 1947).

DANIEL, SAMUEL, *First Fowre Bookes of the Civile Wars Between the Two Houses of Lancaster and York* (1595).

A Description of the Arches erected at The Hague, for the reception of William the Third . . . (1691; *The Harleian Miscellany*, 8 vols. (1744–6), v. 368–9.

A Dialogue Between Tom and Dick . . . (1660), Thomason Tracts, BL 669, fo. 24 (49).

DRYDEN, JOHN, *Works*, ed. Sir Walter Scott, Bart., Revised and Corrected by George Saintsbury, 18 vols. (Edinburgh, 1882–93).

—— *Works*, ed. E. N. Hooker, H. T. Swedenberg, *et al.*, 20 vols. (Berkeley and Los Angeles, 1961–   ).

—— *Poems*, ed. James Kinsley, 4 vols. (Oxford, 1956).

—— *Letters*, ed. Charles E. Ward (Durham, NC, 1942).

—— *Four Tragedies*, ed. L. Beaurline and Fredson Bowers (1967).

D'URFEY, THOMAS, *Wit and Mirth: Or Pills to Purge Melancholy, Edited by Thomas D'Urfey* (1719–20), introd. Cyrus L. Day, 6 vols. in 3 (New York, 1959).

ELLWOOD, THOMAS, *The History of the Life of Thomas Ellwood*, ed. C. Y. Crump (1910).

ELYOT, Sir THOMAS, *The Boke Named the Governour*, ed. H. H. S. Croft (1880).

EUSEBIUS, *The Ancient Ecclesiasticall History* . . . , trans. Meredith Hanmer (1577).

EVELYN, JOHN, *Diary*, ed. E. S. De Beer, 6 vols. (Oxford, 1955).

The Famous Victories of Henry V, in *The Oldcastle Controversy*, ed. Peter Corbin and Douglas Sedge (Manchester, 1991).

FILMER, Sir ROBERT, *Patriarcha and Other Political Works*, ed. Peter Laslett (Oxford, 1949).

FOXE, JOHN, *Actes and Monuments* . . . (1563).

FRENCH, J. MILTON (ed.), *The Life Records of John Milton* (New Brunswick, 1949–58).

GOLLANCZ, ISRAEL (ed.), *The Sources of Hamlet* (1926).

GOODMAN, CHRISTOPHER, *How Superior Powers Ought to be Obeyed* (1558).

GORDON, JOHN, *Henrici Scotorum Regis Manes and Jacobum VI^{ivm} Filium* (1587).

HAKLUYT, RICHARD, *The Principal Navigations* . . . *of the English Nation* (1598–1600).

HALL, EDWARD, *The Union of the Two Noble and Illustre Famelies of Lancastre and Yorke* (1548).

HARINGTON, Sir JOHN, *A Tract on the Succession to the Crown* (1602; 1880).

The Harleian Miscellany: Or, A Collection of Scarce, Curious, and Entertaining Pamphlets and Tracts, As Well in Manuscripts as in Print . . . , 8 vols. (1744–6).

HARRINGTON, JAMES, *Works*, ed. J. G. A. Pocock (Cambridge, 1977).

HARRISON, G. B., *An Elizabethan Journal* . . . *1591–94*, 3 vols. (1928).

HAWKINS, EDWARD (with Augustus W. Franks and Herbert Grueber) (eds.), *Medallic Illustrations of the history of Great-Britain and Ireland to the Death of George II*, 2 vols. (1885).

HAYWARD, Sir JOHN, *The First Part of the Life and Raigne of King Henrie the IIII* . . . (1599).

—— *An Answer to* . . . *Dolman* (1603).

HOBBES, THOMAS, *The English Works*, ed. W. Molesworth, 11 vols. (1839–45).

HOLINSHED, RAPHAEL, *The Chronicles of England, Scotland and Ireland* (1587).

Certayne Sermons appoynted by the Queenes Maiestie . . . [*The Book of Homilies*] (1569).

HUTCHINSON, LUCY, *Memoirs of the Life of Colonel Hutchinson with the Fragment of an Autobiography of Mrs Hutchinson* . . . , ed. James Sutherland (Oxford, 1973).

KING JAMES VI, of Scotland, *Basilikon Doron* (1603).

—— *Political Works of James I*, ed. C. H. McIlwain (Cambridge, Mass., 1918; repr. 1965).

—— 'Lepanto'; *The Poems of King James VI of Scotland*, ed. James Craigie, 2 vols. (Edinburgh, 1955–8), i. 198–257.

JONSON, BEN, *Ben Jonson* [*Works*], ed. C. H. Herford and Percy and Evelyn Simpson, 11 vols. (Oxford, 1925–52).

LAMBIN, G., 'Une Première Ebauche D. Hamlet (mars 1587)', *Les Langues Modernes*, 49 (1955), 37–8.

LAWTON, CHARLWOOD, *A French Conquest Neither Desirable Nor Practicable* (1693).

—— Memoirs Concerning James II, BL Add Mss 40621, fo. 254.

LAUDERDALE, RICHARD MAITLAND, Fourth Earl, *The Works of Virgil, Translated into English Verse* (1709).

—— *The Aeneid of Virgil, Books 4, 6, and 8*, National Library of Scotland, Dept. of MSS 221/62.

LE ROY, LOUIS, *Aristotle's Politiques, or Discourses of Government* . . . *Translated out of French into English* (1598).

LESLIE, JOHN, *A Defence of the Honour of* . . . *Marie Queene of Scotlande* . . . (1569; Liège, 1571).

—— *De Origine, Moribus, et Rebus Gestis Scotorum* . . . (Rome, 1578).

Letters Sent from Venice. Anno 1571 (1571).

LORD, G. de F., *et al.* (eds.), *Poems on Affairs of State, 1660–1714*, 7 vols. (New Haven, 1963–75).

MACHIAVELLI, NICOLO, *Discorsi* (1513–19); trans. Edward Dacre (1636).

—— *Arte Della Guerra* (1519–20); trans. P. Whitehorne (1560–2).

MARVELL, ANDREW, *Poems and Letters*, ed. H. M. Margoliouth and Pierre Legouis with the assistance of E. E. Duncan-Jones, 2 vols. (Oxford, 1927–69).

—— *Complete Poems*, ed. E. S. Donno (Harmondsworth, 1972).

MAY, THOMAS, *Lucan's Pharsalia: or the Civil Wars of Rome, betweene Pompey the Great, and Iulius Caesar* (1627).

MERBURY, CHARLES, *Briefe Discourse of Royall Monarchie, As of the Best Common Weale* (1581).

MILTON, JOHN, *Poems*, ed. John Carey and Alastair Fowler (1968).

—— *Sonnets*, ed. J. S. Smart (Glasgow, 1921).

—— *Sonnets*, ed. E. A. Honnigman (1966).

—— *Complete Prose Works*, ed. Douglas Bush *et al.* (New Haven, 1953–82).

—— *Complete Poems and Major Prose*, ed. Merritt Y. Hughes (New York, 1957).

MONTAIGNE, MICHEL EYQUEM D, *Essaies* (Paris, 1588).

OGILBY, JOHN, *The Entertainment of His Most Excellent Majestie . . .* (1662), introd. Ronald Knowles (Binghampton, NY, 1988).

OLDCASTLE, Sir JOHN, *The Oldcastle Controversy: Sir John Oldcastle, Part I*, and *The Famous Victories of Henry V*, ed. Peter Corbins and Douglas Sedge (Manchester, 1991).

PARSONS, ROBERT (with others?), *A Conference About the Next Succession to the Crowne of Ingland . . . Published by R. Dolman* (1594).

PENN, WILLIAM, the younger, *A Collection of the Works*, 2 vols. (1726, Containing a Life of Penn).

PIKERYNG, JOHN, *Horestes* (1657), in *Three Tudor Classical Interludes*, ed. Marie Axton (Woodbridge, 1982).

Poems on Affairs of State: Augustan Satirical Verse, 1660–1714, ed. G. de F. Lord *et al.*, 7 vols. (New Haven, 1963–75).

PONET, JOHN, *A Short Treatise of Political Power* (1556).

The Roxburghe Ballads, ed. William Chappell (1871).

SANDYS, GEORGE, *A Relation of a Iourney . . . 1610 . . .* (1632).

Don Sebastian King of Portugal: An Historical Novel . . . Done out of French by Mr Ferrand Spence (1683).

SHAKESPEARE, WILLIAM, *The Complete Works: The New Oxford Shakespeare*, ed. Stanley Wells and Gary Taylor (Oxford, 1986).

—— *The New Oxford Shakespeare: The Textual Companion*, ed. Stanley Wells and Gary Taylor *et al.* (Oxford, 1987).

—— *Coriolanus*, ed. G. R. Hibbard, New Penguin Series (Harmondsworth, 1967).

—— *Coriolanus*, ed. Philip Brockbank, New Arden Series (1976).

—— *Hamlet*, ed. Harold Jenkins, New Arden Series (1982).

—— *Hamlet*, ed. G. R. Hibbard (Oxford, 1987).

—— *1 Henry IV*, ed. A. R. Humphreys, New Arden Series (1966).

SELECT BIBLIOGRAPHY265

—— *2 Henry IV*, ed. A. R. Humphreys, New Arden Series (1966).

—— *Henry V*, ed. Gary Taylor, New Oxford Series (Oxford, 1982).

—— *1 Henry VI*, ed. Andrew Cairncross, New Arden Series (1962).

—— *King John*, ed. E. A. J. Honigmann, New Arden Series (1954).

—— *Julius Caesar*, ed. A. R. Humphreys, New Oxford Series (Oxford, 1984).

—— *Julius Caesar*, ed. Martin Spevack, New Cambridge Series (Cambridge, 1988).

—— *The Merchant of Venice*, ed. John Russell Brown, New Arden Series (1964).

—— *Richard II*, ed. Peter Ure, New Arden Series (1958).

—— *Shakespeare's Sonnets*, ed. W. G. Ingram and Theodore Redpath (1964; rev. 1978).

—— *Twelfth Night*, ed. J. M. Lothian and T. W. Craik, New Arden Series (1975).

SMITH, Sir THOMAS, *De Republica Anglorum: A Discourse on the Commonwealth of England* (1583), ed. L. Alston (Cambridge, 1906).

SPENCER, ROBERT, Earl of Sunderland, *The Earl of Sunderland's Letter to a Friend* (1689); *Somers Tracts*, 16 vols. (1748–51), ed. Sir Walter Scott, 13 vols. (1808–15), x. 321–4.

SPENSER, EDMUND, *Works, A Variorum Edition*, ed. Edwin Greenlaw, Charles G. Osgood, and Frederick M. Padelford, 11 vols. (Baltimore, 1932–57).

J. S., *Government Described . . . Together with a Brief Model of the Government of . . . Ragouse* (1659) [By John Streater?]

Royal Archives at Windsor: Stuart MSS 249/113.

THOMAS, WILLIAM, *The History of Italy* (1549), ed. George B. Parks (Ithaca, NY, 1963).

Treatise of the Treasons Against Queen Elizabeth, and the Croune of England . . . (1572).

The Troublesome Raigne of King John of England (1591), in Geoffery Bullough, *Narrative and Dramatic Sources of Shakespeare*, iv (1962), 72–151.

WENTWORTH, PETER, *A Pithie Exhortation To Her Majestie for Establishing Her Successor to the Crowne* (1598).

Thomas of Woodstock (*c.*1591?), ed. George Parfitt and Simon Shepherd (Nottingham, 1977).

SECONDARY

ALVIS, JOHN, and WEST, THOMAS G., *Shakespeare as a Political Thinker* (Chapel Hill, NC, 1981).

AYLMER, G. E. (ed.), *The Interregnum: The Quest for Settlement, 1646–1660* (1972).

BARROLL, J. LEEDS, 'A New History for Shakespeare and His Time', *Shakespeare Quarterly*, 39 (1988).

BARTON, ANNE, 'Livy Machiavelli, and Shakespeare's *Coriolanus*', *Shakespeare Survey*, 38 (1985), 115–29.

BLACK, J. B., *The Reign of Elizabeth* (Oxford, 1936).

BOOTH, STEPHEN, *The Book called Holinshed's Chronicle . . .* (San Francisco, 1968).

BOUWSMA, W. J., *Venice and the Defence of Republican Liberty: Renaissance Values in the Age of the Counter Reformation* (Berkeley and Los Angeles, 1968).

BOXER, C. R., *The Portuguese Seaborne Empire, 1415–1825* (1969).

BROADBENT, J. B., *Some Greater Subject* (1960).

BROWN, PETER, 'Political Thought and Allusion in the Drama of John Dryden', unpublished Cambridge M.Litt. Diss. (1990).

BYWATERS, DAVID, 'Dryden and the Revolution of 1688: Political Parallel in *Don Sebastian*', *JEGP* 85 (July 1986), 363.

—— *Dryden in Revolutionary England* (Oxford, 1991).

CAMPBELL, LILY B., *Shakespeare's 'Histories': Mirrors of Elizabethan Policy* (San Marino, Calif., 1947).

COLLINSON, PATRICK, *The Religion of Protestants* (Oxford, 1982).

—— 'The Elizabethan Exclusion Crisis and the Elizabethan Polity', *Proceedings of the British Academy*, 84 (1993), pp. 51–92.

CORNS, THOMAS M., *Uncloistered Virtue: English Political Literature, 1640–1660* (Oxford, 1992).

CRIBB, T. J. L., 'The Politics of *Richard II*', unpublished paper communicated by the author.

CRUICKSHANKS, EVELINE (ed.), *Ideology and Conspiracy: Aspects of Jacobitism, 1689–1759* (Edinburgh, 1982).

DAVIES, STEVIE, *Images of Kingship in Paradise Lost: Milton's Politics and Christian Liberty* (New York, 1983).

DE LUNA, B. N., *Jonson's Romish Plot: A Study of Catiline and its Historical Context* (Oxford, 1967).

DISALVO, JACKIE, *War of the Titans: Blake's Critique of Milton and the Politics of Religion* (Pittsburgh, 1983).

DOWLING, MARGARET, 'Sir John Hayward's Troubles Over His Life of *Henry IV*', *Library*, 4th ser. 11 (1931).

EDWARDS, THOMAS R., *Imagination and Power: A Study of Poetry on Public Themes* (1971).

ELTON, Sir GEOFFREY, *The Parliament of England, 1559–1581* (Cambridge, 1986).

—— (ed.), *The Tudor Constitution: Documents and Commentary* (Cambridge, 1962).

EMPSON, WILLIAM, *Milton's God* (1961).

ERSKINE-HILL, HOWARD, *The Augustan Idea in English Literature* (1983).

ERSKINE-HILL, HOWARD and MCCABE, RICHARD A. (eds.), *Presenting Poetry: Composition, Publication, Reception* (Cambridge, 1995)

EVERY, GEORGE, SSM, *The High Church Party, 1688–1718* (1956).

FILIPOVIĆ, RUDOLF, and PARTRIDGE, MONICA (eds.), *Dubrovnik's Relations with England: A Symposium* (Zagreb, 1977).

FISH, S. E., *Surprised by Sin* (London and New York, 1969).

FRASER, LADY ANTONIA, *Mary Queen of Scots* (1969).

FRYE, NORTHROP, *Five Essays on Milton's Epics* (1966); first published as *The Return of Eden* (Toronto, 1965).

FRYE, ROLAND MUSHAT, *The Renaissance Hamlet: Issues and Responses in 1600* (Princeton, 1984).

GARRISON, J. D., *Dryden and the Tradition of Panegyric* (1975).

GOLDIE, MARK, 'The Revolution of 1689 and the Structure of Political Argument: An Essay and an Annotated Bibliography of Pamphlets on the Allegiance Controversy', *Bulletin of Research in the Humanities* (Winter, 1980).

GRADY, HUGH, *The Modernist Shakespeare* (Oxford, 1990).

GREENBLATT, STEPHEN, *Renaissance Self-Fashioning* (1980).

—— *Shakespearian Negotiations* (1988).

—— *Learning to Curse* (1990).

—— (ed.), *Representing the English Renaissance* (1988).

HARRISON, T. W., 'Dryden's *Aeneid* ', in Bruce King (ed.), *Dryden's Mind and Art* (Edinburgh, 1969).

HAWKINS, SHERMAN, 'Structural Pattern in Shakespeare's Histories', *Studies in Philology*, 88 (1991), 16–45.

HEXTER, J. H., 'Property, Monopoly and Shakespeare's *Richard II*', in P. Zagorin (ed.), *Culture and Politics* (Berkeley and Los Angeles, 1980), 1–24.

HIBBARD, G. R., '*Othello* and the Pattern of Shakespearean Tragedy', *Shakespeare Survey*, 21 (Cambridge, 1968), 39–46.

HILL, CHRISTOPHER, *Milton and the English Revolution* (1977).

HOLDERNESS, GRAHAM, *Shakespeare's Histories* (1985).

HONIGMANN, E. A. J., 'The Politics, in "Hamlet" and "The World of the Play" ', in John Russell Brown and Bernard Harris (eds.), *Shakespeare Institute Studies* (1963), 129–47.

HUFFMAN, C. C., *Coriolanus in Context* (Lewisburg, NS, 1971).

HUTTON, RONALD, *The Restoration: A Political and Religious History of England and Wales, 1658–1667* (Oxford, 1985).

HUTTON, RONALD, *Charles the Second, King of England, Scotland and Ireland* (Oxford, 1989).

JANNEY, SAMUEL M., *The Life of William Penn* (1851; repr. New York, 1970).

JOHNSON, SAMUEL, *Johnson on Shakespeare*, ed. Arthur Sherbo (vols. vii and viii of the Yale Edition of the *The Works of Johnson* (New Haven, 1968); *Lives of the Poets*, ed. G. Birkbeck Hill, 3 vols. (Oxford, 1905).

JONES, EMRYS, *The Origins of Shakespeare* (Oxford, 1977).

—— 'Stuart Cymbeline', *EC* 2 (1961), repr. D. J. Palmer (ed.), *Shakespeare's Later Comedies* (Harmondsworth, 1971), 248–62.

—— '*Othello, Lepanto*, and the Cyprus Wars', *Shakespeare Survey*, 21 (Cambridge, 1968), 47–52.

JORGENSEN, P. A., 'A Formative Shakespearian Legacy: Elizabethan Views of God, Fortune and War', *PMLA* 40 (1975).

KELLY, H. A., *Divine Providence in the England of Shakespeare's Histories* (Cambridge, Mass., 1970).

KENDRICK, CHRISTOPHER, *Milton: A Study in Ideology and Form* (New York and London, 1986).

KENYON, J. P., *Revolution Principles: The Politics of Party, 1689–1720* (Cambridge, 1977).

KINSLEY, JAMES, 'Dryden's Characters of a Good Parson and Bishop Ken', *RES* ns (1952), 155–8.

KOSTIĆ, VESELIN, *Cultural Relations between Yugoslavia and England before 1700* (Belgrade, 1972).

LEGGATT, ALEXANDER, *Shakespeare's Political Drama: The History Plays and the Roman Plays* (1988).

MCCABE, RICHARD A., *Incest, Drama and Nature's Law, 1550–1700* (Cambridge, 1993).

—— 'The Masks of Duessa: Spenser, Mary Queen of Scots, and James VI', *ELH* 17 (1987), 224–42.

—— 'Edmund Spenser, Poet of Exile', Chatterton Lecture on Poetry, 1991, *Proceedings of the British Academy*, 80 (1991), 73–103.

MACCAFFREY, WALLACE T., *The Shaping of the Elizabethan Regime* (Princeton, 1968).

—— *Queen Elizabeth and the Making of Policy, 1572–1588* (Princeton, 1981).

—— *Elizabeth I: War and Politics, 1588–1603* (Princeton, 1992).

—— *Camden's The History of the Most Renowned and Victorious Princess Elizabeth . . . Selected Chapters* (1970).

MACKENZIE ROSS, MALCOLM, *Milton's Royalism: A Study of the Conflict of Symbol and Idea in the Poems* (Ithaca, NY, 1943).

MASSON, DAVID, *The Life of John Milton, Narrated in Connexion with the Political, Ecclesiastical, and Literary History of his Time* (1859–94).

MERRIX, ROBERT P., 'Shakespeare and the New Bardolaters', *Studies in English Literature*, 19 (1979), 179–96.

MILLER, ANTHONY, '*Henry IV Part I* and Renaissance Ideologies', *Sydney Studies in English*, 16, (1990–1), 35–53.

MILLER, JOHN, *James II: A Study in Kingship* (Hove, 1978).

MILNER, ANDREW, *John Milton and the English Revolution* (Totowa, NJ, 1981).

MINER, EARL, *The Restoration Mode from Milton to Dryden* (Princeton, 1974).

MIOLA, ROBERT S., *Shakespeare's Rome* (Cambridge, 1983).

MOORE, J. R., 'Political Allusions in Dryden's Later Plays', *PMLA* 73 (Mar.–June 1958).

—— '*Windsor Forest* and William III', *MLN* 66 (1951), 451–4.

MORRILL, JOHN, *The Revolt of the Provinces: Conservatives and Radicals in the English Civil War, 1630–1650* (1976).

MYERS, WILLIAM, *Dryden* (1973).

NEALE, Sir JOHN, *Elizabeth I and Her Parliaments, 1584–1601* (1957).

NETHERCOTT, A. H., *The Muse's Hannibal* (1931).

NORBROOK, DAVID, 'Macbeth and the Politics of Historiography', in Kevin Sharpe and Stephen N. Zwicker (eds.), *The Politics of Discourse* (1987).

—— *Poetry and Politics in the English Renaissance* (1984).

—— and WOUDHUYSEN H. R. (eds.), *The Penguin Book of Renaissance Verse, 1509–1659* (Harmondsworth, 1992).

NOSWORTHY, J. M., *Shakespeare's Occasional Plays* (1965).

ORNSTEIN, ROBERT, *A Kingdom for a Stage* (Cambridge, Mass., 1972).

PARKER, W. R., *Milton: A Biography*, 2 vols. (Oxford, 1968).

PATTERSON, ANNABEL, *Censorship and Interpretation: The Conditions of Writing and Reading in Early Modern England* (Madison, 1984).

—— *Shakespeare and the Popular Voice* (Oxford, 1989).

PAUL, H. N., *The Royal Play of Macbeth* (New York, 1950).

PEARE, CATHERINE OWENS, *William Penn: A Biography* (Philadelphia and New York, 1957).

PENN, GRANVILLE, *Memorials of the Professional Life and Times of Sir William Penn, Knt.*, 2 vols. (1833).

PHILLIPS, J. E., *Images of a Queen: Mary Stuart in Sixteenth-Century Literature* (Berkeley and Los Angeles, 1964).

POCOCK, J. G. A., *The Ancient Constitution and the Feudal Law* (Cambridge, 1957).

—— *The Machiavellian Moment* (Princeton, 1975).

POTTER, LOIS, *Secret Rites and Secret Writing: Royalist Literature, 1641–1660* (Cambridge, 1989).

PROFFITT, BESSIE, 'Political Satire in *Alexander's Feast*', *Texas Studies in Literature and Language*, 11 (1970), 7–16.

PROUDFOOT, L., *Dryden's Aeneid and its Seventeenth-Century Predecessors* (Manchester, 1960).

RACKIN, PHYLLIS, *Stages of History* (1991).

RADZINOWICZ, M. A., *Towards Samson Agonistes: The Growth of Milton's Mind* (Princeton, 1978).

—— 'The Politics of *Paradise Lost*', in Kevin Sharpe and Stephen N. Zwicker (eds.), *The Politics of Discourse* (1987), 204–29.

REESE, M. M., *The Cease of Majesty* (1961).

RIBNER, IRVING, *The English History Play in the Age of Shakespeare* (Princeton, 1957; rev. 1965).

ROPER, ALAN, *Dryden's Poetic Kingdoms* (1965).

RUSSELL, CONRAD, Second Earl RUSSELL, *The Crisis of Parliaments* (Oxford, 1971).

—— *The Causes of the English Civil War* (Oxford, 1990).

—— *The Fall of the British Monarchies, 1637–1642* (Oxford, 1991).

SALZMAN, PAUL, *English Prose Fiction, 1558–1700* (Oxford, 1985).

SCHAAR, CLAES, *The Full Voic'd Choir: Ventrical Context Systems in Paradise Lost* (Lund, 1982).

SCHOENBAUM, SAMUEL, ' "Richard II" and the Realities of Power', *Shakespeare Survey*, 28 (1975), 1–13.

SHARPE, KEVIN, *The Personal Rule of Charles I* (1992).

—— and ZWICKER, Stephen N. (eds.), *The Politics of Discourse: The Literature and History of Seventeenth-Century England* (Berkeley and Los Angeles, 1987).

SKINNER, QUENTIN, *The Foundations of Modern Political Thought*, 2 vols. (Cambridge, 1978).

STABLER, A. P., 'The Histoires Tragiques de François de Belleforest', University of Virginia Ph.D. Diss. (1959).

—— 'King Hamlet's Ghost in Belleforest', *PMLA* 77 (Mar. 1962), 18–20.

STONE, DONALD, 'Belleforest's Bandello: A Bibliographical Study', *Bibliothèque d'humanisme et renaissance*, 34 (1972), 489–99.

STRIBRNY, ZDENEK, 'The Idea and Image of Time', *Shakespeare Jahrbuch*, 110 (1974), 129–38.

—— 'The Idea and Image of Time in Shakespeare's Second Historical Tetralogy', *Shakespeare Jahrbuch*, 111 (1975), 51–66.

TALBOT, E. W., *The Problem of Order: Elizabethan Political Commonplace and an Example of Shakespeare's Art* (Chapel Hill, NC, 1962).

THAYER, C. G., *Shakespearian Politics: Government and Misgovernment in the Great Histories* (Athens, Oh., 1983).

TILLYARD, E. M. W., *Shakespeare's History Plays* (1944).

TREVOR ROPER, HUGH, LORD DACRE, *Queen Elizabeth's First Historian: William Camden and the Beginnings of English Civil History* (1971).

TYACKE, NICHOLAS, *Anti-Calvinists: The Rise of English Arminianism, circa 1590–1640* (Oxford, 1987).

WAITH, EUGENE M., *The Herculean Hero* (1962).

WALLACE, JOHN, 'John Dryden's Last Plays and the Conception of a Heroic Society', in Perez Zagorin (ed.), *Culture and Politics from Puritanism to the Enlightenment* (Berkeley and Los Angeles, 1980), 113–34.

WICKHAM, GLYNNE, 'From Tragedy to Tragi-Comedy: *King Lear* as Prologue', *Shakespeare Survey*, 26 (Cambridge, 1973), 35–43.

WILDERS, JOHN, *The Lost Garden: A View of Shakespeare's English and Roman History Plays* (1978).

WINN, JAMES ANDERSON, *John Dryden and His World* (1987).

WINSTANLEY, LILIAN, *Hamlet and the Scottish Succession, Being an Examination of the Relations of the Play of Hamlet to the Scottish Succession and the Essex Conspiracy* (Cambridge, 1920; repr. New York, 1970).

—— 'Hamlet and the Essex Conspiracy', *Aberystwyth Studies*, 6 (1924), 47–66; (1925) 37–50.

WITTREICH, J. A., *Milton and the Lines of Vision* (Madison, 1976).

WOMERSLEY, DAVID, 'The Politics of King John', *RES* NS 40 (1989), 497–515.

—— 'Sir Henry Savile's Translation of Tacitus and the Political Interpretation of Elizabethan Texts', *RES* Ns 42: 167 (1991), 313–42.

—— 'Sir John Hayward's Tacitism', *Renaissance Studies*, 6: 1 (1992), 46–59.

WOOLRYCH, AUSTEN, 'The Date of the Digression in Milton's *History of Britain*', in R. Ollard and P. Tudor Craig (eds.), *For Veronica Wedgwood, these* (1986), 217–46.

—— 'Dating Milton's *History of Britain*', *Historical Journal*, 36: 4 (1993), 929–43.

WORDEN, BLAIR, *The Rump Parliament, 1648–1653* (Cambridge, 1974).

—— 'Classical Republicanism and the Puritan Revolution', in Hugh Lloyd-Jones, Valerie Pearl, and Blair Worden (eds.), *History and Imagination: Essays in Honour of H. R. Trevor-Roper*, (1981), 181–200.

—— 'The Politics of Marvell's Horatian Ode', *The Historical Journal*, 27: 3 (1984), 525–47.

ZAGORIN, PEREZ (ed.), *Culture and Politics* (Berkeley and Los Angeles, 1980).

ZWICKER, S. N., *Politics and Language in Dryden's Poetry: The Arts of Disguise* (Princeton, 1984).

INDEX

Notes: 1. Monarchs, other than those with qualification, are those of England.
2. Page references in *italics* indicate illustrations.

INDEX 281

Peare, Catherine O. 259
Pecarone, Il (Giovanni) 127, 128
Peele, George 14
Penn, Granville 259
Penn, Admiral Sir William 234, 250
Penn, William (son of Sir William)
  234, 250, 259
Perrot, Sir John 65
Peters, Hugh 225
Petrarch 152-3, 157, 163
Pharsalia (Lucan) 133
Philip II, King of Spain 39
  Armada 28, 38, 65-6, 96
  marriage to Mary I 25
Pikeryng, John: *Horestes* 21-2, 99, 111
Pilgrimage of Grace 199
Pindar 159
Pithie Exhortation to Her Maiestie
  (Wentworth) 35-7
Pius V, Pope: *Regnans in Excelsis* 23,
  64
Plantagenets (and Angevins) 14, 26,
  36, 38, 39, 51, 54
  see also John
Plautus: *Menaechmi* 257
Plutarch 140, 141, 142, 144, 172
Poetaster, The (Jonson) 135, 136
Poetry of Opposition and Revolution
  (Erskine-Hill) 3, 10
poetry and politics, *see* political
  allusion
Poland, King of 18
political allusion in poetry, *see* political
  foreground; post-revolutionary;
  republicanism; tetralogies
political foreground 13-45
  Camden's *Annales* and Elizabeth I
    15-29
  kingship and succession 29-45
Politics (Aristotle) 117, 142
Polybius 219
Ponet, John 30
Pope, Alexander 4
popular poetry, *see* ballads
post-revolutionary:
  epics, *see* defeat and relevance
  tragedy 4, 216-51; Dryden 216,
    220-1, 226-40, 241; Milton 216,
    221-6, 229, 240-6
Prerogative of Popular Government
  (Harrington) 166-7
Pro Populo Anglicano Defensio
  (Milton) 189

*Prosopopoia Or Mother Hubberd's
  Tale* (Spenser) 2, 58
Protectorate 175
Protestantism 1, 29-30, 35, 37-8, 134
  post-revolutionary 186, 199, 217-18
  see also Elizabeth I *and under*
    Catholicism
Proverbs (Old Testament) 190
puritanism 218

queens see *de jure* queens; Elizabeth;
  Mary; monarchy
Quintilian 158

Radzinowicz, Mary Ann 189-90, 191
Ragusa, Republic of 115, 131-2,
  257-8
Ralegh, Sir Walter 2
Ranters 199
*Readie and Easie Way to Set Up a Free
  Commonwealth* (Milton) 9-10,
  166, 175, 176, 181, 185, 189,
  190, 198, 223
Realm of Politics 5
regicide 197
  Charles I 28
  Mary, Queen of Scots 27, 28, 37,
    66-7, 103
  see also under Darnley
Regnans in Excelsis (Pius V) 23, 64
Reign of King Edward III 14
religion, *see* Catholicism; Protestants
René,, Duke of Anjou 47
Republica Anglorum, De (Smith) 9,
  123-5, 130, 143, 145-6, 149-50
republicanism and republican
  government 5, 8-10, 115-67,
    177, 252, 253
  and kingship 137-8, 140-2
  see also commonwealth; Italy;
    Parliament; Rome
Restoration of monarchy 7-8,
  116-17, 180, 225, 234, 259
revenge plays 21-2, 99, 111
  see also *Hamlet*
revolutions, rebellions and revolts:
  (1660) 10, 171, 185
  (1688) (Glorious) 7-8, 171, 185,
    206 *see also* post-revolutionary
  Catholic–Huguenot conflicts 48
  French 82
  Irish 41, 42
  Midlands 143-4